HEIDEGGER'S WAYS

D1592865

SUNY Series in Contemporary Continental Philosophy
Dennis J. Schmidt, editor

Heidegger's ways

Hans-Georg Gadamer

Translated by
John W. Stanley

State University of New York Press

Published by
State University of New York Press, Albany

© 1994 State University of New York

For information, address State University of New York Press,
State University Plaza, Albany, N.Y., 12246

Production by Marilyn P. Semerad
Marketing by Dana E. Yanulavich

Library of Congress Cataloging-in-Publication Data

Gadamer, Hans Georg, 1900–
  [Heideggers Wege. English]
  Heidegger's ways / Hans-Georg Gadamer ; translated by John W.
Stanley ; with an introduction by Dennis J. Schmidt.
      p.   cm. — (SUNY series in contemporary continental
philosophy)
  Translation of: Heideggers Wege.
  Includes bibliographical references and index.
  ISBN 0-7914-1737-9 (HC : alk. paper). — ISBN 0-7914-1738-7 (PB :
alk. paper)
  1. Heidegger, Martin, 1889–1976.   I. Title.   II. Series.
B3279.H49G24613   1993
193—dc20   93-24934
                                              CIP

10   9   8   7   6   5   4   3   2   1

CONTENTS

PREFACE

The Heidegger Studies presented here are a collection of essays, lectures, and speeches written in the course of the last twenty-five years, the majority of which have already been published. The fact that these are all relatively recent works should not be taken to mean that my engagement with Heidegger is recent as well. Rather, I received impetuses for thinking from Heidegger very early on, and I attempted from the very beginning to follow such impetuses within the limits of my capabilities and to the extent that I could concur. It set a standard that I had to learn to meet. However, as is always the case when one is attempting to find one's own position, some distance was needed before I was able to present Heidegger's ways of thinking as his; I first had to distinguish my own search for my ways and paths from my companionship with Heidegger and his ways.

This process had its beginning with Heidegger's request that I write the introduction to the Reclam edition of his "Artwork" essay. Basically, this collection of works is only a continuation of what I first undertook in 1960 with that introduction. I was actually in my own element, for I took it as encouragement and confirmation of my own efforts when Heidegger introduced the work of art into his own thinking in the 1930s. Thus, my relationship to this short introduction to the "Artwork" essay of 1960 was not so much that of one "commissioned" to write it, rather I recognized in Heidegger's thought some of the very questions I had voiced in *Truth and Method*. All of my later Heidegger essays are an effort—although one framed by my own assumptions and capabilities—to offer a view of the task for thinking that confronted Heidegger; they attempt to show that especially the Heidegger who had made this "turn" [*Kehre*] after *Being and Time* was in truth continuing down the same path when he encountered questions probing the underpinnings of metaphysics and attempted to think an unknown future.

All of the works assembled here pursue in essence the same goal—to introduce the independent, unconventional thought of Martin Heidegger, thought that renounced all previously existing ways of thinking and speaking. Above all, these works are intended to prevent the reader from the error of supposing that a mythology or poetizing gnosis is to be found in Heidegger's renunciation of the customary. The fact that all of my studies are confined to a single task entails that each one of them contains an occasional element. Variations on a single theme are what confront the eyewitness who attempts to give an account of the thought of Martin Heidegger. Thus, I must accept the consequently unavoidable repetitions as a part of the terrain.

The first essay introduces the situation into which Heidegger entered. The following articles form a continuum as regards content. The memorial address that I gave in Freiburg after Heidegger's death serves as the conclusion.

HGG

TRANSLATOR'S PREFACE

The approach that I have taken in this translation is in essence a compromise between two conflicting interests. On the one hand, I had a strong interest in rendering a translation that would allow as much of the "otherness" of the German text as possible to shimmer through in the English. Yet, on the other hand, I wanted the translation to mirror the exceptional eloquence of Gadamer's prose. That these two interests conflict and the way that they conflict may not be readily apparent to one who has not previously worked with translations and, therefore, may warrant a short explanation.

My interest in languages, especially my interest in the German language, was transformed into a passion when I first encountered *Being and Time* as an undergraduate in 1982. In an effort to better understand Heidegger's thought, I spent an inordinate amount of time trying to work through what I deemed to be key passages in the German text. That experience was exceptionally rewarding, not so much because I was able to gain an understanding of *Being and Time,* but because, in facing the otherness of the German text, I was forced to begin thinking differently; I had to somehow integrate this otherness into my own thinking, which meant that I myself had to assume some of these ways of thinking as my own—a part of me became "other." It was always with a sense of loss and some frustration that I returned to the translation of *Sein und Zeit* because the experience of this otherness was necessarily greatly diluted. The frustration is that which brought about the transformation of my interest into a passion for language; I vowed then to try to bring as much of the otherness over into a translation if I ever had the chance to do one.

I interpret Gadamer's cautious enthusiasm for Heidegger's interpretation of the Greeks as a confirmation of my own perspective, for Gadamer praised these interpretations precisely because they were able to break through the scholarly overlay and allow one to sense the otherness of Greek thinking (see Chapter 12 of this book). Yet, implicit in both the description of my experience of "otherness" with reference to Heidegger's *Sein und Zeit* and in Gadamer's motto "to think the Greeks more Greeklike" is a certain grievance against translation: The experience of this otherness seems to require that one be intimately proximate to it. Thus, when translation is necessary, then the rendition with the least translating would be the best; that is, the most literal translation possible would be the one most desirable because it remains as close as possible to the original text—hence Gadamer's passing definition of translation as a "word-for-word rendition of an assigned text" (see the end of Chapter 3).

Here, the conflict is already beginning to show itself. A "word-for-word" translation is really no translation at all, for the text of the translation would be unintelligible to any reader, probably even to the translator. The linguistic structures of the original language that support the words and lend them their meaning cannot be translated without the target language losing its integrity: Frequently the grammatical structures that show gender, case, and number simply cannot be translated; and the effort to mirror the syntactical order of the original language in the target language results in babble. Therefore, the translator is forced to do some interpreting, thereby distancing the translation from the original text and, hence, from the otherness embedded in the linguistic structures of the original language. This is where the freedom of the translator that Gadamer often mentions comes into play—and yet, if one translates in accord with this first interest, then the freedom of the translator is exceedingly limited; one can deviate from the original text only enough to make the translation intelligible.

My second interest, the one in allowing Gadamer's eloquence to show through, is not merely motivated by a sense of aesthetics.

Much of the power and force of Gadamer's thinking is lent by his prose, which often verges on the poetic. Not only does one not have to struggle with Gadamer's text, but, moreover, it works on the reader like a magnet. To offer a translation of Gadamer's text that seemed awkward to the English speaker would be to ignore a fundamental element of Gadamer's thought. Gadamer himself is quite aware of this; he encouraged me in one conversation to take as much freedom as I wanted, going so far as to say, "Herr Stanley, vergessen Sie den Text" (Mr. Stanley, forget the text). Yet, to render a translation of Gadamer's text that is as eloquent in English as it is in German is to move it completely away from its home, to erase its otherness. An eloquent speaker is one who is completely at home in a language, who inhabits it to the fullest extent possible, who knows all of its avenues and pathways and can even sometimes cut new ones that mesh so well with the old that they seem neither strange nor new. This second interest, then, demands that I make Gadamer's thought at home in a foreign country, that I strip it of all strange elements so that the natives (native speakers) do not even notice that it had at one time had this character of "otherness."

Obviously, no single principle or simple guideline could meet the demands of both interests; the approach to this translation, like the translation itself, has more of the character of a sheaf of uneasy compromises. On the one hand, I have endeavored to find a language at home in the structures of the English language, a language the English speaker would find enticing. On the other hand, I have sometimes strained against the constraints of English and tried, at least at some sights, to find a language that would "let thinking break through" (see the end of Chapter 11), to find expressions unusual enough that they did not always fall squarely into the typical linguistic "tracks" our thinking usually follows. My goal was to find a language that stretched over into the German world of Gadamer's thought without being distorted, a language that rings of another culture and way of thinking and yet is devoid of the clashing sounds of discord.

As Gadamer mentions in his preface, the chapters of this book consist of essays published over the last twenty-five years. Subsequently, seven of these essays have already been translated into English. Among those already translated, four have been reprinted here; they are Chapters 7, 8, 9, and 11 (the acknowledgments appear on the first page of each chapter). I have made some revisions in these translations to bring some of the technical terms in line with the conventions I have been using and to accommodate revisions Gadamer himself made in the German text of these essays before they were published in this book. The three chapters that have not been reprinted are as follows: (1) Chapter 3, *"Die Marburger Theologie"* was translated as "Heidegger and the Marburg Theology" by David Linge and appears in *Philosophical Hermeneutics,* which he edited; (2) Chapter 13, *"Die Geschichte der Philosophie,"* was translated by Karen Cambell as "Heidegger and the History of Philosophy" and published in *The Monist* (64, no. 4); (3) Chapter 15, *"Sein Geist Gott,"* was translated by Steven Davis and appears in *Heidegger's Memorial Lectures,* edited by Werner Marx. I have retranslated these three chapters from the German and all other translations are mine, including quotes and excerpts from other sources as well as Celan's poem.

I have adopted conventional translations of key words coined by Gadamer and Heidegger; I was helped in this endeavor by the aforementioned translations as well as other sources. With reference to Heidegger's terminology, I have relied to a large extent upon John MacQuarrie and Edward Robinson's translation of *Sein und Zeit* as a canonical source. A glossary of important German terms and their translations has been included at the end of the text. The footnotes in this book, with exception of the acknowledgments, are Gadamer's; the notes, which are explicative comments made by either myself or other translators (in the case of reprints), are designated with letters. (In general, the contents of the notes have been restricted to comments intended to explain the meaning of non-English terms; I had wanted to provide bibliographical notes, but I have been living in Germany for the last one-and-a-half years and do not have access to the English translations of Heidegger's works.) To distinguish between different kinds of explanatory or qualifying remarks within the texts, I have used a system employing parentheses and two kinds of brackets. Parentheses are used to mark comments that Gadamer made and usually that he himself put in parentheses in the German text. Square brackets are used to give the German, Latin, or Greek word from which an English word was translated, or to give an English translation of a word left in a foreign language. Angle brackets, < >, are used to bracket a word or words that I inserted in the English text that did not exist in the German.

I am indebted to such a large number of people for their help with this translation that I cannot thank them all here. However, I would like to thank Professor Gadamer for our conversations and Dennis Schmidt for his help in arranging this translation. I would also like to express my gratitude to Jason Wirth and Andreas Engler for their frequent help with difficult passages in the text. Finally, I wish to thank my parents and especially my spouse, Jan Robert, for their financial and emotional support, without which this translation would not have come to be.

John Stanley

INTRODUCTION

by Dennis J. Schmidt

AMONG THE WAYS

Anyone who has ever attempted it will confirm that writing about one's teacher, while a joy, poses a special difficulty. The difficulty is clear: in writing about someone whose lasting influence finds its roots in one's own formative years—a time that one never quite leaves—one necessarily writes out of a curious entanglement and a debt that can never be repaid. In such cases the hermeneutical situation of the interpreter takes on a peculiar sharpness as one learns that writing such a text entails, in large measure, a very real, yet thoroughly mediated, self-confrontation. When Gadamer writes about his teacher Heidegger, the stakes of this engagement are raised and rendered more complex still by virtue of the impact that each has had upon the direction of thinking—and not only in philosophy—in these times. The effective history of Heidegger's work, the often independent afterlife of his texts, the new directions his questioning has opened, and the controversies of his life that have intensified since his death all contribute to the process whereby Heidegger has come to be rendered larger than life, a figure, an abstraction, a proper name on the way to some sort of allegorization in history. Whatever Heidegger is coming to mean for thinking at this historical juncture—and of course he will mean many and frequently conflicting things for thinking—one must recognize its distance from the Heidegger who, in a lecture course on Aristotle, first ignited the philosophical imagination of Gadamer during his student years.

In turning to write about Heidegger, Gadamer not only elucidates some of the paths of Heidegger's thinking, but also, in a quiet and unthematized manner, Gadamer confronts himself and the evolution in his relationship with Heidegger. Indeed, as one reads these essays and follows Gadamer's reflections upon Heidegger's texts, one soon understands that Gadamer is driven by a question that he formulates at the time of his first encounter with Heidegger but asks only many years later in his autobiography: what is the secret of Heidegger's enduring presence? The impact and profound impression of Heidegger upon Gadamer is expressed in Gadamer's sense that there is some "secret" in Heidegger. Not a secret kept and jealously guarded, but the most haunting of secrets, namely an open secret in which something is found somehow apart from the language in which we know how to tell what we know. The remarks about Heidegger that Gadamer makes in his autobiography (which bears the revealing and ironic epigram "De nobis ipsis silemus") provide ample evidence of the force of Heidegger in Gadamer's life as the one who introduced him to an experience of philosophizing that Gadamer likens to "an electric shock." Those remarks also give some indication of the extent to which his early encounter with Heidegger drove Gadamer to stretch his own language in an effort to respond to the challenge that this secret posed. Of course, the secret and the shock was not about Heidegger the man, but about the body of questions and texts that signaled a breakthrough to a new philosophic experience. Consequently, while Gadamer speaks about the personal dimensions of his engagement with Heidegger in his autobiography, it is in these essays that he makes a sustained effort to understand the radicality and originality of the philosophic experience found in Heidegger. Here Gadamer calls our attention to Heidegger's place in the history of philosophy by repeatedly emphasizing the shock and radicality of his approach to thinking and to the remarkable synthesis of conceptual rigor and a wide concern with the questions of human existence beyond the sphere of consciousness: "in a whirl of radical questions—questions that Heidegger posed, that posed themselves to Heidegger, that he posed to himself—the chasm that had developed in the course of the last century between academic philosophy and the need for a world-view seemed to close" (19).

It should be noted that Gadamer refrained from writing about Heidegger for quite some time and the long silence that precedes the essays in this volume, essays written over the course of some twenty-

essays in this volume, essays written over the course of some twenty-five years, needs to be heard as the true preface to what is said here. Gadamer did not write about Heidegger until 1960, almost four decades after his first, and lasting, encounter with Heidegger. It is a remarkable period of silence, a period during which Heidegger's work became the focus of intense debate and discussion around the world. But it should be obvious that such a stunning silence is not an indication that Gadamer had forgotten Heidegger during those years; it is not a period during which Gadamer neglects Heidegger, as if such neglect were even an option. Rather, those years proved to be the time in which Gadamer pursued, with imagination and rigor, what he describes as the "impulse" he received from Heidegger. During those years Gadamer worked through figures and themes akin to those animating Heidegger at the time, but he carried out his own philosophical projects—especially the project of thinking through Greek and poetic texts, and the formulation of hermeneutics after the philosophical shock of Heidegger's hermeneutics of facticity—with a remarkable independence from Heidegger's explicit efforts along similar lines. That independence is most evident in the extent to which Gadamer, himself a writer of extraordinary philosophical prose, avoided the seductions of Heidegger's language and style during that period. For those years served as the period in which Gadamer found the requisite "distance" needed if he was to write "about" Heidegger. Gadamer describes this situation by saying that "I received an impetus for thinking from Heidegger early on. . . . However, as is always the case when one is attempting to find one's own position, some distance was needed before I was able to present Heidegger's ways of thinking as his; I first had to distinguish my own search for my ways and paths from my companionship with Heidegger and his ways." (vii) It is important to realize what this "distance," the distance requisite for these essays, means. Of course it refers to a certain critical and creative distance from his first encounter with Heidegger. But it is a distance measured in several manners. Yet, however its measure is taken, it would be misleading to think that this distance marks a simple departure in which Gadamer becomes remote from Heidegger's work. Quite the contrary; a fundamental empathy with Heidegger prevails in all of Gadamer's writings. The last words of the introduction to *Truth and Method* acknowledge this debt: there Gadamer announces the standards to which he wants to submit his own work by referring first to Husserl, then to Dilthey, then finally to Heidegger, by speaking of the impulse he found in Heidegger's innovative advance of the phenomenological-hermeneutical tradition in his development of the hermeneutics of facticity. So Gadamer presents his own achievements in *Truth and Method* along with an expression of the debt of those achievements to Heidegger. But it should also not escape notice that *Truth and Method* was published in the same year as the first text that Gadamer wrote on Heidegger, a circumstance indicating that the distance from which Gadamer writes these studies of Heidegger is the distance found in the achievements of Gadamer's own work, in some respects elaborations of possibilities first opened by Heidegger, in other respects departures from and alternatives to Heidegger. But, however it is situated with respect to Heidegger, Gadamer's work always manifests a deep fidelity to the continuing effort of thinking out of a sense of the finitude of understanding and the enigmas of factical life.

While this distance is to be understood as the creative distance which Gadamer needed to travel in order to be able to take up Heidegger as a theme for his own work, it is also a distance measured by history, a distance not simply of four decades but one that might also be designated as a moral distance. When Habermas entitles his laudatio of Gadamer on the occasion of Gadamer's receipt of the Hegel-Prize "The Urbanization of the Heideggerian Province" he makes a gesture toward one way in which this distance between Heidegger and Gadamer can be conceived: Gadamer's work is responsive to the events of the historical present in a manner that indicates an aspect of the distance taken from Heidegger. From the time of Jean Beaufret's question that Heidegger took as the occasion for his "Letter on Humanism"—namely, how are we to give a sense to the word 'humanism' after the events of our age?—up to the celebrated *Spiegel* interview in which Heidegger laments that "only a god can save us," there is a conspicuous absence of any overt concern with the immediate demands of political life on Heidegger's part. This devotion to the provinces, this apparent strange provincialism of such a sweeping and original mind, has infuriated many and frustrated some of Heidegger's most sympathetic readers. Heidegger knew well that our historical juncture needs to be thought as a period of profound and protracted crisis, and his commitment to taking up this crisis as a crisis of the "roots" of inherited forms of thinking and cultural practices is unquestionable. But it is precisely the single-mindedness of the drive to interrogate the roots of contemporary problems that gives Heidegger's thought a legitimate claim to radicality and, equally, lets it be criticized for its oblivion to the dangerous configuration of those "roots" in the contemporary world. One could argue that the absence of an overt and immediate concern does not so much signal an oblivion to such concerns on Heidegger's part as it does an abiding and overriding sense that a radical refunctioning of the terms of political discourse is needed before any amelioration of the injustices of political life could become thinkable. Gadamer himself interprets Heidegger's work in just that way when he writes that "what distinguishes his thinking is the radicality and boldness with which he depicted the progression of occidental civilization into the technical omniculture of today as our fate and the necessary consequence of occidental metaphysics. But this means that all the benign attempts to slow down this gigantic process of calculating, empowering and producing—which we call cultural life—did not have a place in his thought." (193) That such seems to be Heidegger's conviction—wisely or not—becomes evident when one thinks, for instance, of his 1946 text on Anaximander, a text that takes up the question of rendering justice in time by means of an interpretation of what he says is the "oldest text of the occident," a text written in the aftermath of the war and the revelations of the Holocaust, and while Freiburg lay in ruins. For Heidegger such events are best understood as the visibility and violence of the end of metaphysics and those events are to be confronted as such. Gadamer, on the other hand, driven by a deep ethical and political sensibility, one remarkably akin to that which continually inspired Kant, never lets his work become so stubbornly remote from the exigencies of historical life. As one reads these essays one discovers Gadamer's deep engagement with his topic and one discovers that his engagement is not just with texts, but with the time of the texts at hand, so that there emerges a vivid sense of the stakes of what is thought and said—for philosophy, of course, but also for history and the life of culture and peoples.

So when reading the essays collected in this volume one is well advised to remember the distances that Gadamer has crossed from Heidegger in a time of protracted silence. But, every distance notwithstanding, there remains a deeper kinship between them and so these essays are best read as emerging from a shared sense that thinking that lives up to its name is responsive to the finitude of factical life and understanding, to, in other words, the self-renewing capacity of life to throw itself into darkness. Such a sensibility is well expressed in a phrase that Gadamer is fond of citing from Heidegger and that Heidegger himself loved to repeat: "Das Leben ist diesig, es nebelt sich immer ein." For both the ambiguity and withdrawal of the grounds of what can be thought and spoken is a decisive experience which tinges all that can be thought and said. For both this means that philosophy always thinks and speaks *out of* and, when it is strict in its reflexivity, *to* limits. For Heidegger this means attentiveness to the end of philosophy, an event which is never a simple cessation but an experience of limits, while for Gadamer this means attentiveness to the hermeneutic play of finite truth as forging the openness of traditions. But however they specify this experience of limits, both regard it as the task of thinking to solicit, even to love, the limit. Given this kindred sensibility, it is no surprise then that once Gadamer has found the distance appropriate to such a profound affinity, once he turns to write about Heidegger, he does so by taking up a theme that marks perhaps their point of closest contact and, arguably, a point that Gadamer had explored with more persistence even than Heidegger, namely, the question of the work of art. Both Gadamer and Heidegger begin with, and see themselves as going significantly beyond, "the idealistic aesthetics that had ascribed a special significance to the work of art as the organon of a nonconceptual understanding" (101). So, in 1960, when Gadamer writes the introduction to the Reclam edition of Heidegger's "Origin of the Work of Art" he is able to conclude by saying that "the thinking that conceives all art as poetry and that discloses that the work of art is language is itself still on the way to language" (109).

Many themes run through the essays collected here—one reads about the existential and religious dimensions of Heidegger's thought, about Heidegger's efforts to out-Greek the Greeks, about Heidegger's relation to metaphysics and its language, as well as about Kant and the turns in Heidegger's thought—but among the issues that simultaneously unite and divide Gadamer and Heidegger, three can be singled out as forming the most pervasive and significant axes of their relationship and as providing a tension propelling these essays forward in a creative manner: the relation of art and truth, the limits of the claims of language, and the aporias of history and tradition. But it is the last theme—the question of history at the present historical juncture—that marks the point of the most severe dispute between Heidegger and Gadamer, and so a few comments about it are in order.

Gadamer is one of the few figures in the last two hundred years of the continental tradition who does not advertise his thought as the overcoming of metaphysics and the inauguration of a new beginning. That does not mean that he understands himself as a metaphysical thinker. Far from it. Gadamer's hermeneutics is not metaphysics by another name; rather it is a reply to two of the most prominent concerns—namely the question of the universal claims of language and the discovery of the force of history and factical life— that have come forward with the decision that metaphysical assumptions have lost their tenability. But, since hermeneutic theory takes to heart the weight and power of history—as a dual and conflicted movement of the future and the past—it can make no claims to be the signal of a new beginning. The claims that have been made in that direction are well rehearsed: Kant's claim to be instituting a Copernican revolution in philosophy begins this tendency, Hegel's claim to think out of the exhaustion of his age to the perfection of the possibilities of history accelerates the question of metaphysics, and the intentions guiding a wide range of philosophers from Marx through Kierkegaard and Nietzsche only magnify the project of overcoming metaphysics. Heidegger's project of the destruction of metaphysics belongs to this tradition as its summit. Gadamer takes up the first formulations of this project in Heidegger in discussing the text "What is Metaphysics?," showing that Heidegger's first attempt at overcoming metaphysics "was still couched in the language of metaphysics" (46). In his text Heidegger relies upon the self-interrogating question that serves as the title of that essay—as Heidegger indicates "what is it," "*ti estin*," is the preeminent metaphysical question—to dislodge his own analysis of metaphysics from the empire of metaphysical representation. But, as Gadamer notes, Heidegger's own returns to this text (he wrote an epilogue in 1943 and a preface in 1949) are themselves indicators that his early attempts to ask a question completely outside the orbit of metaphysical reflections, the question of 'the nothing,' fail because "the question concerning "nothing" was introduced expressly as a metaphysical question" (46). Nonetheless, the project of the destruction of metaphysics remains "the monumental theme" and "subject of Heidegger's later thought experiments" (46). To understand Heidegger one needs to understand how crucial the destruction of metaphysics is. On the other hand, to understand Gadamer one needs to understand the power of sedimentation that leads him to suggest that such destruction is never fully realizable.

   In this a difference between Heidegger and Gadamer is manifested. Gadamer himself is alert to this difference and so in the preface to *Truth and Method* acknowledges that "Heidegger, like many of my critics, might see in this a lack of ultimate radicality in the drawing of conclusions." But Gadamer is undeterred by such criticisms and insists rather that "the finitude of understanding is the manner in which the reality, resistance, the absurd and the unintelligible find their validation. One who takes this finitude seriously must take the reality of history seriously." In other words, in his notion of effective historical consciousness, Gadamer understands himself as maintaining Heidegger's early insights into the finitude of factical life and as giving history its due. And so Gadamer understands this apparent difference with Heidegger as more a matter of a difference of emphasis than as a fundamental dispute. That is part of what he means when he says that "the break with tradition that took place in Heidegger's thought represented just as much an incomparable renewal of tradition" (70). Such a comment is not in the least a retreat from the radicality of the criticisms that Heidegger levels against the tradition he characterizes as ontotheological; rather, it serves as a reminder of the complications of the ineluctibility of history for thinking.

   The discovery that thinking is never unenvironed and that history has always already registered itself as a necessary topic for philosophy entails the radical problematization of the relation of thinking and its history. That is why the question of the nature of tradition—the forces whereby canons and disciplines are formed and submitted to scrutiny—has emerged with such prominence today. One might even say that this question of history is among the defining questions of what has come to be called "continental philosophy"—a phrase that should not be understood as a geographical designation, but as naming this readiness to index thinking to the reality of history. Both Heidegger and Gadamer address this topic of history and tradition, and both do so with a keen sense of the crisis and extremity of the present age. But, in the end, there remains the matter of this difference of emphasis: while Heidegger prefers to see in the present historical situation the signals of "another beginning" and the end of a long, exhausted tradition, Gadamer is inclined to take this situation as the moment in which the past becomes visible in a different light. Gadamer's sense then is that there are surprises to be found in history—in the future, of course, but not only there.

Much more could be said about the relation between Gadamer and Heidegger. The issues that surface between them are among the most pressing and difficult questions of this era which their work has helped define. But there is perhaps no better way to begin to take up those matters than by reading the essays that follow. In them one reads Gadamer reading Heidegger. But one finds more than even a highly original and insightful examination of Heidegger's work: one witnesses the complex event of a subtle interpreter of philosophic texts and movements interpreting a set of texts and a movement that gave shape and impulse to his own beginnings.

Reading these essays one senses that they are also an act of homage of one philosopher to another, of a student to his teacher. Written from a distance and after a prolonged silence, these pieces provide testimony of the abiding affinity of the philosophical projects animating Heidegger and Gadamer. They are not uncritical of Heidegger, but the critique here arises out of an uncommon alchemy of imagination, rigor, and insight and a fidelity so deep that, as Nietzsche says, it must include some element of treason.

CHAPTER ONE

EXISTENTIALISM AND THE PHILOSOPHY OF EXISTENCE (1981)

Nowadays, when existentialism is spoken of in philosophical circles, its meaning is taken for granted. Yet, quite a few different types of things fall under this heading, although they are certainly neither without a common denominator nor lacking an internal coherence. With existentialism one thinks of Jean-Paul Sartre, Albert Camus, and Gabriel Marcel; of Martin Heidegger and Karl Jaspers; perhaps also of the theologians, Bultman and Guardini. Actually, the word *existentialism* was a French creation. It was introduced by Sartre in the 1940s—during the very period that Paris was occupied by the Germans—as he was developing the philosophy that he later presented in his voluminous book *Being and Nothingness*. He was acting on the stimulus he had received from his studies in Germany during the 1930s. One could say that a special constellation led to his new, productive response—a constellation in which his interest in Hegel, Husserl, and Heidegger had been awakened in the same way and at the same time.

But it must be made clear that the German stimulus standing behind this, which is mainly associated with Heidegger's name, was in essence completely different from that which Sartre himself had produced from it. At that time one referred to such things in

1

Germany with the expression *philosophy of existence,* and the word *existential* was quite in vogue during the late 1920s. If it was not "existential," it simply did not count. It was primarily Heidegger and Jaspers who were known as the representatives of this movement, although neither of them met this characterization with real conviction or approval. After the war, Heidegger delivered a thorough and well-founded rejection of the Sartrean brand of existentialism in the well-known "Letter on Humanism"; and in the middle of the 1930s, after observing the devastating consequences of the uncontrolled existential emotionalism that had strayed into the mass hysteria of the National Socialist movement, the horrified Jaspers hurriedly moved the concept of "the existential" back to its secondary position and return reason to a position of primacy. *Reason and Existence* was one of the most beautiful and effective publications of Jaspers to come out of the 1930s. In this work he made an appeal to the exceptional cases of Kierkegaard and Nietzsche and sketched out his theory of the "encompassing," which incorporated both reason and existence. What bestowed the word *existence* with such power then? Certainly not the usual, normal grade-school use of the word, meaning "to exist," "existent," or "existence," as it would be found in phrases such as *the question of the existence of God* or *the existence of the external world.* No, a special expression lent the word *existence* its then-new conceptual character. This took shape under some specific conditions that need to be brought into view. The use of the word in this new, emphatic sense can be traced back to the Danish writer and thinker Søren Kierkegaard. He wrote in the 1840s, but his effect on the world and especially on Germany was not felt until the beginning of this century. A Swabian minister by the name of Christoph Schrempf arranged a translation of the complete works of Kierkegaard with Diederichs. The translation had a somewhat loose style but was exceptionally readable. As this translation became well known, it contributed a great deal to the movement that was later given the name the *philosophy of existence.*

Kierkegaard's own situation in the 1840s was determined by his critique of Hegelian speculative idealism, a critique motivated by his Christian faith. It was out of this context that the word *existence* gained its specific *pathos.*[a] Schelling's thought had already brought a new element to bear on the matter when, in his profound speculations about the relationship of God to his creation, he postulated a distinction within God himself. He spoke of the foundation in God and of the existence in God, which in turn allowed for the discovery that freedom was firmly rooted in the Absolute and provided for a deeper understanding of the nature of human freedom. Kierkegaard picked up this thought-motif of Schelling's, and he transplanted it into the polemical context of his critique of Hegel's speculative dialectic, a dialectic in which all is mediated and united in syntheses.

But what presented a particular challenge to Christianity—and especially to the Protestant church—was Hegel's claim to have raised the truth of Christianity to the level of an intellectual concept and to have completely reconciled faith and knowledge to one another. This challenge was taken up on many sides. Feuerbach, Ruge, Bruno Bauer, David Friedrich Strauss, and finally, Marx come to mind. But it was Kierkegaard who, driven by his own religious distress, had the deepest insight into the paradox of faith. His famous first work had the challenging title *Either/Or*. It programmatically expressed what was lacking in Hegel's speculative dialectic: the decision between "either/or," upon which human existence—and Christian existence in particular—is actually based. Nowadays one uses the word *existence* spontaneously in such contexts—as I just did—with an emphasis that translocates it completely from its scholastic origins. This usage can certainly be found in other expressions, such as in the phrase *the struggle for existence*—in which we are all engaged—or when one says, "my existence depends on it." These are phrases with a special emphasis, yet one that certainly reminds us more of the religion of hard cash [*harte Taler*] than the fear and trembling of the Christian heart. But when someone like Kierkegaard says of Hegel, the most famous philosopher of his time, that the absolute professor in Berlin has forgotten "to exist" [*das Existieren*], one finds in this sarcastic polemic a clear and emphatic reference to the basic human situation of choosing and deciding—one whose Christian and religious gravity cannot be muddled or played down by reflection and dialectical mediation.

How is it that this critique of Hegel, which came out of the first half of the nineteenth century, was instilled with new life in our century? To grasp this one must visualize the catastrophe of World War I and what its outbreak and development meant to the cultural consciousness of European humanity. The bourgeois society, spoiled by the long period of peace, had developed a belief in progress and a cultural optimism that came to characterize the liberal age. All of this collapsed in the storm of the war, which in the end was completely different from all those that had preceded it. The course of the war was not decided by personal courage or military genius but, rather, by the outcome of the competition between the heavy industries of all the different countries. The horror of matériel battles [*Material-schlachten*], in which innocent nature, fields and woods, villages and cities were devastated, in the end left those in the trenches and dug-outs with no room for any thought except "one day, when everything is over," as Carl Zuckmayer had expressed it then.

The extent of this insanity outstripped the youth's powers of comprehension. They had come to the struggle with an idealistic enthusiasm and a willingness to make sacrifices, but it soon became clear to the youth on all sides that the old forms of chivalrous—if often cruel and bloody—honor had lost their place. What remained was a nonsensical and unreal event—one that was also founded on the unreality of the overheated nationalism that had in turn caused the workers' movement, the internationale, to explode. It was no wonder that the intellectual leaders of that time asked, "What has gone astray with our belief in science, with our belief that the world was being made a more humane place and that its safety was being insured by the increasing amount of regulation? What had gone astray with the presumed development of society towards progress and freedom?"

It is obvious that the profound cultural crisis that came over the whole European culture at that time would have to express itself philosophically, and it is just as obvious that this would be especially pronounced in Germany, whose radical transformation and collapse was the most visible and catastrophic expression of the general absurdity. The critique of the reigning educational idealism [*Bildungs-idealismus*], which was supported primarily by the continuing presence of Kantian philosophy in academia, pervaded during these years and stripped academic philosophy as a whole of its credibility. A consciousness of this complete lack of orientation filled the spiritual situation of 1918, a situation into which I myself had begun to peer.

One can imagine how the two men, Jaspers and Heidegger, first encountered and approached one another when they first met in Freiburg in 1920. That meeting was occasioned by the sixtieth birthday of the founder of phenomenology, Edmund Husserl. Both viewed from a critical distance the academic hustle and bustle and the academic style of affected behavior. A philosophical friendship was founded then—or was it an attempt at a friendship that was never a complete success? It was motivated by a shared resistance to the old and a common will to new, radical forms of thinking. Jaspers had just begun to mark out his own philosophical position. In *The Psychology of World Views,* he devoted a lot of space to Kierkegaard (among others). Heidegger pounced upon Jaspers with his own peculiar form of sinister energy—and simultaneously radicalized him. He wrote a long, critical exposé of Jaspers's *The Psychology of World Views,* in which he followed Jaspers's thought to its bold and extreme consequences. This critique remained unpublished at that time, but it has since been published.

In the aforementioned book Jaspers analyzes the different world-views of representative figures [*Gestalten*]. His intention was to show how the different ways of thinking are played out in the praxis of life, because even world-views extend beyond the binding generalities of the scientific orientation to the world. World-views are dispositions of the will that rest, as we now say, upon "existential decisions." Jaspers described what all of the different forms of existence that can be differentiated in this way have in common with the concept of boundary situation [*Grenzsituation*]. By boundary situations he meant such situations whose boundary character demonstrated the limits of scientific mastery of the world. One such boundary situation is the appearance of something that no longer can be conceived of as just another example of a general rule and, hence, a case where one can no longer rely on the scientific control of calculable processes. Some examples of such a situation would be death, which we all must face; guilt, which everyone must carry; or the whole formation of a person's life, in which each of us as an individual—that one and only individual—must come to realize himself or herself. It is meaningful to say that it is precisely in these boundary situations where what one is first really emerges. This emerging, this stepping out of the controllable, calculable reactions and ways of behaving of social beings, constitutes the concept of existence.

Jaspers had stumbled upon the thematization of the boundary situation in his critical appropriation of science and in his recognition of its limits. He had the good fortune of being in the proximity of Max Weber, a figure of truly giant scientific stature whom he admired and followed, although ultimately with critical and self-critical questions. This great sociologist and polyhistorian represented, not only for Jaspers but also for my own generation, the grandeur and complete absurdity of the internal asceticism of the modern scientist. His incorruptible scientific conscience and his passionate impetus compelled him to a downright quixotic self-restriction. This consisted of the fact that he detached completely from the scientific, objective realm of knowledge the living, acting human beings, the very human beings who were confronted by these ultimate decisions; but at the same time he gave them the duty to know, that is, they were to pledge themselves to an "ethics of responsibility." Max Weber became the advocate, founder, and harbinger of a value-free sociology. But this did not mean at all that a colorless and bloodless scholar pushed his spiel about methodology and objectification but that this was a man of powerful temperament whose boundless political and moral passion demanded of himself and others such self-restriction. In the eyes of this great researcher, to go so far as to make armchair prophecies was absolutely the worst thing one could do. However, Max Weber was not only a model for Jaspers; he also served as a counterexample that led Jaspers to explore more deeply the limits of the scientific orientation to the world and to develop, if I might say so, a version of reason that transcends these limits. That which he presented in his *Psychology of World Views* and later in his three-volume magnum opus, *Philosophy*, was—even if directed by his personal passions—an impressive philosophical recapitulation and conceptual unfurling of the negative and positive <elements> aroused by the gigantic figure of Max Weber. He was constantly dogged by the question of how the incorruptible purity of scientific research, on the one hand, and the imperturbability of the will and feelings that he encountered in the existential weight of this man, on the other hand, could be grasped and gauged within the medium of thought.

Heidegger started from completely different assumptions. Unlike Jaspers, he had not been educated in the spirit of the natural sciences and medicine. Although one would generally not have guessed it, his genius had allowed him to keep up with academic developments in the natural sciences as a young man. The minor subjects that he chose in his examination for his doctorate were mathematics and physics! But his real focus lay elsewhere—in the historical world. Above all, the history of theology, which he had intensively pursued, and philosophy and its history captured his interest. He had been a student of the neo-Kantians Heinrich Rickert and Emil Lask. Then he found himself under the influence of the masterful art of phenomenological description, and he took as his model the superb analytical technique and the concrete, factual approach [Sachblick] of his master, Edmund Husserl. But beyond this, he had been schooled by yet another master—Aristotle. He had become familiar with Aristotle quite early on, but as one would expect, the modern interpretation of Aristotle that had served as his introduction quickly began to appear questionable to him. This interpretation had been rendered by Catholic neo-Scholasticism, and on the basis of his own religious and philosophical questions, it appeared inappropriate to the subject matter. So, he attended school with Aristotle once again—this time alone—and gained for himself an immediate, living understanding of the beginnings of Greek thinking and questioning, an understanding that transcended all mere erudition, was immediately evident, and possessed the compelling power of the simple. In addition, this young man, who at this time was slowly freeing himself from and extending himself beyond his own narrow regional environment, found himself confronted by a new climate: The rages of World War I ushered in a new spirit that demanded expression everywhere. The currents of Bergson, Simmel, Dilthey, maybe not Nietzsche directly but certainly philosophy beyond the scientific orientation of neo-Kantianism flowed in on him, and so, with all of the qualifications of the inherited and acquired erudition and with an innate, deep passion for questioning, he became the authentic spokesman of the new thinking taking shape in the field of philosophy.

Certainly Heidegger was not alone. This reaction to the disappearing educational idealism of the era preceding the war revealed itself in many fields. One thinks of the dialectical theology, which in Karl Barth raised the talk of God to a new problem and with Franz Overbeck threw out the calm balance that had been established between Christian proclamation and historical research—a balance represented by liberal theology. And one thinks in general of the critique of idealism connected with the rediscovery of Kierkegaard.

But there were still other crises in the life of science and culture that could be felt everywhere. I remember that van Gogh's correspondence was published at that time and that Heidegger loved

quotations from him. The appropriation of Dostoyevsky also played
an immense role at this time. The radicality of this portrayal of
human beings, the passionate questioning of society and progress,
the intensive fashioning and suggestive conjuring up of human ob-
sessions and labyrinths of the soul—one could continue endlessly. It
is easy to see how the philosophical thought that was compressed
into the concept of existence was the expression of a newly released,
very prevalent *Dasein*-emotion. One recalls the then-contemporary
poetry, the expressionistic stammering of words, or perhaps the bold
beginnings of modern painting, all of which demanded a response.
One thinks of the virtually revolutionary effect that Oswald Spengler's
The Decline of the West had on everyone's souls. So it was in the air
and Heidegger was uttering the word of the hour when he, in a
radicalization of Jaspers's thought, characterized human existence as
such by way of a reference to the notion of a boundary situation and
brought it newly in view.

Actually, they approached the feeling of existence of those
years from two completely different points of departure and with
two completely different thought impulses, when Jaspers, on the one
hand, and Heidegger, on the other, elevated this feeling to the level
of a philosophical concept. Jaspers was a psychiatrist and apparently
an astonishing, wide-ranging reader. When I first came to Heidelberg
as a follower of Jaspers, someone showed me the bench in the
Koestersschen Bookstore where Jaspers sat for exactly three hours
every Friday morning and had all of the new releases laid out before
him. And without exception he ordered a large package of books to
be delivered to his house every week. With the self-confidence of an
important spirit and the posture of a schooled, critical observer, he
was able to find nourishment in any of the diverse areas of scientific
research that had some import for philosophy. He was able to mesh a
conscience or, better, the conscientiousness of his own thought with
the awareness of his own participation in the actual research. This
gave him the insight that scientific research meets up with insur-
mountable boundaries when it encounters the individuality of existence and the obligatoriness of its decisions.

Thus, in essence Jaspers reestablished in the context of our
time the old Kantian distinction that critically marked the boundaries
of theoretical reason, and he refounded in practical reason and its
implications the actual realm of philosophical and metaphysical truths.
By making an appeal for the grand tradition of occidental history, its

metaphysics, its art and religion, in which human existence became aware of its own finitude, its release into boundary situations, and its surrender to its own existential decisions, Jaspers made metaphysics possible once again. In the three lengthy volumes of his *Philosophy,* the "World Orientation," "Existential Elucidation," and "Metaphysics," he circumscribed the entire area of philosophy in meditations possessing a uniquely personal tone and stylistic elegance. One of his chapter headings reads "The Law of the Day and the Passion for the Night"—those are sounds that one was not accustomed to hearing from the philosophical lectern in the era of epistemology. And Jaspers's comprehensive picture of the situation in 1930, which was presented in *Die geistige Situation der Zeit* [*Man in the Modern Age*] as the thousandth small volume from the Göschen Press, was also impressive because of its terseness and powerful observations. In those days, when I myself was still a student, it was said of Jaspers that he had a superiority that reigned supreme when it came to leading discussions. By contrast, his style of lecturing sounded like noncommittal chatter or a casual talk with an anonymous companion. Later, when he moved to Basel after the war, he constantly followed contemporary events with the attitude of the moralist. He frequently made an existential appeal to the public consciousness and argued philosophically for positions on such controversial issues as collective guilt or the atom bomb. His thinking always seemed to transpose the most personal experiences into the communicative scene.

The young Heidegger's appearance and bearing was completely different: A dramatic entrance, a diction with great force, the focus with which he lectured—he cast a spell over the entire audience. The intention of this teacher of philosophy was in no way to make a moralistic appeal to the authenticity of existence. He certainly took part in such an appeal, and a good deal of his almost magical effect came from his natural gift to radiate such an appeal from his very being as well as in his lectures. But his real intention was a different one. How should I say it? His philosophical questioning was undoubtedly motivated by a desire to clarify the deep disquiet that had been aroused by his own religious calling and by his dissatisfaction with the then-contemporary theology and philosophy. From early on Heidegger strove toward a completely different, radical commitment for thinking, a commitment for thinking that referenced existence, and this gave him his revolutionary force. The question that so moved him and to which he brought the entirety of

the troubled self-esteem of those years was the oldest and first question of metaphysics: the question of Being. He asked how a finite,
frail human Dasein—one whose death is certain—could understand
itself in its Being in spite of its temporality; indeed, how it could
experience Being, not as a privation, as a defect, or as a merely fleeing
pilgrimage of earthlings journeying through this life toward a participation in the eternity of the divine, but rather as the distinguishing
feature of being human. It is astonishing how this fundamental intention of Heidegger's questioning, which presupposed a constant
dialogue with metaphysics and with the thinking of the Greeks, as
well as with the thinking of St. Thomas, Leibniz, Kant, and Hegel,
was completely missed at first by many contemporaries who shared
Heidegger's philosophical interest.

The friendship that had begun to form between Heidegger
and Jaspers was certainly based primarily upon their common rejection of the settled academic teaching, upon the bustle of "idle talk,"
and upon the anonymity of its responsibility. As both began to articulate their own thinking more clearly, the tensions between Jaspers's
personalized manner of thinking and that of Heidegger, who devoted
himself completely to his mission for thinking, to the "matter" for
thinking, began to show themselves in an ever-sharper form. Jaspers
often employed the critical expression *encasement* [*Gehäuse*] in reference to all didactically hardened thought, and he did not hesitate to
use this against Heidegger's effort to revive the question of Being. In
spite of this, Jaspers wrestled during his whole life with the challenge
that Heidegger presented to him. This has just recently been impres-
sively documented by the publication of Jaspers's notes on Heidegger.

However, it is correct that *Being and Time,* Heidegger's great
firstborn, presented two very different aspects. What brought about
its revolutionary effect was the temporally critical timber and the
existential engagement, which were expressed in a vocabulary emu-
lating Kierkegaard's. On the other hand, Heidegger leaned so heavily
on Husserl's phenomenological idealism that Jaspers's resistance is
understandable. But as Heidegger pursued his way of thinking, he
was truly led beyond any dogmatic "encasement." He had himself
spoken of the "turn" [*Kehre*] that befell his thinking, and in fact his
thinking shattered all academic standards because he attempted to
find a new language for his thought as he pursued the theme of art,
the Hölderlin interpretations, and the extreme thought of Friedrich

Nietzsche. He never claimed to espouse a new doctrine. When the large edition of his writings, the one that followed his own arrangement, began to appear, he gave it the following epigraph: "Ways, not works"; and his later works did in fact always present new ways and new thought experiments.[b] He began working on these ways years before his political involvement, and after the short episode of his political blunder, he continued without a visible break in the direction he had already begun.

Of course, the most astonishing aspect of Heidegger's great effect was that in the 1920s and early 1930s, before he fell into political disfavor, he was able to generate such an unheard-of enthusiasm among his auditors and readers and that, after the war, he was able to regain that effect. This took place after a period of relative seclusion. He was unable to publish during the war because, after he had fallen into political disfavor, no one would give him any paper. After the war he could not teach because he had been suspended due to his involvement as a former Nazi chancellor. But, in spite of all this, he developed an almost overpowering presence during the postwar period when the German material and spiritual life was being reconstructed. He did not do this as a teacher; he spoke only rarely before students. But he entranced an entire generation with his lectures and publications. It was almost life threatening—and presented the organizer with nearly unsolvable problems—when Heidegger would announce one of his cryptic lectures. No lecture hall was large enough during the 1950s. The excitement that emanated from his thinking was picked up by everyone, even by those who did not understand him. One could no longer call what he was voicing in the profundity of his later speculations and in the solemn pathos of his interpretations of poetry (Hölderlin, George, Rilke, Trakl, and so on) *philosophy of existence.* The previously mentioned "Letter on Humanism" was a formal rejection of the irrationalism of the pathos of existence [*Existenzpathos*], which had earlier accompanied the dramatic effect of his thinking but which was never his actual aim. What he saw at work in French existentialism was very distant from his thinking. The "Letter on Humanism" addresses that in very clear language. It was the theme of ethics that the French readers missed in Heidegger— as did Jaspers as well. Heidegger defended himself against this expectation and demand, not because he underestimated the question of ethics or the social plight of Dasein, but rather because his mission in thinking compelled him to ask more radical questions. "For some time we have not considered the nature of action decisively enough" reads the first sentence of the "Letter on Humanism," and it becomes clear what this sentence, written in an age of social utilitarianism and completely "beyond good and evil," means: The task of thinking cannot be to run along behind self-dissolving ties and self-weakening solidarities and hold up the admonishing finger of the dogmatist. Rather, the task was much more to think about what lies at the bottom of this disintegration that has been brought about by the industrial revolution and to call thinking back to itself, thinking that had otherwise been reduced to calculating and producing.

It is the same with the alleged inattention to the social problems of the "we," which is known in philosophy as the problem of intersubjectivity: Heidegger first displayed in his ontological critique the prejudices contained the concept of the subject, and therewith he incorporated into his thought the critique of consciousness practiced by Marx, Nietzsche, and Freud. This means, however, that *Dasein* and "Being-with" [*Mit-Sein*] are equally primordial, and "Being-with" does not signify the being together of two subjects. Rather, "Being-with" is a primordial mode of "Being-we"—a mode in which the I is not supplemented by a you; instead, it encompasses a primary commonality that cannot be reached by the Hegelian thought of "Spirit." "Only a god can save us."

We ask in closing, what in the thinking of these men is still alive and what is dead? This is a question that every present must put to the voices of its past. It is true that since the 1960s a new mood has entered the spiritual life. The mood of the younger generations is characterized by a new feeling of disenchantment, a new inclination toward technical certainty and control and an avoidance of risks and uncertainties. The pathos of "existence" sounds as strange to these people as the pathos of the great poetic gestures of Hölderlin and Rilke, and the figures who presented us with the so-called philosophy of existence are today almost completely dormant. The fine structure of the movement of Jaspers's reflection with its intense personal pathos will scarcely be able to have an effect in the age of mass existence and emotional solidarity. Heidegger, on the other hand, remains surprisingly present in spite of all this. Indeed, for the most part he is rejected with an haughty air—or celebrated in an almost ritualistic recapitulation. Both responses go to show that one cannot easily get around him. It is not so much the pathos of existence found in his beginnings that allows him to maintain his presence as it is the unflagging perseverance with which a natural genius in thinking pursued his own religious and philosophical questions—his own expressive gestures often pushed to the point of unintelligibility and yet maintaining the unmistakable signet of a genuine perplexity in thinking. One must think in global terms if one wants to properly grasp Heidegger's presence. Whether in America or the Far East, whether in India, Africa, or in Latin America—the impetus for thinking that emanated from him is to be found everywhere. The global destiny that mechanization and industrialization holds has found its thinker in Heidegger, but at the same time, the multiplicity and multivocity of the human legacy has won through him a new presence, one that will be brought into the world conversation of the future.

So one can say in closing, the greatness of spiritual figures can be measured by their ability to overcome, by virtue of what they have to say, the stylistic resistance and stylistic distance that separates them from the present. Not the philosophy of existence, but the men who have gone through this phase of existential and philosophical pathos and then proceeded beyond it belong among the philosophical partners in a philosophical conversation that is not only of yesterday; it will continue through tomorrow and the days after.

CHAPTER TWO

MARTIN HEIDEGGER—
75 YEARS (1964)

On the 26 September 1964, Martin Heidegger turned 75. When a man who achieved world renown so early in his life lives to such a biblical age, his life serves as a standard against which we measure the passage of time. Soon it will be a half-century that this intellect has been having its effect on us. As it tends to be in the rhythm of time, so too is it in Heidegger's case; the revolutionary impetus that emanated from him has receded from the surface of our consciousness. New tendencies are emerging in our temporal consciousness that resist the power and force of an intellect that once permeated everything. His prodding gestures are beginning to encounter a dulled sensibility, one that has become receptive to another trend. Words that were once so vibrant now seem manneristic, artificial, and rigid. Things tend to go that way. The spiritual tends to pass away, perhaps to return one day and speak its word anew in a changed world.

The further we enter into the second half of the twentieth century, the greater our awareness becomes that an epochal break separates our own age, and what it accepts as valid, from all times past. A new phase of the industrial revolution, introduced by modern physics with its promising and yet threatening development of atomic energy, has enveloped the earth. The rational regulation of the economy and politics, of our living together with other human

15

beings, of our living together with other peoples, and of the interactions of the political power groups of today, defines the spirit of our age. The hopes and expectations of the younger generation are no longer directed toward the undetermined, the unmeasured, or the uncanny, but toward a functional, rational administration of the world. Sober planning, sober calculation, and sober observation exert a constant and coercive force on the forms that our spiritual expressions now take. The speculative profundities, dark oracles, and prophetic emotionalism that once held us captive are now shunned. In philosophy this manifests itself in a growing trend toward logical clarity, exactness, and verifiability of all assertions. Once again science is adorned with an unconditional faith, be it in the form of Marxist atheism or a belief in the technical perfectionism of the Western world; once again an unconditional faith in science demands of philosophy a justification of its very existence.

One must be aware of this if one does not want to understand Heidegger's work merely from a historical perspective, if one does not want to view it as a slow movement of thinking from the recent past that grows ever more strange as it develops. An awareness of this shift allows for a placement of Heidegger next to the present, or better, it allows for an understanding his work as a question posed to the present. The technical perfectionism of our age is not a refutation of Heidegger's philosophy; on the contrary, he thought it with a rigor and radicality that remains unequaled in the academic philosophy of our century.

Of course, a great deal of both the early and later Heidegger sounds like cultural criticism. This is one of the most peculiar concomitants of the technological age; our confidence in technological progress is called into doubt by the plaintive cries concerning the uniformity, the leveling and flattening taking hold in every aspect of our lives. These critiques of contemporary culture accuse the technological culture of reducing and repressing freedom, and yet their very existence proves the contrary. Heidegger, on the other hand, is much more ambiguous. From the beginning his sharp and vehement critique of the "they," of "curiosity" and "idle talk," and therefore of the "publicness" and "mediocrity" in which the human Dasein "for the moment and for the most part" remains was only a secondary motif (although one that could not be ignored). To be sure, at first this shrill critique drowned out the basic motif and focus of Heideggerian thought. Still, the necessary concomitance of authenticity with inauthenticity, of the essential [*Wesen*] with the inessential [*Unwesen*], of truth with error [*Irre*] defined his task. Indeed, Heidegger is not to be placed in the ranks of the romantic critics of technology—he attempts to seize the very essence of technology, even to think in advance of that essence, because he attempts to think what is.

Whoever knew the young Heidegger could even attest to this based upon his external appearance: It did not correspond in the least to our usual image of a philosopher. I remember how I first met him in the Spring of 1923. I had already heard murmurs in the academic circles at Marburg of a genius who had surfaced in Freiburg, and handwritten reports concerning the unconventional diction of a certain assistant to Husserl were being passed from hand to hand. I went to visit him in his office at the University of Freiburg. Just as I turned into the corridor I saw someone coming out of his office who was accompanied by someone else—a small, dark man. I waited patiently outside because I assumed there was another person still with Heidegger. But this other person was Heidegger. Of course, he was quite different from those whom I had heretofore known as professors of philosophy. He appeared more like an engineer or a technician: brief, matter of fact, aloof, full of bound energy and without the glib cultivation of *homo literatus* [educated human being].

However, if one wants to stick with the physiognomical, the first time one caught a glimpse of his eyes one knew who he was and is: a visionary. A thinker who sees. Indeed, as I see it the basis for Heidegger's uniqueness among all of the philosophical teachers of our time is that the things, which he portrays in a language that is highly unconventional and that often offends all "cultivated" expectations, are always depicted in a way in which they can be seen intuitionally. And this "seeing" occurs not only in momentary evocations in which a striking word is found and an intuition [*Anschauung*] flashes for a fleeting moment. The entire conceptual analysis is not presented as an argued progression from one concept to another; rather, the analysis is made by approaching the same <thing> from the most diverse perspectives, thus giving the conceptual description the character of the plastic arts, that is, the three-dimensionality of tangible reality.

The fundamental teaching of Husserl's phenomenology was that knowledge [*Erkenntnis*] is first and foremost viewing or intuition [*Anschauung*];[a] that is, it is achieved when a thing is seen

comprehensively with one beholding. Sense perception, which places
the object before the eye in its incarnate givenness, is the model
according to which all conceptual knowledge is to be thought. Everything hinges upon the intuitional fulfillment of what is intended
[*des Gemeinten*]. Indeed, we had already learned from Husserl's honest craft of thinking the art of description, in which one began by
patiently referring to and comparing the most varied and disparate
perspectives and then brought the intended phenomenon to a well-
rounded presentation through masterly stippling. What Husserl's phenomenological working method opened up seemed to be something
new—something new, because it strove to regain with new means
something of old that had been forgotten (and unlearned). No doubt,
the great ages of philosophizing, for instance that of Athens in the
fourth century or of Jena around the turn of the nineteenth century,
knew how to combine the same fullness of an intuition [*Anschauung*]
with the use of philosophical concepts so that the fullness of this
intuition would be engendered in the readers and auditors. When
Heidegger took the lectern, his thoughts were always prepared to the
last detail and, in the moment of the lecture, were brought to life in
the greatest detail. During the lecture, he would glance up again and
again and look sideways out of the window; he saw what he was
thinking, and he made us see. When asked about phenomenology,
Husserl was quite right to answer as he used to in the period directly
after World War I: "Phenomenology, that is me and Heidegger."

     I do not believe that Husserl followed the civil custom and
said, 'Heidegger and me.' He took his task with too much missionary
seriousness for that. It is quite possible that in the course of the
1920s he got the feeling that his student Heidegger was no collabora-
tor who was going to continue the patient work of his life. His rash
ascent to the top, the incomparable fascination he aroused, and his
stormy temperament surely must have made Husserl, the patient
one, as suspicious of Heidegger as he always had been of Max Scheler's
volcanic fire. And indeed, the student of this masterly technique of
thinking was different from his master. Heidegger was a person beset
by great questions and final things, a person who was shaken down
to the last fibers of his existence, who was concerned with God and
death, with Being and "nothing," and who had been called to thinking as the mission of his life. These were the burning questions of an
aroused generation whose pride in their cultural and educational

tradition had been shaken, the questions that plagued a generation crippled by the horrors of the materialistic slaughter of World War I, and these questions were also Heidegger's questions.

It was precisely at that time that van Gogh's correspondence appeared, whose picturesque turbulence mirrored the feeling of life [*Lebensgefühl*] of these years. Excerpts from these letters lay on Heidegger's desk under his inkwell and were quoted occasionally in his lectures. Dostoevski's novels also stirred us; the red Piper volumes flashed like beacons from every desk. One could sense the same distress in the lectures given by the young Heidegger, and this gave him an incomparable power of suggestion. In a whirl of radical questions—questions that Heidegger posed, that posed themselves to Heidegger, that he posed to himself—the chasm that had developed in the course of the last century between academic philosophy and the need for a world-view seemed to close.

Yet another aspect of Heidegger's external appearance revealed something most inward: his voice. This voice, which was then very strong and rich at lower pitches, seemed confined and, without being too loud, overtaxed when pushed to higher pitches during the excitement of the lecture. It always seemed to be near the edge, about to tumble over itself, alarming as it was itself alarmed. Obviously no deficiency in the voice or breathing techniques used in speaking pushed him to the outermost edge and final limit of speech. Rather, precisely the *being driven* to the outermost edge and the final limit of thinking seemed to be responsible for the loss of voice and breath.

People tell me that today this voice and way of giving lectures can be heard on recordings. I can well understand how the printed word gains a new dimension and becomes easier to comprehend when one hears the voice of the author in this way. In spite of this, I think that a member of the older generation who has personally experienced the exciting reality of one of Heidegger's lectures will excuse me for saying that this kind of technical reproduction of his self-disclosing thought experiment comes across like a mummification. There is no life in a mummy of thought. But in Heidegger's thought there was and is life. Life—trials and temptations, wagers, ways. One of the most peculiar paradoxes concerning the effect of Heidegger's thinking, so it seems to me, is that it has elicited a constantly growing stream of interpretations dedicated to his thinking but that attempt with the most meticulous care to order his thinking and systematically reconstruct his "teachings." This strikes me as paradoxical, regardless of whether it is done in an honest effort to understand his work or if it is the consequence of a bitter or perhaps hesitant rejection; to attempt to write a systematically developed summary of Heidegger's thought is not only futile but even pernicious. After his *Being and Time* in 1926—in which a single question is posed and explored—none of Heidegger's later works operate on a single, unified plane; they belong to different planes. They are like a constant ascent, in which all vantage points and perspectives are continuously shifted, an ascent in which one can easily lose one's way and then must retreat to the solid ground of the phenomenological intuition—only to set off again with a new ascent.

The power of the phenomenological intuition—people generally recognize that the analysis of world found in *Being and Time* is a masterpiece of phenomenological analysis, but at the same time they tend to think that his later writings become caught up more and more in inescapable, mythological skeins of concepts. There is something to that, insofar as these writings document a deficiency in language, one that led to some rather questionable rescue attempts. However, one should carefully avoid suggesting that this proves that Heidegger was losing his phenomenological power. One needs only to read the chapter on affect, passion, and feeling in the *Nietzsche* volumes to put any such suspicions to rest. Rather, the question to be asked is much more, "Why is Heidegger's power of phenomenological intuition, whose continuity we experience with astonishment in every encounter with Heidegger through the present day, still insufficient? What kind of task has he gotten himself into? From what kind of deficiency is he trying to save himself?"

His critics are in the habit of saying that after the so-called turn [*Kehre*] Heidegger's thinking no longer stood on solid ground. *Being and Time* is said to be a magnificent liberation, a work through which the call to the authenticity of Dasein was made and the business of philosophical thinking gained a new intensity and responsibility. But it is also said that after the turn, which is tied up with his topsy-turvy political folly brought on by his own ambition for power and his intrigue with the Third Reich, he no longer spoke of demonstrable things. Rather, like one initiated in the secrets of his God, he speaks only of "Being." A mythologist and Gnostic, he speaks as an initiate [*ein Wissender*]—without knowing what he is saying. Being withdraws. Being presences. "Nothing" nothings. Language speaks. What kind of beings are acting here? Are these names—perhaps code names—for a divinity? Is a theologian talking here—or better, a prophet who is foretelling the arrival of "Being?" And with what legitimation? Where in such indemonstrable chatter is the conscientiousness expected of thinking?

People ask such questions without recognizing that all of these Heideggerian expressions speak from the antithesis. They have been set with a provocative pungency *against* a certain habituation of thought, one that holds that it is the spontaneous activity of our thinking which "posits" something as an entity, negates something, or "coins" a word. The famous turn, of which Heidegger spoke to show the inadequacy of his transcendental conception of the self in *Being and Time,* is anything but an arbitrary reversal of a habit of thinking brought about by some voluntary decision. Rather, this was something that happened to him. It was not a kind of mystical inspiration, but a simple matter of thinking—something so simple and compelling, as it can sometimes happen with thinking, that it dares to push itself to the edge. It is therefore necessary to comprehend this matter of thinking [*Sache des Denkens*] that had come to Heidegger in a way that is true to the inner dynamics of the matter itself.

In the turn, Being becomes the point of departure; one no longer takes one's start from the consciousness that thinks Being, or from the Dasein that depends on Being, understands itself in its relationship to Being, and is concerned about its Being. Thus, Heidegger does not so much pose the question of Being in *Being and Time* as prepare for it. Then, after 1930, Heidegger began speaking of the "turn," although the first time he did this publicly was after World War II in his "Letter on Humanism"—perhaps one of his most beautiful essays due to its exceptionally relaxed style, written as though he meant to use the informal form of you [*du*]. This was, of course, preceded by a series of Hölderlin interpretations that indirectly bear witness to the fact that his thinking was in search of a new language more suited to new insights; these explications of Hölderlin's difficult poems and verses were in fact a process of identification. But to try to give an account of the violence he used to bring about such an identification would be a miserable undertaking. It could tell us only what anyone who has been following Heidegger's thought knows only too well; namely, that Heidegger resounded only what stood before him as his task, and as one truly obsessed with his own affairs [*Sache*], he was able to hear only what promised to be an answer to his own questions. What is much more astonishing is that Hölderlin's works were able to maintain such a presence for a thinker that he tried to think them as his own matter [*Sache*] and according to his own measure. It seems to me that no encounter with Hölderlin since Hellingrath's compares to Heidegger's in intensity and therewith also in disclosive power—in spite of all of the distortions and misrepresentations. It must have been a genuine release for Heidegger—a type of freeing of his tongue—when he found himself free to pursue new ways of thinking as an interpreter of Hölderlin. Now he could speak of heaven and earth, of mortals and gods, of parting and arriving, and of the desert and home—as well of that which had been thought and will be thought [*von etwas Gedachtem und zu Denkerdem*]. Later, when the lectures entitled "The Origin of the Work of Art" were published [1950], about which a great deal had already been heard back in 1936 in Freiburg, Zurich, and Frankfurt, one could indeed detect a new tone. The use of word *earth* gave the Being of the work of art a conceptual characterization that showed that Heidegger's Hölderlin interpretations (and these lectures) were stages on his way of thinking.

Whence came this way? Where did it lead? Was it a deadend, or did it lead to a destination? Certainly, it did not lead to a mountain peak from which one would be granted an unobstructed view of the surroundings, disclosing effortlessly the furrowed formations of the landscape. And certainly, it was also not without detours, backtracking, and false starts. In spite of this, Heidegger's later works do not present us with an aimless series of efforts that in the end prove to be a failure, simply because he is never able to state clearly what Being is—this Being that is not supposed to be the Being of a being [*Seiende*] is sometimes said to be able to be without a being and, at other times, is said to be unable to be without a being (or not: to "be?"). In every case, there is a beginning and a series of steps following a way.

The first question of the first beginning was: What is the Being of the human Dasein? Certainly not mere consciousness. But what kind of Being is this that neither lasts nor counts the way that the stars or mathematical truths do, but rather constantly dwindles like all life caught between birth and death, and yet in spite of its finitude and historicity is a "there" [*ein Da*],[b] a here, a now, a presence in the moment [*Gegenwart im Augenblick*], not an empty point, but a saturated temporality and a collected totality? The Being of the human Dasein is said to be just such a *"Da"* in which the future and past are not simply moments rolling toward and then away from the present; rather, the future is each individual's own future, and each individual's own history constitutes its own Being from the accident of birth on. Because this Dasein, which projects itself into its own future, must accept itself in its own finitude—a kind of discovery of oneself as "thrown" into Being—facticity becomes the key word, and not self-consciousness, reason, or spirit, that Heidegger used when he first introduced the question of Being.

But what is this *"Da"* that Heidegger was immediately to name "the Dasein in human beings," words that ring of gnostic mystery? Certainly this *"Da"* does not mean merely being present; rather, it signifies an event. Every *"Da,"* like all things earthly, dwindles, passes away, and is carried off into oblivion—yet, it is a *"Da"* precisely because it is finite, that is, aware of its own finitude. What is happening there [*da*], what happens as a *"Da,"* is what Heidegger later calls the *clearing of Being* [*Lichtung des Seins*]. A clearing is that into which one enters after walking endlessly in the darkness of a forest when, suddenly, there is an opening in the trees letting in the light of the sun—until one has walked through the clearing as well and the darkness envelops one anew. Certainly not a bad illustration of the finite fate of human beings. When Max Scheler died in 1927, Heidegger gave a speech in his honor during a lecture that ended in the words, "A way of philosophy falls into darkness once again."

But Heidegger's question concerning the Being of Dasein was not geared toward a new "characterization of human beings" or a new ontological founding of a philosophical anthropology. Certainly, such an anthropology could not have been based solely on *Angst* and death, or on boredom and nothing; it would obviously have to take into account pleasant emotions and constructive moods as well. However, because the question is concerned with "Being," it must linger at those sites where the *"Da"* stands out in relief before the receding beings, such as in the "nothing" of *Angst* or the emptiness of boredom. But the self-clearing of Being occurs not only in the *"Da"* that is the human being. It seems to me that Heidegger took a very important step in designating the work of art as an event of truth. He shows that the work of art is not merely the product of an ingenious creative process, but that it is a work that has its own brightness in itself; it is there [*da*], "so true, so fully existing [*so seiend*]." Anyone who has seen a Greek temple in the splendid mountain ranges of Greece will be able to follow Heidegger on this point: It is precisely in the small, almost delicate dimensions of these Greek temples, from which an elemental world of overpowering greatness appears to have been wrestled, that Earth and Heaven, the Stone and the Light are more authentic; they come forth into the *"Da"* of their true essence.

And again with the essay "The Thing" we reach a new plateau, one that offers another view. In this essay not only the artwork, that is, the event that opens up and supports a world, but also things used by human beings [*dem von Menschen Gebrauchten*] are granted existence and truth. Yet the thing only *is*—existing in itself and pressed toward nothing—because there *is* a clearing in the ancient forest of Being that encloses itself within itself.

Finally, the word, "Where the word breaks off, no thing can be." Heidegger has put even this poem by Stefan George [*"Das Wort"*] on the rack in his self-inquisition to interrogate "the word"—this most mysterious oddity that lies at the very heart and soul of the human spirit—about Being. One may be ill-disposed toward all of the Heideggerian formulations such as fate [*Geschick*] of Being, withdrawal of Being, forgetfulness of Being, and so on; but anyone who is not blind should be able to visualize what Heidegger sees, and in particular with reference to the word. We all know that there are words that function merely as signals (even if that which has been signaled is a real "nothing"), and then there are other words—and this is not confined to poetry—that bear witness *themselves* to that which they communicate. These words are, so to speak, proximate to something that is; they are neither replaceable nor exchangeable, a *"Da"* that discloses itself in its own act of speaking. It is obvious in this case what *empty* or *full* means. That it is "Being" that is absent or present there can be learned from carrying Heidegger's way of thinking to its conclusion.

To be sure, one must make an effort to see contemplatively [*denkend*] if one wants to discern the path that Heidegger's thinking takes and understand it as the unwavering pursuit of one thinker's question. Otherwise, Heidegger's thinking comes across as a hopeless meandering through the lightless twilight of a metaphysics forsaken by God. For it is true: this thinking lacks a language. Yet this "lack" itself will completely convince him that this thinking attempts its reflections in the midst of a forgetfulness of Being. It is enmeshed in our technical age, an age that views even language as a technical tool. Language has become a tooth on the cog of the "information theory." One encounters with Heidegger a deficiency of language—a linguistic impass that he himself ran up against. However, in the final analysis this deficiency is not merely the end result of a thinker's attempt to think the unconventional and unthought. Perhaps it has more the character of an occurrence, drifting in from the distance; a predicament in which we have all found ourselves at one time or other. Words no longer emerge like flowers. Instead, ways of talking become widespread, as schematic as the situations they are designed to control. And precisely the most abstract language of mathematical symbolism seems to be uniquely suited to the task of technically controlling and managing the world. A deficiency of language as such is not encountered at all. Obviously, there is a forgetfulness of this deficiency of language that is a type of counterpart to the forgetfulness of Being that Heidegger speaks of; indeed, the former may be the very expression and general proof of the latter.

Perhaps it was not to be avoided that this thinker's language often resembles a tormented stammering, for it is a language struggling to awaken from the forgetfulness of Being and to think only that which is worthy of thought. The same man whose words and phrases could be of such visual force and power that they were unparalleled by those of his philosophical contemporaries, whose words allowed us to think of materialized phenomena, whose words made something spiritual tangible—this same man extracts out of the shafts of language the most peculiar lumps, breaks up the extracted stones so that they completely lose their usual outline, and moves around in a world of fragmented word-rocks, searching, checking. These facets, artificially produced in this manner, carry his message. Sometimes he makes a real discovery; then the words spark suddenly, and one sees with one's own eyes what Heidegger is saying. Sometimes a tragic struggle for the right language and a concept with the ability to speak permeates Heidegger's work—in which case anyone wishing to think with him is necessarily drawn into the struggle.

Why this impass, this deficiency? Typically the philosopher's language is that of Greek metaphysics and its legacy, a language that has been passed on through the Latin of antiquity and the Middle

Ages to the national languages of contemporary times. Therefore, many conceptual words in philosophy are foreign words. But the great thinkers usually have the power to find new ways of expressing what they want to say—ways that their native tongue held ready for them. Plato and Aristotle, for example, created a conceptual language drawn from the living, flexible language of their contemporary Athenians. Likewise, Cicero came up with certain Latin words that could pass on Greek concepts. Similarly, Meister Eckhart at the beginning of the Middle Ages, Leibniz, Kant, and above all Hegel were able to develop new ways of expressing the conceptual language of philosophy. The young Heidegger was also able to draw upon the linguistic resources of his native Alemannic home and release new linguistic forces that have enriched our philosophical language.

However, the later Heidegger found himself in a much worse predicament. Not only the conceptual and linguistic habits of others continuously attempted to push him off the course set by his own questions, but even his own conceptual and linguistic habits exerted this pressure, habits that were determined by the tradition of occidental thought. His thinking is threatened in this way because his question is really a new one. It is not a metaphysical question concerning the highest being (God) and the Being of all beings. Rather, the concern is much more about what first opens up the area for such questions and forms the space in which these metaphysical questions move about. Indeed, Heidegger's question is concerned with something that the tradition assumes to be unquestionable: What is Being in the first place [überhaupt]? All of the great metaphysicians were unable to reply to this question because they always asked what made an entity an entity or what entities ultimately are. The conceptual tools that they had developed for use in their answers could offer Heidegger limited assistance with reference to his question. They always give a false appearance, as if it were somehow valid to offer assurances that the being that stood behind all of those previously known would one day show itself. But Heidegger's task was much more to become aware of that which, more than anything else, can become the object of knowledge, of that which first makes the knowledge itself, questioning itself, or thinking itself possible. Whoever attempts to think the area in which the relationship between thinking and that which has been thought first disintegrates, seems to get lost in the unthinkable.[c] That there is something at all and not nothing—this most radical exaggeration of the question of metaphysics speaks of Being as if it were something known. Is there a way of thinking that brushes against this unthinkable? Heidegger calls it "rememberance" [*Andenken*] and the dubious echo of "reverence" [*Andacht*] may well have been intended, in as much as the religious experience touches this unprethinkability [*Unvordenkliche*] of Being more than metaphysical thinking. And what can be said of thinking can also be said of the language of thinking. Language names the thinkable and that which has been thought; it has no word for the unprethinkability of Being. "Being is itself" said Heidegger, frustrating those curious about Being. Is "Being" nothing? Is "nothing" nothing? The paths Heidegger has taken, some of which were described previously, permit one to think what he has called *Being*. But how can it be said?

Heidegger's rescue attempts are violent. He is constantly rupturing the natural understanding of familiar words and forcing new meanings upon them—often basing this on etymological connections that no one else sees. The products of this approach are extremely manneristic expressions and provocations of our linguistic expectations.

Must it be so? Does not the natural language in its universal malleability always offer a new way to express what one has to say? And is it not the case that whatever does not allow itself to be said has been insufficiently thought? Perhaps. But we have no choice. Now that Heidegger has posed the question, we are obligated to continue our inquiry in the direction it delineates; we can only hope to be assisted by that found in his works which is accessible to our understanding. It is easy to poke fun at things unusual or violent. To improve on it is much more difficult. Certainly the game in which participants shove around the little ivory discs inscribed with Heidegger's conceptual jargon—a form of following Heidegger that is very common—should not be played. This type of scholasticism blocks the way into the opening formed by the question asked no less than the most caustic polemics.

But either way, Heidegger is there [*da*]. One cannot get around him nor—unfortunately—can one progress beyond him in the direction of his question. He blocks the path in a most disturbing way. He is an erratic block awash in a stream of thinking rushing toward technical perfection. But he is a block that cannot be budged from its place.

CHAPTER THREE

THE MARBURG
THEOLOGY (1964)

Let us think back to the 1920s, to that great, tension-filled time when the theological turn away from the historical and liberal theology was made, when the philosophical rejection of neo-Kantianism took place, when the Marburg school was dissolved, and when new stars rose in the philosophical heavens. At that time Eduard Thurneysen delivered a lecture to the community of Marburg theologians. For those of us who were younger, it was one of the first harbingers of the dialectical theology in Marburg. Upon its conclusion, it received the more or less hesitant blessings of the Marburg theologians. The young Heidegger also took part in this discussion. He had just come to Marburg as an associate professor, and to this day it is unforgettable to me how he closed his contribution to the discussion on the Thurneysenian lecture. After evoking the Christian skepticism of Franz Overbeck, Heidegger said that it was the true task of theology—a task that theology must find its way back to—to search for the word that was capable of beckoning one to and preserving one in faith. A genuine Heidegger sentence, full of ambiguity. As Heidegger said this sentence, it sounded as if he was setting forth a task for theology. But perhaps he was expressing a thought even more radical than the one he had just quoted; perhaps he was voicing a skepticism concerning the possibility of theology itself that transcended Franz Overbeck's attack on the theology of his time.

A stormy epoch of philosophical-theological debates broke forth then. On the one hand, there was the dignified coolness of Rudolf Otto, on the other, the sharp, aggressive exegesis of Rudolf Bultmann; on the one hand, Nicolai Hartmann's astute, refined art of chasing, on the other, the breathtaking radicalism of Heidegger's questions that also cast a spell over theology. The prototype of *Being and Time* was a lecture given to the community of Marburg theologians in 1924.

That which was first voiced in Heidegger's discussion of the Thurneysenian lecture can be followed as a central motif of his thinking until the present day [1964]: the problem of language. There was no foundation for this in Marburg. The Marburg school, which had been distinguished for decades within the then contemporary neo-Kantianism because of its methodological rigor, concentrated primarily on the foundations of science. For them it was completely self-evident that the complete acquisition of all that is knowable could take place only in the sciences, that the objectification of experience through science fulfilled completely the meaning of knowledge. The purity of the concept, the precision of the mathematical formula, the triumph of the infinitesimal method—this, not the midworld of unstable linguistic shapes, defined the philosophical orientation of the Marburg school. Even when Ernst Cassirer included the phenomenon of language in the topic of the neo-Kantian idealism, he did so methodically with the methodical idea of objectification. To be sure, his philosophy of the symbolic forms had nothing to do with a methodology of the sciences; rather, in this theory myth and language were viewed as symbolic forms, that is, as shapes [*Gestalten*] of the objective spirit and, moreover, in such a way that they were to find their methodical basis in the primary stream of the transcendental consciousness.

Well, it was then that phenomenology began to mark an epoch in Marburg. Max Scheler's founding of the ethics of material value, which was connected with a overly angry and blind criticism of the formalism of the Kantian moral philosophy, made a lasting impression on Nicolai Hartmann early on, who was then the avant-gardist within the Marburg school.[1] It was convincing—as it had

---

1. See N. Hartmann's review in the *Jahrbuch für Philosophie und phänomenologische Forschung*, 1 (1914): 35, 97 ff. See also Hartmann, *Kleine Schriften II* (Berlin: DeGruyter, 1958), pp. 365 ff.

been for Hegel a century earlier—that one cannot approach the totality of ethical phenomena from the phenomenon of an "ought,"
that is, as in the imperative form of an ethics. Therefore, a first
limit to the subjective, fundamental basis of the transcendental
consciousness appeared in the field of moral philosophy: the "ought-
consciousness" could not cover the whole scope of moral value. But
the phenomenological school had still a more powerful impact in
that it did not share the Marburg school's orientation toward the
"self-evident" facts of science. Instead, it went behind the scientific
experience and the categorical analysis of scientific methods and
moved the natural life experiences—that which the later Husserl
named with the now-famous term *life world*—into the foreground of
the phenomenological research. Both of these, the moral-philosophical
turn away from the imperative ethics and the turn from
methodologism of the Marburg school, had their theological coun-
terparts. The difficulty of speaking of God became a new issue, and
as a consequence, the foundations of systematic and historical theology came upon shaky ground. Rudolf Bultmann's critique of myth
and his concept of the mythical world image, especially insofar as it
still held sway in the New Testament, was also a critique of the claim
to totality made by objectifying thinking. Bultmann's concept of "having at one's disposal" [*Verfügbarkeit*], with which he attempted to
encompass in identical ways both the process of historical science
and that of mythical thinking formed a concept that was precisely the
opposite of the actual theological testimony.

　　　Then Heidegger entered the scene at Marburg, and immediately, whatever he read—whether it was Descartes, Aristotle, Plato,
or Kant who formed the link—his analysis always pressed on to the
most original experience of Dasein, which he disclosed from behind
the concealment of traditional concepts. Theological questions motivated him from the start. An early manuscript, which Heidegger had
sent to Paul Natorp in 1922 and I had a chance to read, shows this
really well. It was a basic introduction to an Aristotle interpretation
that Heidegger had prepared, and above all it dealt with the young
Luther, with Gabriel Biel, and with Augustine. Heidegger would
certainly have named it an exposition of a hermeneutical situation; it
attempted to make the reader aware of the questions and intellectual
expectations with which we approach Aristotle, the master of the
tradition. Today no one would doubt that the fundamental intention which guided Heidegger in his engrossment with Aristotle was

critical and de<con>structive. At the time, this was not so clear at all. Heidegger brought superb powers of phenomenological intuition [*Anschauungskraft*] to his interpretations and, in so doing, freed the original Aristotelian text so thoroughly and effectively from the overlay of the scholastic tradition and from the miserable, distorted picture the critical philosophy of the period had of Aristotle (Cohen loved to say, "Aristotle was a pharmacist.") that he began to speak in an unexpected way. Perhaps the strength of opponent was such that it dominated not only those learning but even Heidegger himself for a while. Or perhaps the strengthening of the opponent that Heidegger, true to the Platonic principle that one should strengthen the opponent's position,[2] was willing to dare in his interpretations gave Aristotle such a dominating presence.[3] But what else is there to interpret in philosophy if not to engage thoroughly with the truth of the text and to risk exposing oneself to it?

I became aware of something like this for the first time when I met Heidegger in 1923—still in Freiburg—and took part in a seminar on Aristotle's *Nicomachean Ethics*. We were studying the analysis of *phronesis* [thinking, practical wisdom]. Heidegger showed us with reference to Aristotle's text that all *techne* [(technical) skill] contained an internal limit: Its knowledge never entails a complete disclosure because the work that it knew how to produce is released into the uncertainty of a use that was not at one's disposal [*eines unverfügbaren Gebrauchs*]. And then, as a topic for discussion, he presented the distinction that separated all knowledge—especially that of mere *doxa* [opinion]—from *phronesis*: λήθη της μὲν τοιαύτης εξεως ᾽έστιν, γρονήσεως δὲ ουχ ᾽έστιν (1140 b 29).[a] As we groped for an interpretation, uncertain about the sentence and completely unfamiliar with the Greek concepts, Heidegger explained curtly, "That is the conscience!" This is not the place to reduce the pedagogical exaggeration contained in this claim to its appropriate dimensions, and even less the place to point out the logical and ontological weight that Aristotle's analysis of *phronesis* in fact carries. But what Heidegger found in this, which was also what fascinated him so with Aristotle's criticism of Plato's idea of the Good and with Aristotle's concept of practical

---

2. Plato, *Sophist*, 246d.
3. Consider in this respect the reference to Aristotle's *Nicomachean Ethics* VI and *Metaphysics* I (*Sein und Zeit*, p. 225, footnote 1).

knowledge, is clear today: Here a type of knowing (a ειδος γνωσεως)[4] is described that admits of no reference to a final objectivity in the sense of a science—a knowing in the concrete situation of existence. Indeed, could Aristotle perhaps have helped to overcome the onto-logical prejudices of the Greek concept of the *Logos,* which Heidegger later interpreted temporally as being present-at-hand [*Vorhandenheit*] and presentness [*Anwesenheit*]? This violent appropriation of the Aristotelian text for use with his own questions reminds one of how the call of the conscience in *Being and Time* is what first makes the "Dasein in human beings" visible in its ontological and temporal event-structure. It was much later that Heidegger, when rethinking the concept of Dasein in the light of the "clearing," dissolved all connections with any transcendental reflective thinking.[5] Could it be that in the final analysis the word of faith has found a new philo-sophical legitimation through the critique of *logos* and the under-standing of Being, much in the same way that the later Heidegger's "rememberance" [*Andenken*] never allows one to completely forget the nearness to the old "reverence" [*Andacht*], which Hegel had al-ready observed? Had that been the gist of Heidegger's ambiguous contribution to the Thurneysenian discussion?

Later, in Marburg, a similar instance drew our attention. This time Heidegger was concerned with a scholastic contradiction and spoke of the distinction between *actus signatus* [an act that has been explicitly designated as spontaneously executed] and *actus exercitus* [a spontaneously executed act].[b] These scholastic concepts correspond roughly to the concepts *reflexive* and *directe* and refer, for example, to the distinction between the act of questioning itself and the possibility of concentrating on the question as a question. The transition from one to the other can be easily made. One can designate the question as a question and, thus, not only question but also point out that one is questioning and that such and such is questionable. This ability to reverse the transition from that which is immediate and direct into the reflexive intention seemed to us then to be a way to freedom. This promised to liberate thinking

---

4. Aristotle, *Nicomachean Ethics* VI 9, 1141 b 33f.
5. That the Aristotelian concept of φύσις [nature] was also important for Heidegger in this development can be seen in his interpretation of Aristotle, *Phys* B 1 *Wegmarken,* pp. 309–371.

from the inescapable circle of reflection; it also pledged a way to regain both the evocative power of conceptual thinking and a philosophical language that had the ability to secure for thinking a position next to poetic language.

Certainly Husserl's phenomenology had moved beyond the sphere of explicit objectivizations in its analysis of the transcendental constitution. Husserl talked of anonymous intentionalities, that is, conceptual intentions in which something was intended and posed as ontically valid, but that no one person intends and carries out consciously, thematically or individually—intuitions that are nonetheless basic for everyone. This is more or less how the phenomenon that we refer to as the *stream of consciousness* is developed in the inner time consciousness. The horizon of the lived world is yet another example of a product of anonymous intentionalities. However, both the scholastic distinction with which Heidegger was concerned and Husserl's constitutional analysis of the anonymous achievements of the transcendental consciousness share a basic assumption. They both presuppose an unlimited universality of reason that can clarify each and every thing intended in a constitutive analysis—an analysis that transforms these things anonymously intended into objects of an explicit act of intending, that is, objectifies them.

Heidegger himself moved resolutely in another direction. He pursued the inner inextricability of authenticity and inauthenticity, of truth and error, and the concealment that necessarily accompanies all disclosure and shows the internal contradiction in the idea of total objectifiability. Where this led him can already be seen in the insight that was then the most moving and instructive to us: The most original way in which the past *is* is not in memory but in forgetting.[6] Here Heidegger's ontological protest against Husserl's transcendental subjectivity shows up most visibly at a point most central to the phenomenology of inner time consciousness. Certainly Husserl's phenomenological analysis is more precise than Brentano's analysis of the role of memory in time consciousness. Husserl differentiated explicit recollection, which always accompanies the act of intending "a perceived entity," from the entity of the present, which is held fast in the process of sinking away. Husserl named this process of sinking away *the retentional consciousness,* and he based all time consciousness

---

6. Compare *Sein und Zeit*, p. 339.

and consciousness of entities in time on its performance.[7] These were certainly "anonymous" performances, but their goal was nevertheless to bring about a retention-of-the-present or, so to speak, to arrest the movement into the past. The now, this rolling into the present from the future and rolling away into the past, was always understood from the vantage point of "being currently present-to-hand." Heidegger, on the other hand, had in view the original ontological dimensionality of time that is fundamental to the motility of Dasein. From this vantage point, light is shed not only on the enigmatic irreversibility of time—in that it never emerges, it only passes away—but it also becomes obvious that time does not have its Being in the now or in a series of nows; rather it has its Being in the futurity [*Zukünftigkeit*] that is essential to Dasein. This is obviously true to the real experience of history, to the way in which historicality happens with us. Forgetting attests to the fact that something happens to us—rather than that we *do* it. It is a way in which the past and passing away show their actuality and power. Clearly Heidegger's thinking moved in a direction away from Husserl's transcendental philosophy of reflection, which—as in Husserl's case—thematized with the help of anonymous intentionalities these structures of temporality as inner time consciousness as well as the self-construction of inner time consciousness. In the end, the critique of both the modern concept of the subject and the ontological prejudices found in the Aristotelian concepts of being and substance put asunder the idea of transcendental reflection.

Every *actus exercitus* in which reality is experienced in a completely unreflective manner, such as the reality of the tool in inconspicuous service or the past as it inconspicuously fades away, disallows its conversion into a designated act unless it is provided with a new covering. This can be found in a stronger form in Heidegger's analysis of Dasein as being-in-the-world, in that the Being of the beings experienced in this way—especially the worldhood of world—is not encountered "objectively" [*gegenständlich*], but rather conceals itself in an essential way. Already the character of ready-to-hand as a "holding within," upon which the "Being-in-itself" was ultimately based

---

7. Compare the *Vorlesungen zur Phänomenologie der inneren Zeitbewusstsein*, ed. Martin Heidegger, in the *Jahrbuch für Philosophie und phänomenologische Forschung*, 4 (1928): 395 ff.

(the "Being-in-itself" could not be explained from the present-at-hand), had been discussed in *Sein und Zeit* (p. 75). The Being of ready-to-hand is not simply concealment and seclusion, upon whose unconcealment and disclosure everything depended. Its "truth," its authentic, undisguisable Being lies manifestly in its inconspicuousness, unobtrusiveness, and nonobstinacy. Already here in *Being and Time* are preludes to the radical turn away from the "clearing" and "disclosedness" that were oriented to the self-understanding [*Selbstverständnis*] of Dasein. Even though the "holding within of that which is ready-to-hand" may well have been based ultimately on Dasein as the "for-the-sake-of-which" of all involvement, it is obviously due to the nature of being-in-the-world itself that "disclosedness" does not imply a complete transparency of Dasein, but rather entails an essential being-thoroughly-ruled by the indeterminate (*Sein und Zeit*, p. 308). This "holding within" of the ready-to-hand is not so much withholding and concealment as being included and being sheltered in the fabric of the world in which it had its Being. The internal tensions not only between "unconcealment" and "concealment" but also between "unconcealment" and "sheltering" determine the dimension in which language can become visible in its elusive, unmanageable Being, a dimension that also can be useful for the theologians in their understanding of God's word.—

In the area of theology the concept of self-understanding experienced a corresponding transformation. It was evident that the self-understanding of faith, which is the fundamental aim of Protestant theology, could not be appropriately grasped with the transcendental concept of self-consciousness. We are familiar with this concept from transcendental idealism. Fichte, in particular, had proclaimed the *"Wissenschaftslehre"* as the single consistent realization of the self-understanding transcendental idealism. Perhaps one remembers his criticism of Kant's concept of the "thing in itself."[8] At this point Fichte said with his characteristic base roughness, "If Kant had understood himself, then the 'thing in itself' could have only meant something or other. If Kant had not thought that, then he would have only been a half wit and no thinker at all."[9] It is fundamental to the concept of self-understanding that all dogmatic presuppositions

---

8. Fichte, *Die Zweite Einleitung in die Wissenschaftslehre*, WW I, 471 f.; 474 ff.; 82 f.
9. Ibid., p. 486.

are eliminated through the internal self-production of reason, so that upon completion of this self-construction of the transcendental subject a total transparency of the self is rendered. It is astonishing how close Husserl's transcendental phenomenology comes to meeting this demand set forth by Fichte and Hegel.

Such a concept could not be maintained in theology without a reformulation. For if something is indispensable to the idea of revelation, then it is precisely this: Human beings are incapable of obtaining a understanding of themselves solely from themselves. It is an ancient motif of the experience of faith—a motif that is ever-present in Augustine's reflections on his life—that all attempts of human beings to understand themselves from themselves and from the world that they have at their disposal are ill-fated. Indeed, it appears that the word and concept "self-understanding" owes its first formulation to the Christian experience. We find intimations of this in the correspondence between Hamann und his friend Jacobi. In these letters Hamann approaches his friend from the standpoint of pietistic certain faith and attempts to convince him that he would never be able to reach a pure self-understanding with his philosophy and with the role that faith played in it.[10] What Hamann had in mind was obviously more than the complete self-transparency of a think-

---

10. See "Renate Knoll, J. G. Hamann und Fr. Jacobi," in the "Heidelberg Forschg. 7," 1963. See also my work, "Zur Problematik des Selbstverständnisses" (*Kleine Schriften* I, pp. 70–81). My train of thought in both works shows that I had just begun to concern myself with the novelty of the morphology of "self-understanding" and the difficulties that surround it. In the first edition I expressed myself incorrectly, an error I have since corrected. The word *self-understanding* is indeed young. F. Tschirch (*Festschrift Eggers*, 1972) presented an extensive collection of evidence for that. He had obviously either not read or not understood my own works; otherwise he would have silently corrected this mistake, which went unnoticed by me. Etymologists should also take note of the following observations about the history of the concept:

1. The collection of words presented by Tschirch indirectly confirms the pietistic origin of the concept as put forth by myself: Both Erwin Metzke and Hans R. G. Günther dealt as researchers with pietism (Hamann, Jung-Stilling).

2. Tschirch is not justified in tracing the modern, theological use of the word back solely to Karl Schumann. *Self-understanding* was already a favorite word of Rudolf Bultmanns in the 1920s—as I have shown with the contribution quoted previously.

3. Also, Theodor Litt is correct when he wrote in 1938, " 'Self-understanding' is sought after the 'self-evidence' of *Dasein* is gone."

ing that has obtained a state of consistent and continuous harmony with itself. Self-understanding has much more than a determining moment of historicality. Anyone who has achieved true self-understanding has had something and is having something happen to him. The modern discourse concerning the self-understanding of faith is concerned precisely with this: The believer has become aware of his or her dependence on God. The believer gains an insight into the impossibility of knowing oneself from that which one has at their disposal.

With the concept of having something at one's disposal [*Verfügen*] and the necessary shattering of any self-understanding based upon that which one has at one's disposal, Rudolf Bultmann turned Heidegger's critique of the philosophical tradition on theology. In keeping with his own scientific origins, he sharply distinguished the Christian orientation to faith from the self-consciousness of the Greek philosophy. However, Greek philosophy was for him, as one focused not so much upon the ontological bases as upon the existential statements, the philosophy of the Hellenic age and especially the stoic ideal of self-sufficiency. This ideal was in turn interpreted as the ideal of having oneself completely at one's disposal [*volle Selbstverfügung*] and was criticized as being untenable from the Christian point of view. From this point of departure and under the influence of Heideggerian thinking, Bultmann explicated his position through the concepts of inauthenticity and authenticity. This Dasein, which has fallen into the world and understands itself only through that which it has at its disposal, is called upon to convert, and the shattering of the illusion that it had itself completely at its disposal [*Selbstverfügung*] brings about a turn to authenticity. For Bultmann, the transcendental analytic of Dasein seemed to describe in neutral terms a basic anthropological constitution that allowed for an "existentiell"[c] interpretation of the call to faith—irrespective of its content—within the fundamental movement of existence. It was precisely this transcendental-philosophical conception found in *Being and Time* that was integrated into theological thinking. Certainly the old, idealistic concept of self-understanding and its culmination in "absolute knowledge" could no longer depict the a priori <nature> [*das Apriori*] of the experience of faith. Indeed, it was the a priori <nature> of an event, the a priori <nature> of the historicality and finitude of the human Dasein, that was to make the conceptual explication of the

event of faith possible. And this is precisely what Heidegger's interpretation of Dasein accomplished via temporality.

It would exceed my competency to attempt a discussion of
the exegetic richness of Bultmann's approach here. But one can certainly say that his new existentiall exegesis was a triumph. It allowed
the Letters of Paul and the Gospel of John to be interpreted in terms
of the self-understanding of their faith with the rigorous methods of
historical philology, and precisely this method of interpretation of
the kerygmatic meaning of the New Testament brought it to its
highest realization.

Meanwhile, Heidegger's way of thinking led him in the
opposite direction. The transcendental-philosophical conception of
the self began to show itself to be less and less in keeping with the
inner concern of Heidegger's thinking that had stirred him from the
beginning. The later talk of a turn [*Kehre*], which eradicated all existential overtones from the talk of the authenticity of Dasein and,
thus, the concept of authenticity itself, could no longer be brought
into harmony, so it seems to me, with the fundamental theological
concerns of Rudolf Bultmann. Only after this turn did Heidegger
truly begin to approach a dimension in which his earlier demand on
theology—that it find the word that not only called one to faith but
was also capable of preserving one in faith—could be met. If the call
to faith, the summons that challenged the self-sufficiency of the ego
and made it necessary that the ego become an issue for itself in faith,
was to be able to be interpreted as self-understanding, then the language of faith—a language that could preserve one in faith—was
perhaps something quite different. It was exactly this for which
Heidegger's thinking sketched out an increasingly more visible new
foundation: Truth as an event that contained within itself its own
error [*Irre*], the unconcealment, the concealment, and with it the
sheltering, also the well-known phrase from the "Letter on Humanism" in which language is the "house of Being"—all of this points
beyond the horizon of any self-understanding, be it one shattered
and historical.

Progress can also be made by proceeding along the same
lines from the experience of understanding and from the historicality
of self-knowledge, and my own attempts at a philosophical
hermeneutics begin at this point. First of all, the experience of art
presents us with an irrefutable evidence that one's self-understanding

does not offer an adequate horizon for interpretation. This is certainly nothing new with reference to the experience of art. Nevertheless, the concept of a genius, which has served as the basis of the more recent philosophy of art since Kant, contains an essential element of the unconscious. For Kant, the internal correspondence to a creative nature, whose formations bestow us with and confirms in a human way the wonder of beauty, follows from the fact that the genius, as a favorite of nature, creates exemplary works with neither awareness nor application of rules. It is a necessary consequence of this conception of the self that the artist's own interpretation loses its legitimation. The artist's self-interpretive statements ensue from a position of subsequent reflection, and the artist is not entitled to a privileged position over the others who stand before his work. Such self-interpretive statements are certainly documents and, in some circumstances, key clues for interpreters who follow, but they are not of canonical status.

The consequences become even more significant if one extends this beyond the boundaries of the aesthetics of the genius and *Erlebnis*-art and takes into account the internal affiliation of the interpreter with the movement of meaning in the work. Then the standards of an unconscious canon, which are perceived in the wonder of a creative spirit, must be given up. The universality of the hermeneutic phenomenon surfaces in its entirety behind the experience of art.

Indeed, this leads to a deeper penetration into the historical nature of all understanding. A momentous insight comes to the fore particularly when one studies the older hermeneutics of the seventeenth and eighteenth centuries. Can the *mens auctoris*,[d] that which the author intended, be recognized in an unrestricted way as the standard for understanding a text? If one interprets this hermeneutic principle in a broad and charitable way, then there is certainly something convincing about it. Namely, if one understands "what the author intended by this" as "what he or she could have intended by this in general [*überhaupt*]," that is, what lay in the author's own individual and temporal-historical horizon, and one excludes that "which could not have occurred to the author at all," then this principle seems sound.[11] It keeps the interpreter from making anachronisms, from inserting

---

11. Compare Chladenius, quoted in *Wahrheit und Methode*, p. 172 (*Ges. Werke*, vol. 1, S. 187).

things arbitrarily and making illegitimate applications. It seems to provide a formula for the moral of a historical consciousness and for the
conscientiousness of historical meaning.

However, if one associates the interpretation of texts with
the understanding and the experience of the work of art, then this
principle also contains something fundamentally questionable. Perhaps there are historically appropriate and, in this sense, authentic
ways to experience the work of art, but the experience of art certainly
cannot to be restricted to them. Even those who do not want to
embrace fully a Pythagoreanizing aesthetic because they want to em-
phasize the historical task of integration—a task that all experiences
of art as human experiences involve—even those will have to recognize that the work of art depicts a peculiar type of structure of meaning whose ideality approaches the ahistorical dimensions of the
mathematical.[12] Obviously, its experience and explication [*Auslegung*]
can in no sense be limited by the *mens auctoris*. If we now add that the
internal unity of understanding and explication—a unity already
pointed out by German Romanticism—brings every object we are
trying to understand, regardless of whether it be a work of art, a text,
or any part of a tradition, into the movement of the present and
allows it to speak again in the language of the present, then I believe
one can see certain theological consequences being sketched out.

The kerygmatic meaning of the New Testament, which lends
the form of application of *pro me* [for or according to me] to the
gospel, cannot, in the end, contradict the legitimate investigations of
the historical sciences. As I see it, this is an indispensable require-
ment of the scientific consciousness. It is impossible to assume that
there is a mutually exclusive relationship between the meaning and
the salvation-meaning of a scriptural text. But could a relationship of
mutual exclusion be the issue here in the first place? Does not the
intended meaning of the New Testament authors, an intended meaning that they were certainly able to imagine in great detail, move in
the direction of the meaning of salvation *for which* one reads the
bible? This is not to say that their statements are to be granted the
status of an adequate, appropriate self-understanding. They certainly

---

12. In my opinion, O. Becker was unable to raise any real issue for a dispute when
he tried to play the "Pythagorean" truth off against my attempts to interpret the
aesthetic experience hermeneutically (see *Philosophische Rundschau* 10 [1969], beginning on p. 225, see especially p. 237).

belong to the genre of "original literature" [*Urliteratur*], as characterized by Franz Overbeck. If the meaning of a text is understood as
mens auctoris, that is, the "actual" horizon of understanding of the
Christian authors of the day, then the authors of the New Testament
are given a false honor. Their actual honor lies precisely in the fact
that they are the herald for something that surpasses their own horizon of understanding—even if they are called John or Paul.

We are in no way propagating a theory of uncontrollable
inspiration and pneumatic exegesis. This would squander the knowledge won by the science of the New Testament. What we are dealing
with here is in truth not a theory of inspiration. This becomes clear
when one links the hermeneutical situation of theology together with
hermeneutical situation of jurisprudence, of the humanities, and of
the experience of art, as I did in my attempt at a philosophical
hermeneutics. Understanding is never simply regaining that which
the author "intended," regardless of whether the author was the creator of a work of art, perpetrator of some act, the writer of a book of
law or whatever. The *mens auctoris* does not limit the horizon of
understanding in which the interpreter moves, indeed, in which the
interpreter must necessarily move if, instead of parroting, he truly
wants to understand.

The most definitive evidence of this, so it seems to me, lies
in language. Interpretation does not merely take place in the medium
of language; interpretation deals with linguistic forms, and by transforming these forms into its own understanding, it carries the form
over into its own linguistic world. This is not an act that is secondary
to understanding. After Schleiermacher, the old distinction between
"thinking" (νοεῖν) and "speaking" (λέγειν), which was always held
by the Greeks (a distinction that first appeared in a didactic poem by
Parmenides[13]), has been unable to confine hermeneutics to the
preliminariness of merely removing occasional difficulties. Also, we
are in essence not dealing with a "carrying over" or a "transferal" at
all, at least not from one language into another. The hopeless inadequacy of all translations shows this distinction very clearly. One
who "understands" is not bound by the constraints of a translator—
where one must give a word-for-word rendition of an assigned text—
when one tries to explicate one's understanding. Rather, one takes

13. See H. Diels, *Fragmente der Vorsokratiker,* 5th ed., pp. 2, 7 f., 8, 35 f.

part in the freedom that comes with true speaking, with saying what is meant or intended. Certainly every understanding is always "underway"; it never comes completely to a close. And nevertheless, a totality of meaning is present in the free execution of saying what is meant, and this includes what is meant by an interpreter. Any understanding that articulates itself in language finds itself surrounded by a free space—a space that reverberates with the continuous reply of the understanding to the words spoken to it, but a space that it is never completely filled up. "There is much to say"—this is the fundamental axiom of hermeneutics. Interpretation is no more the subsequent fixing of fleeting opinions in language than is speaking. That which comes to language, and this is also the case in our literary tradition, is not merely a collection of opinions as such; rather an experience of the world itself is given through this medium, and the totality of our historical tradition is enclosed within it. A tradition is always permeable to that which is carried [*tradiert*] within it. Every reply to the call of the tradition, and not only the word that theology is searching for, is a word that preserves.

CHAPTER FOUR

WHAT IS
METAPHYSICS? (1978)

Heidegger's Freiburg inaugural lecture of 1929 occupies
a distinctive place in his work. It is an academic lecture delivered to
the professors and students of his old alma mater, an institution that
he had left after his stay as a student, assistant, and unsalaried lecturer and to which he was returning then in 1929—but at that time,
after the sweeping success of *Sein und Zeit,* as the most famous thinker
of his time. The response to this lecture was also exceptional. Translations into French, Japanese, Italian, Spanish, Portuguese, English,
and Turkish followed immediately, and I do not know how many
translations into still other languages have ensued since. But the
rashness and broadness of the first dissemination of this lecture into
other cultures is itself noteworthy. A translation of *Sein und Zeit*
obviously could not follow so quickly due to its size, but the fact that
the lecture "What Is Metaphysics" received such a peculiarly turbulant
and broad response simply cannot be ignored. Especially the fact that
translations into Japanese and later into Turkish appeared so early on
says something, for these translations extended beyond the sphere of
the Christian languages of Europe. Heidegger's ability to think beyond metaphysics obviously came across a special readiness in re-
gions where the Greek-Christian metaphysics did not form a
self-evident and fundamental background. Conversely, this lecture

45

and its discussion of "nothing" [*das Nichts*][a] was the explicit target of
an extreme, logical critique presented by Rudolf Carnap in *Erkenntnis*[b]
in 1932. In his critique, Rudolf Carnap repeated and critically sharpened all of the objections Heidegger himself had discussed in the
section of the lecture where he prepared for the question concerning
"nothing" and expressed his doubts about such a question.

But Heidegger himself had also distinguished this small publication by twice adding detailed commentaries to later editions of
the document: first in the epilogue of the 1943 edition and then in a
longer preface in the 1949 edition. Today's text amounts to more
than double the original size. Furthermore, it is noteworthy that
Heidegger himself added all three parts [1929, 1943, 1949] to the
collection called *Wegmarken,* a collection of smaller works published
between 1929 and 1964—obviously as *Wegmarken* <markers on the
way of his thinking>.

In fact, the monumental theme of overcoming metaphysics
and metaphysical thinking, which was the subject of the later
Heidegger's thought experiments, emerged for the first time in this
lecture. However, due to the way that the issue emerged, the lecture
itself was still couched in the language of metaphysics. The question
concerning "nothing" was introduced expressly as a metaphysical
question—a question into which one is necessarily drawn if one
decides to dispense with the well-known system of logical defences.

In fact, the question concerning "nothing" and the thought
provoking, fundamental experience of "nothing" were brought up so
that thinking would be forced to think the *Da* of Dasein. This is the
mission that Heidegger, in an ever more-conscious turn away from
the metaphysical question concerning the Being of beings and the
language of metaphysics, recognized as his own. This question preoccupied him his entire life. In a notable entanglement and in a
complete disclosure of his deficiency of language, Heidegger ventured this challenging sentence in the epilogue of 1943: "It belongs
to the truth of Being that Being certainly essences [*west,* i.e., is present]
without beings, but there is never a being without Being." But
Heidegger then changed this sentence in the fifth edition into precisely its contrary: "Being never essences without beings; there is
never a being without Being." (The latter rendering is the text that
served as the basis for the Italian translation.) The two contradictory
versions span the tense space in which Heidegger's questioning
moved. Both versions make perfectly good sense. The internal inex-

tricability of the being [*das Seiende*] from Being's dimension of essence [*Wesensdimension*] is expressed in both variants, but the reversed dependency of Being on the being is expressed only in the second and final version. Well, this is a question of perspective. Does one think the dimension of "essence" in which Being "essences" as such, as if it "had" "Being" (apart from all beings)? Or, even though this means that Being is thought in such a way that it can be only when there are beings, does one think of it merely as the dimension in which Being "is?" To think Being itself—one senses here the pressure of reifying thinking. Is this Being, which "is not a thing" but rather "essences," a possible subject of thinking and speaking at all? The ancient seductiveness of the *Chorismos* [separation]—which Plato recognized as the seduction of the thinking of the Ideas and yet just did not know how to avoid completely—tangles up Heidegger's analysis of metaphysics here.

The modification of the text that we took as our point of departure was made in the fifth edition (1949)—to which Heidegger added yet another new introduction. This is in itself significant enough. The difference between the tone of this new introduction and the tone of the older epilogue, however, is no less than the difference between the two variants of the text as it is there expressed. The epilogue from 1943 is introduced as if its purpose were only to put aside a few hinderances that might get in the way of following the train of thought in the lecture, hinderances connected with the task of thinking "the 'nothing' that attunes angst in its essence." In posing the question concerning "nothing," the lecture inquires into Being—that which is not a "what," a *ti*, and therefore cannot be thought by metaphysics as "Being." This epilogue presents this new questioning as the "essential thinking" and juxtaposes it against logic and calculative thinking. The apologia, in words and images trembling with the eschatological emotionalism of those years of the German catastrophe, comes down in its appeal on the side of those who attempt to describe from the vantage point of Being itself a thinking that is determined by the "other to the being." Here the talk is of the need for sacrifice, of a gratitude [*der Dank*] that thinks of Being and preserves its rememberance, of the "echo of the favor of Being," and of the urgency in Dasein to find the word for Being: It comes across like a confirmation of this sonerous imagery when, in the end, the epilogue itself draws the speaking of the thinker and the naming of the poet close together. In contrast to this, the later

introduction attempts to present the lecture as an internal consequence of the rupture in thinking that first broke open with *Being
and Time* and continued beyond this lecture to other thought experiments after the so-called turn. In the meantime, not only did
Heidegger's Hölderlin interpretations begin to have a general effect,
but the "Letter on Humanism" and *Holzwege* also began to make the
ways traveled by Heidegger's thinking more visible. With precise
references to *Being and Time* and to the history of philosophy, especially to Aristotle and Leibniz, the introduction elucidates the mission of overcoming metaphysics that held Heidegger's thinking captive
after the "turn." Again Heidegger's thinking took its start from a
metaphor, but this time one known in the history of philosophy
itself—the *arbor scientiarum* [the tree of knowledge], the image of a
tree reaching upward from the ground. Using this image Heidegger
illustrated his point that metaphysics does not think its own foundation, and then he proposed the mission of clarifying the essence of
metaphysics by returning to and examining its own foundations—
foundations that have heretofore remained hidden from metaphysics
itself. In making metaphysics itself an object of inquiry, in questioning the way that metaphysics "is" and inquiring about the way that
thinking itself began, Heidegger expressly ran up against metaphysics
and its claim that it thinks Being. What does the question concerning
the Being of beings mean for Being itself and for its relation to
humans? The question of metaphysics, "Why are there beings at all
and not rather 'nothing?'" turned into the question, Why does thinking concern itself more with beings than with Being? Unlike the
question concerning "nothing" as posed in the lecture, the question
posed here is obviously no longer a metaphysical question; it is rather
a question put to metaphysics itself. Not, What does metaphysics
itself intend? but rather, What *is* metaphysics really? What sort of fate
[*Geschick*]? And how does this event determine our destiny? The
introduction that was added to the lecture of 1949 no longer leads
into the situation of the sciences and the task of the *Universitas literarum,*
as the programistic lecture of 1929 did; rather, it leads into the situation of the contemporary world and of humanity as a whole as limned
against the advent of the postwar era and the explosive progression of
the industrial revolution into the second half of the twentieth century.

Chapter Five

Kant and the Hermeneutical Turn (1975)

Kant's place in contemporary thought is virtually unique. He is more or less a common prerequisite for the most opposed philosophical tendencies. On one side, there are the empiricists, who credit themselves with Kant's destruction of "dogmatic metaphysics," this work of the "crusher of everything" (Mendelssohn)—even if they are still dissatisfied with the large portion of the remaining dogmatic stock of the rationalistic way of thinking, such as Kant's derivation of the three-dimensionality of space. And, on the other side, there are the apriorists, who certainly understand themselves transcendentally and frequently reference Kant, but who, in the end, all follow Fichte and would gladly leave the dogmatic remainder of the thing-in-itself behind in favor of deriving of all validity from the highest principle, that is, from the ego. As is well known, even the contrast between idealism and materialism, as seen from the Marxist perspective, was redefined by Kant in the sense that Marx himself viewed all pre-Kantian materialism as dogmatic. Around 1860 the slogan "back to Kant" was used to introduce neo-Kantianism and, in so doing, was also used to attack not only the dominance of the Hegelian school of speculative idealism, but also the victorious materialism, naturalism, and psychologism, which had come on the scene as a countermovement to Hegel. Yet, the fact remains that this slogan was much more firmly rooted in the tradition of Fichte and Hegel than those following this slogan were aware.

There is still another area in which Kant's empirical tendency together with the neo-Kantian apriorism led to a modification of Kant's image in the post-Kantian and post-Hegelian age: Kant's establishment of a moral philosophy based on the rational fact of freedom tends to fade into the background behind the destruction of dogmatic metaphysics by the *Critique of Pure Reason*. Indeed, Kant's founding of a moral philosophy based on his concept of the autonomy of practical research and on the categorical imperative was correctly seen as the greatest contribution of Kantian philosophy. But that this founding was a founding of a metaphysics of morals and that it validated a "moral metaphysics" concerned few.

Certainly Kant's orientation to the pure natural sciences in the Newtonian sense had little to offer the world of history, especially when compared to Hegel's magnificent and yet violently construing philosophy of world history. Kant's moral philosophy rejected all anthropological foundations and expressly claimed to be valid for rational beings as such. Even in an age that claimed proudly to have overcome metaphysics, there were still attempts to carry the idea of a transcendental method over into other areas whenever Kant was interpreted along epistemological lines. Thus, precisely the ingenious element of Kant's moral philosophy was interpreted epistemologically, and a theory was sought that would provide a foundation for our knowledge of the historical world as well as for the natural sciences. Dilthey's ambition to place a critique of historical reason alongside the Kantian critique, and the Windelband-Rickert neo-Kantian theory that subsumed historical knowledge under the systematic-theoretical idea of a realm of values, each testifies in it's own way to the supremacy of the Kantian critique. But they are quite a way from Kant's self-conception, according to which he wanted to point out the limits of knowledge in order to create a place for faith.

Thus, it was a strangely diluted Kant that, in the age of neo-Kantianism, was developed into a general system of thought either as critique or as transcendental philosophy. And it is precisely this neo-Kantianism—especially in its Marburg form, where the idea of a transcendental psychology (Natorp) was developed as a counterpart of a transcendental "general logic"—which lent support to the philosophical self-understanding of Husserl's budding phenomenology.

The twentieth century, and especially the philosophical movement after World War I, is tied to the concept of phenomenology, and what one now calls *hermeneutical philosophy* is based to a large extent on a phenomenology. But when viewed retrospectively and historically from a contemporary vantage point, the question arises, What was phenomenology? It was certainly not primarily a variation on—or the most consistent implementation of—the Marburg variety of Neo-Kantianism. As the word itself implies, phenomenology was a methodical manner of describing phenomena without biases, one in which there was a methodological renunciation of all explanations of physiological-psychological origins and of all attempts at derivations from preconceived principles. Thus, the mechanism of sensations (Mach), the English utilitarianism of social ethics (Spencer), James's American pragmatism, and Freud's hedonistic school of deep psychological drives all collapsed under the weight of Husserl's and Scheler's phenomenological critiques. When compared with these explanative schemata, one could call phenomenological research as a whole as well as Dilthey's descriptive and analytical psychology, which was oriented towards the liberal arts, "hermeneutical"—in a very broad sense—insofar as the meaning or essence contained in a phenomenon or the structure of the phenomenon is not "explained" [*erklärt*], but rather is to be "explicated" [*zur Auslegung gebracht werden soll*]. Indeed, the word *explicate,* in the sense of a detailed description, is found in Husserl's usage of language quite early on, and in the final analysis, Dilthey's formation of theories in the liberal arts is based completely on the "hermeneutical" character of *understanding meaning and expressions* [*Sinn- und Ausdrucks-Verstehens*].

Nevertheless, the conscious reliance on Neo-Kantianism, which Husserl used for the purpose of providing a theoretical justification for his art of description and his theory of evidence, meant a renewal of a highly one-sided conception of a system, a system based less on Kant than on Fichte and Hegel. Certainly, it was a transcendental effort at justification that Husserl undertook with the motto, "How do I become a honest [*ehrlich*] philosopher?" but the transcendental reduction leading back to the apodicticity of self-consciousness, which was to transform philosophy to a "rigorous science," and his program of a "constitutive" phenomenology, which was erected upon the evidence of a transcendental ego, did not correspond in the least bit to transcendental deduction in the Kantian sense. For Kant, the deduction was given as "proof" of the validity of the categories after the metaphysical deduction of the table of categories had been derived from the "table of judgments." Husserl's "constitutive" phenomenology resembled much more the Fichtean ideal of a "derivation"; that is, obtaining the categories from the actions of an ego [*Tat-Handlung des Ichs*]. Of course, Husserl may have well been aware that the concept of a system as found in the Fichtean-Hegelian idealism or in the Neo-Kantianism (of the Marburg school) was lacking a genuine foundation "from underneath" and that only a phenomenological clarification of the correlation between an intentional act and an intentional object could make the transcendental thought of the "production" or of the "constitution" feasible. The well-known paradigm of an investigation of the correlation between an intentional act and an object was the phenomenology of perception. Here the decisive improvement over Natorp's concept of correlation became apparent in the rich differentiation of the acts in intentional life, a differentiation that offered itself over and against the same object as a theme for phenomenological analysis. This led to a new phenomenological clarification of Kantian insights in the sense of a consistently near-Fichtean Neo-Kantianism.

Take, for example, the old crux of Kantianism, the doctrine of a "thing-in-itself," which Fichte saw as a metaphor that needed to be explained away, and which the Marburg Neo-Kantianism (Natorp) had transformed into the "endless task" of determining the object of knowledge. Husserl clearly saw through the naiveté of those who wanted to preserve here in Kant a "realistic" element in his idealistic philosophy, and he elucidated even this "realistic" element of being-in-itself [*Ansichsein*] through his masterly analysis of the phenomenology of perception. The continuum of shadings, through which an object of perception is presented according to its essence, is implied in the intention belonging to every act of perception—and precisely that is the meaning of the being-in-itself of a thing.

Husserl could have unequivocally thought himself to be the consummator of transcendental thought, inasmuch as he attempted in his *Phenomenology of Internal Time Consciousness* to display in dazzling phenomenological analyses the transcendental synthesis of apperception and its connection to the "internal sense." By constantly reformulating and refining his questions, he proceeded from this basis to design the whole system of a phenomenologically based philosophy as a rigorous science, in which he set about solving the most difficult problems from the standpoint of the transcendental ego [*Ich*], namely, the problem of consciousness of the body, the problem of constituting the other (the problem of intersubjectivity), and the problem of the historically varying horizons of the "lived world." These are without doubt the three cases that put up the stiffest resistance to constitution by self-consciousness. Husserl's later works were dedicated more than anything else to overcoming these sites of resistance. Whoever allowed himself or herself to be led astray in carrying out transcendental phenomenology by these opposing cases had, in his eyes, not understood the transcendental deduction. This was something that Husserl later said not only about the Munich phenomenologists and Scheler, but ultimately also about the Heidegger of *Being and Time*. This is admittedly not clear at first glance, if one takes Heidegger's transcendental self-conception into view. Even in the year 1929, a year after the publication of *Being and Time*, Oskar Becker still thought Heidegger's "transcendental analytic of Dasein," as an investigation of the hermeneutical dimension of the "life-world," belonged in Husserl's program of transcendental phenomenology.

Nevertheless, Heidegger's true intention, which converged with his linking of the hermeneutical problematic to the theological and historical sciences, was quickly carried through; and with this the original Kant was awakened to a new actuality and relevance in an astonishing way, albeit one that challenged his speculative followers. In truth, the categorization of *Being and Time* as fitting into the Husserlian transcendental phenomenology must have ruptured the Husserlian framework, and in the long run, Husserl himself could no longer conceal the fact that the profound and thoroughly successful work of Heidegger's was no contribution to "philosophy as a rigorous science." Heidegger's talk of the "historicality" of Dasein pointed in a totally different direction. The tradition of the historical school as reflected in the works of Dilthey and Grafen Yorck stood quite some distance from the transcendentalism of Neo-Kantianism. Under the influence of the historical school and, also, with Schopenhauer's reformulation of Kant into a metaphysics of the blind will, the basis of the philosophy of self-consciousness had been shifted during the nineteenth century to "the thought-forming work of *life*." More than all others, the budding influence of Friedrich Nietzsche, which was conveyed through the great novelists of the day as well as through Bergson, Simmel, and Scheler, moved "life" into the fore-ground at the beginning of our century—as it did into the psychology of the unconscious. One was no longer concerned with that which was given phenomenologically by consciousness, but rather with the interpretation of the phenomena that arose out of hermeneutical movement of life and that must be subject to inter-pretation.

　　　Thus, a complicated constellation gave Heidegger's intellec-tual contribution its special effect. Reared in Rickert's Neo-Kantianistic apriorism and developed by way of a Kantian interpretation of Husserl's phenomenology, Heidegger nevertheless brought this other tradition, the "hermeneutical" tradition of the humanities and social sciences, to bear on the fundamental questions of contemporary thought. In particular, the irrationality of life presented a type of counterinstance to Neo-Kantianism. Even the Marburg school itself attempted to break the spell of transcendental thought then, and the aging Natorp left all logic to return to the underlying "primal con-creteness" [das "Urkonkrete"]. The sentence, "Life is hazy [diesig]," is given to us by Heidegger in his earliest lectures. Hazy has nothing to do with the "this" [Dies]; rather it means misty, foggy. Thus, the sentence means that it belongs to the essence of life that no complete enlightenment can be gained within self-consciousness; rather it is constantly being reenshrouded in fog. This was thought much more in the spirit of Nietzsche. By comparison, the internal consistency of Neo-Kantianism, as it then existed, was at best able to recognize the irrational and extratheoretical types of validity as only a kind of bound-ary concept of their own logical system. Rickert offered his own critical account of the "philosophy of life." And Husserl's idea of "philosophy as a rigorous science" stood with firm resolve against all irrational trends of the day, especially against the philosophy of the Weltanschauung. What Heidegger carried out with the call of the historicality of Dasein was in the final analysis a radical turn away from idealism. It was a recapitulation in our century of the same criticism of idealism that the young Hegelians had leveled at the speculative encyclopedism of Hegel's system after his death. This recapitulation was mediated especially through the influence of Kierkegaard. He was the one who had accused Hegel, the absolute professor in Berlin, of having forgotten "to exist" [das "Existieren"]. In the liberal translation into German by Christoph Schrempf,

Kierkegaard's work effected an epoch in Germany in the years before and after World War I. Jaspers conveyed his teaching through an exceptional work, *"Referat Kierkegaards,"* and the so-called philosophy of existence emerged. The criticism of idealism found in this work was widely used by philosophers and theologians. Such was the situation in which Heidegger's work came to have an effect.

This criticism of idealism was obviously much more radical than the critical differences that existed between the Neo-Thomists, Kantians, Fichteans, Hegelians, and logical empiricists. Also, the contrast between the systematic thinking of the Neo-Kantians and Dilthey's attempts at a critique of historical reason was one that remained within a framework of common assumptions about the task of philosophy. The critique of philosophy found in Heidegger's new contributions was the only one that shared the radicality of the young Hegelians. It is obviously no coincidence that the revival of Marxist thinking could not simply ignore Heidegger's contribution to thought, and indeed, Herbert Marcuse attempted to unite these two.

The slogan that the young Heidegger proclaimed was itself paradoxical enough, and it was critical of all factions. It was the slogan of a hermeneutics of facticity. Of course, to speak of a "hermeneutics of facticity" is to speak of something like "wooden iron." For facticity means precisely the unshakable resistance that the factual puts up against all grasping and understanding, and in the special phrasing in which Heidegger couched the concept of facticity, it meant the fundamental determination of human Dasein. This is certainly not merely consciousness and self-consciousness. The understanding of Being, which distinguishes Dasein from all beings and constitutes its hermeneutical structure, could not be fulfilled by the projection of an intellectual constitution through which it raised itself above all natural beings. The understanding of Being, which distinguishes the human Dasein by compelling it to question the meaning of Being, is itself in the highest degree a paradox. For the question concerning the meaning of Being is not like other questions concerning meaning, in which "something given" is understood through a comparison with that which constitutes its meaning. Rather, the human Dasein, which is concerned with the meaning of its own Being, sees itself confronted with the ungraspable nature of its own Dasein <in the sense of "existence," see note a in Chapter 2>. Regardless of how much certainty human beings are capable of gaining

concerning the sensibleness of everything and anything in understanding, the question of meaning with reference to its own Dasein
and regarding its own ability to understand itself, a question it must
pose to itself, runs up against an impassable boundary. Dasein is not
only the open horizon of its own possibilities, onto which it projects
itself. Rather, it encounters in itself the quality of an impassable
facticity. Dasein may well choose its Being, as with Kierkegaard where
the thought of the "either/or" of choice designated the actual ethical
character of Dasein—but in truth, with this choice Dasein only overtakes its own existence into which it had already been "thrown."
Thrownness and projection make up the unitary fundamental constitution of the human Dasein.

With this a critique of two factions is implied: of Husserl's
transcendental idealism, on one side, and of the philosophy of life
[*Lebensphilosophie*] as formulated by Dilthey and even Max Scheler
himself, on the other side. Ultimately, this two-pronged critique also
opens up a new passage way to the original Kant.

Heidegger's critique of Husserl was directed more than anything else toward the unidentifiable character [*Unausgewiesenheit*] of
the being of consciousness. Heidegger, who had grown up with
Aristotle, discovered the unknown, potent legacy of Greek thought
in the modern philosophy of consciousness. The analysis of the actual human Dasein, with which Heidegger began the exposition of
the question concerning Being, expressly condemned the "fantastical,
idealized subject" that the modern philosophy of consciousness had
consistently referred back to when justifying objectifying. This was
obviously not an immanent criticism that Heidegger was giving.
Rather, Heidegger had his eye on an ontological deficiency when he
criticized Husserl's analysis of time- and self-consciousness as being
prejudiced. Behind this lay a criticism of the Greeks themselves. A
criticism of their "superficiality" lurked in the background, a criticism of the one-sidedness of their perspective in which the outline
and form of a being is grasped and in this invariable "Being" its
Being is then thought. By contrast, the question concerning Being,
which dictates in advance all questions concerning the Being of
beings, was never posed. Spoken with reference to the temporal
horizon, "beings" are what are present contemporarily [*das Gegenwärtig-
Anwesende*]—and this is obviously inappropriate to the genuine constitution of human Dasein, which is not contemporariness, nor the

contemporariness of an intellect, but rather is futurity and care—in spite of all facticity.

And in the other direction, the new Heideggerean approach was not simply directed toward the foundation of Dilthey's concept of life. Indeed, he recognized in Dilthey's incessant search for the ultimate grounding of life a move toward a deeper understanding of what one usually calls *intellect* or *consciousness,* but his own intentions were ontological. He wanted to grasp the constitution of the Being of human Dasein in its internal unity, not simply as dualistic tension between the dulled impulse for life and the brightness of the self-consciousness of spirit. And he criticized Scheler precisely because he too remained in such a dualism. Then, during the period when he was on the way to an ontological deepening of his own approach to a philosophy of life and when he was immersed in these criticisms of modern philosophy of consciousness, Heidegger suddenly discovered Kant. And, indeed, it was precisely the Kant that the Neo-Kantianism and its phenomenological elaboration had concealed: the reference [*Angewiesenheit*] to that which is given. The human Dasein is neither a free self-projection nor a self-realization of an intellect, but rather a Being toward death—and that means that it is essentially finite. It was precisely due to this finitude of Dasein that Heidegger was able to recognize a premonition of his own insights in Kant's doctrine of an interaction between the understanding and intuition and of the restriction of the use of the understanding to the realm of possible experience. Especially the transcendental imagination, this puzzling mid-ability of the human soul in which intuition, the understanding, receptivity, and spontaneity cooperate, allowed Heidegger to interpret Kant's own philosophy as a finite metaphysics. The Being of an object is not defined though a reference to an infinite spirit (as in the classical metaphysics). Precisely the human understanding in its openness to accepting that which is given defines the object of experience.

Gerhard Krüger then interpreted Kant's moral philosophy with a loose application of the impulse that had come from Heidegger. According to this interpretation, the famous autonomy of practical reason is seen less like the self-legislation of morals than the free acceptance of law or, indeed, the obedient submission to the law.

Of course, Heidegger later viewed Kantian philosophy as having been determined much more by the forgetfulness of Being, and he gave up any attempts at a metaphysical understanding of his new exposition of the question of Being based upon the finitude of the human Dasein. This happened with the abandonment of the concept of transcendental reflection in Heidegger's "turn." After that, the Kantian tone disappeared from his thought experiments and with it all links to Kant's critique of rational metaphysics. However, the concept of critical philosophy still remains as a constant methodological corrective that philosophy cannot be allowed to forget.

If one follows the intentions of Heidegger's late philosophy, as I have done in my own hermeneutical philosophy, and attempts to use them as a proof of the hermeneutical experience, then one finds oneself again in the danger zone of the modern philosophy of consciousness. In this regard, it is certainly convincing that the experience of art conveys more than aesthetic consciousness is capable of grasping. Art is more than an object of taste, even of the most refined taste for art. The experience of history, which we ourselves have, is also covered only to a small degree by that which we would name *historical consciousness*. It is precisely the mediation between past and present, the reality and the effective power of the past, that determines us historically. History is more than the object of historical consciousness.—Thus, the only referential basis for this experience is one that shows itself in the thorough reflection of the procedures of the hermeneutical sciences and that we could characterize as the effective historical consciousness. This has more Being than being conscious; that is, more is historically affected and determined than we are conscious of as having been effected and determined.

It is inevitable that this kind of reflection about the hermeneutical experience must be understood as an abandonment of the claim of reflection [*Reflexionsanspruch*] made in Hegel's speculative dialectics—especially if one does not restrict it to the hermeneutical sciences, but rather recognizes the hermeneutical structure inherent in all of our worldly experiences and their explication. The original motive, which is captured in the term *effective historical consciousness,* is given its character precisely by the finitude of the results of reflection, results that can be gained by a consciousness reflecting on its determinedness. Something always remains in the background, regardless of how much one brings to the fore. Being historical means never being able to pull everything out of an event such that everything that has happened lies before me. Thus, that which Hegel named the *bad infinity* is a structural element of the historical experience as such. Hegel's claim to have finally disclosed reason even in history and to have thrown all mere contingencies onto the rubble heap of Being corresponds to an immanent tendency of movement found in reflective thought. A movement toward a purpose that can never be thought as being completely realizable does indeed seem to be a bad infinity—one to which thought is not capable of adhering. But which goal could history possibly contemplate—regardless of whether it be the history of Being or the history of the forgetfulness of Being—without straying again into the realm of simple possibility and phantasmal irrealities? Regardless of how great the temptation might be to think along with the reflective movement of our thought beyond every knowable limit and determinedness and to call real that which can be thought only as possible, in the end Kant's warning remains justified. He expressly distinguished the ideas that reason can only peer up to from the type whose meaning is constituted by the basic concepts of the understanding and that we therefore are capable of knowing. A critical consciousness of the limits of our *human reason,* which he accentuated in the critique of dogmatic metaphysics, certainly paved the way for a "practical metaphysics" founded upon the "rational fact" of freedom—but this is precisely *for practical reason.* Kant's critique of "theoretical" reason is still a valid argument against all attempts to put technique in the place of praxis and to exchange the rationality of our planning, the certainty of our calculations, and the reliability of our predictions for what we are capable of knowing with unconditional certainly, that is, what we have to do and how we are capable of justifying the decisions that we have made. Kant's critical turn remains unforgotten in hermeneutical philosophy, a philosophy that gained its foundation with Heidegger's reception of Dilthey. This turn is just as present in hermeneutical philosophy as is Plato himself, who understood all philosophizing as an endless dialogue of the soul with itself.

CHAPTER SIX

THE THINKER
MARTIN HEIDEGGER
(1969)

The eightieth birthday of a man whose thought has had its effect on us now for fifty years is an occasion to give thanks. But how should that take place? Should one speak directly to Martin Heidegger?—certainly the issue of thinking has grasped him too strongly for such a direct address to his person to be appropriate. Does one speak with Martin Heidegger?—it sounds a bit presumptuous to dare such a partnership. Or does one speak about Martin Heidegger in front of Martin Heidegger? All of these possibilities are excluded. What remains is that one, who was there from early on, bears witness to all others. A witness says what is and what is true. So the witness, who is speaking here, is permitted to say what everyone who has encountered Martin Heidegger has experienced: He is a master of thinking, of that unfamiliar art of thinking.

This was there [*da*] suddenly, already apparent with the young Heidegger's first appearance at the Freiburg lectern following World War I. Here was something new, something unheard of. We had learned that thinking was charting out relations, and it really seemed to be correct that one should reflectively put a thing in a certain relation and then make a statement about this relation, which one called a *judgment*. Thinking seemed to be process, a proceeding in a

stepwise fashion from relation to relation, from judgment to judgment. But suddenly we learn that thinking is showing and bringing
something to show itself. This was an event of fundamental importance; with one fell swoop Heidegger stepped over the flatness of
this reflective progression and his instructive words led us into a
completely new dimension. This incomprehensible offering by
Heidegger, in which Husserl's phenomenological legacy became more
forceful and was made more effective, led to the very embodiment of
the current object [Sache] of thought—regardless of what it might
be. It became round, three-dimensional; it was there [da]—one was
always facing it, because every turn of thought always referred back
to the same matter [Sache]. Where, in thinking, we would otherwise
be concerned with proceeding from one thought to another, here we
remained steadfastly concerned with the same matter. And it was not
that the matter was simply made visible, that it was merely given a
vivid portrayal such as in Husserl's famous analysis of the thing
[Ding] of perception and its shadings. Rather, the boldness and
radicality of the questions that were imposed on those present would
take one's breath completely away.

    Then one might have fancied that what was going on at the
time must have resembled Athens at the close of the fifth century, as
the new art of thinking, the dialectic, was introduced and the Attic
youth plunged into a enthusiastic mania—Aristophanes depicted that
for us splendidly and made no distinctions with reference to Socrates.
The intoxicating effect of the questions emanating from Martin
Heidegger in the early Freiburg and Marburg years seemed to be like
this, and there was no lack of followers and imitators. They coasted
along behind him, trying to outdo his questions and in the process
furnishing a caricature of the passionate momentum of the
Heideggerean questions and thought. But something like a new seriousness also entered into the business of thinking with Heidegger's
arrival. The subtle technique of academic conceptual exercises suddenly looked to us like pure frivolity, and one is not claiming too
much to say that this has had quite a long lasting effect in the life of
the German universities. Those of us who were younger then had
found a model when we made our own first attempts at teaching. A
new dignity of the vox viva [the living voice] and the complete unifi-
cation of teaching and research came on the scene with the risky
business of these radical philosophical questions, replacing the rou-

tine way of running courses in which the lecture was neglected because the professor was still preoccupied with his own work. This was the event of the 1920s; Martin Heidegger had an effect well beyond the "discipline" of philosophy.

This was not simply a new art, an intuitive power used to prove once again the value of a conceptual craft. It was much more than that. Above all, a new impetus was taking hold in Heidegger's thought that effected a complete transformation. Here was a thinking that attempted to think the very beginning and beginnings—although certainly not in the style of Neo-Kantianism and Husserl's phenomenology "as a rigorous science." There, the search was for a beginning as an ultimate foundation that would allow for a systematic ordering and derivation of all philosophical propositions—a beginning found in the principle of the transcendental subject. But Heidegger's radical questions were aimed at a much deeper originality than that searched for in the principle of self-consciousness. In this regard, he was a child of the new century—a century that had been dominated by Nietzsche, by historicism, and by thought determined by the philosophy of life, a century that doubted the legitimacy of all statements about self-consciousness. In an early Freiburg lecture, which I gained access to from Walter Bröcker's notes, Heidegger spoke of a "haziness" of life instead of the principle of clear and distinct *perceptio* of the *ego cogito*. That this life is hazy does not mean so much that the little ship of life cannot see a clear and free horizon around itself. Haziness does not simply mean the clouding of one's vision; rather, it describes the basic constitution of life as such, the very movement of life itself. It shrouds itself in fog. Here lies the inner tension, the internal struggle [*Gegenwendigkeit*] that Nietzsche had pointed out: Not only to strive toward clarity and to know, but also to conceal in darkness and to forget. When Heidegger named the basic experience of the Greeks' *aletheia,* unconcealedness, he did not simply mean that truth does not lie openly exposed and that concealedness must simply be ripped from it—as if it were some kind of loot. He meant moreover that truth was constantly in danger of receding back into darkness, that efforts at conceptualization must involve efforts to keep truth from receding back, and that even this receding back must be thought as an event of truth.

Heidegger named his first attempt to think the beginnings "ontology"—this was the title of the first lecture that I heard him give in 1923. But this was not an ontology in the traditional sense of Western metaphysics, which gave a first, world-history-making answer to the question concerning Being. Rather, here the sole claim was merely to have made the most rudimentary preparations for a formulation of a question. But what does it mean to formulate a question? It sounds easy, like setting a trap that one falls into with their answer, or something that one falls for because of the way it is posed to them. However, here the questions were not posed in an effort to obtain an answer. Whenever "Being" is questioned, the interrogation is about nothing. And to "pose" the question concerning Being is much more to give oneself over to the question, to à question that allows for "Being" in the first place and without which "Being" would remain an empty linguistic haze. When Heidegger asked the question concerning the beginning of occidental metaphysics, it had completely different meaning than it would have had, had it been posed by a historian. Occasionally—in connection with the issue of overcoming occidental metaphysics, whereby the issue was not so much to put metaphysics behind us as to bring it before us—Heidegger said of this beginning that it has always already passed over and moved beyond us. That is to say, inquiries concerning the beginning are always inquiries concerning ourselves and our future.

Of course, Heidegger's inquiries concerning the beginning have been misunderstood in the most absurd ways. He is often interpreted as if he were trying to escape from the terrible decline that had taken place in history and return to a more pristine time that was still proximate to these beginnings and origins. This misses the seriousness with which that which "is" is questioned. There is nothing mystical about what has come over us as the "destiny of Being" [*Seinsgeschick*]; rather, it is apparent to everyone as a consequence of the way that occidental thinking has played out in the technical civilization of our day—it covers the globe like an all-encompassing net. Here the usual tones of a cultural critique gain a peculiar ambiguity, full of grim forebodings of a disaster but yet anticipating a resistant future that, due to an effort to produce without limits, holds out a radical challenge of Being. But there is no illusion here that one could withdraw from what "is" into a supposed freedom, into a pining for origins that might one day return.

Herein one finds the roots of the second most common misunderstanding, the accusation of historicism: The assumption is that if the historicality of truth is understood as the destiny of Being, then the question concerning truth is lost. This scenario allows for one of two possibilities. It leads either to a renewal of the difficulties of Dilthey's historicism, a historicism that exhausts itself within the question of infinite, self-entangling reflection, or it leads to a socio-ethical emotionalism that demands sociological reflection. In the latter case, one is first made aware of the ideological bias inherent in all knowledge and then, after offering the illusion of a freedom from these biases by way of a dialectic, a call is made for social involvement.

This all seems a bit odd when seen in contrast to a thinking that does not share such worries; this thinking does not see itself as an instrument for some purpose. It is not a thinking in which everything depends on sagacity and a know-it-all attitude; rather, here thinking is experienced as a pure passion. Here "knowing it all" does not help. One must recognize that thinking is always selfless in a deep and final sense—not only in the sense that thinking cannot be guided by a particular interest in an individual or societal gain. It is more that the actual self of whoever is thinking, that individual's personal and historical determinedness, is extinguished. It is true that such thought occurs infrequently—and it must accept the accusation of being socially irresponsible because it does not acknowledge its own convictions—but there have been great models and convincing examples of this kind of thinking. The masters at teaching this great but unfamiliar art of selfless thinking were the Greeks. They even had a word, *nous,*[a] for that which is called (in a rough correspondence) the rational and spiritual in German idealism—thinking in which nothing is meant except that which "is." Hegel can be considered the last Greek precisely because his dialectic demanded a selflessness of this type; it elevated thinking without flaunting his own ideas or a know-it-all attitude. When Martin Heidegger adds his name *nolens volens* to the list of classical thinkers, he does so not so much because he took up the great questions of this great tradition devoid of any "historical" distance and made the posing of the question concerning Being his own, but rather because these questions filled him so completely that there was no longer any space between that which he thought and taught and that which he was himself. The unfamiliar art of thinking is based on such a selflessness, one that no longer knows itself and no longer is entangled in the dialectic of attempting to know oneself better and better.

With this I come to my last point. Here I would like to give a testimony concerning the driving momentum of thought that made its appearance with Martin Heidegger and address a point that is on everyone's lips and—precisely for that reason—elicits misunderstandings. I am talking about Heidegger's language. For Heidegger, more than for the great tradition of metaphysical thought, the material of his thinking is language, this most visible selflessness of thought. People take pleasure in criticizing Heidegger's unconventional language, and it may well be—indeed, it must be—that whoever is not thinking along with Heidegger will be unable to forget that these are not the usual tracks of linguistic construction upon which one usually proceeds. It is certainly not the language of information. The language of Heidegger and of thinking does not simply transmit through linguistic means something that is what it is—something that would be known devoid of all language because in principle it can be known by anyone. In the askant view of sociologist and political scientist, the "straightforwardness" of such thought is certainly not comprehensible, and it comes across as forced mannerisms. But Heidegger found himself challenged more and more as he researched deeper and deeper into the foundations of language and, like a treasure hunter, teased out of those dark shafts and brought to light gleaming and flashing discoveries. What flashed in that strange "darklight"—often very disconcerting and unfamiliar, sometimes generally convincing in the end, like a precious find worthy of a secure setting—certainly cannot be found in the familiar tracks of the polished words and phrases that we use to record our worldly experiences. Also, these are not simply new things that, once unearthed, increase the wealth of our experience. It is "itself" [es selbst] that should be thought in all of this harsh and violent thought-constructions; Being that should come to language. Certainly it is not always the case that subsequent thinking, in its effort to comprehend, knows how to justify the necessity of these breaks from the usual linguistic paths. Language—even the most violent language—always has something binding. In language something shared, something held in common comes into Being. Likewise, Heidegger's radical questioning concerning "Being" is not an esoteric, private activity; rather, the desire was to compel <one> with linguistic force to go along on the search for the word that seizes "itself." This is why he dug through the concealed foundations of language searching for a find. Even the usual relationship between language and what is signified is misleading. Language is not here and Being there, here an opinion and there something opined; rather, in the most violent break-in and rupture, with which he introduced his language, Heidegger draws the "subject" of his questions—"Being"—closer.

This is what binds the language of thinking that Heidegger sought to speak to the language of the poets. It is not just that one finds Heidegger using poetisizing phrases to embellish the barren language of concepts. The language of a poem [*eines Gedichts*], one that is really a poem [*ein Gedicht*], is not poetic [*poetisch*]. Rather, that which the language of thinking has in common with poetic [*dichterisch*] language is that nothing is opined here and, therefore, nothing can be signified. The poetic [*dichterisch*] word, like the word of thinking, "opines" nothing. In a poem, nothing is opined that is not already to be found there [*da*] in its linguistic formation and what is opined cannot exist [*dasein*] in any other linguistic form. Certainly the word spoken by the philosopher is not the incarnate Being of thought, at least not in the same way that the word of the poem embodies the Being of poetry. But in its speaking, the thought itself is not simply realized; rather, the thought is authenticated in it. This could not be more apparent than in the movement of thought that is a dialogue of thinking with itself. In thinking philosophy, thinking itself is transformed completely into thought. One need only recall the way Heidegger approached the lectern—the excited and almost angry seriousness with which his thought was ventured, the way he glanced askant out the window, his eyes only brushing over the audience, and the way his voice was pushed to its very limit in all of the excitement—to recognize that the language in which Heidegger spoke and wrote simply cannot be avoided. One must take it as it is and as it offers itself in its thought. For, in this way is thinking there [*da*]. That is what we have to thank Heidegger for, not only for being one who has thought something important and has had something important to say, but because, in a time that rushed headlong into an arithmetic and calculative approach, he has left something there [*da*] that has set a new standard for thinking for all of us.

CHAPTER SEVEN

THE LANGUAGE OF METAPHYSICS (1968)

The tremendous power emanating from Heidegger's creative energies in the early 1920s seemed to sweep along the generation of students returning from World War I or just beginning its studies, so that a complete break with traditional academic philosophy seemed to take place with Heidegger's appearance—long before it was expressed in his own thought. It was like a new breakthrough into the unknown that posed something radically new as compared with all the mere movements and countermovements of the Christian Occident. A generation shattered by the collapse of an epoch wanted to begin completely anew; it did not want to retain anything that had formerly been held valid. Even in the intensification of the German language that took place in his concepts, Heidegger's thought seemed to defy any comparison with what philosophy had previously meant. And that was in spite of the unceasing and intensive interpretive effort that especially distinguished Heidegger's academic instruction—his immersion in Aristotle and Plato, Augustine and Thomas, Leibniz and Kant, in Hegel and Husserl.

From *Philosophical Hermeneutics*, by Hans-Georg Gadamer, trans. and ed. David Linge, pp. 229–40. Copyright 1976 by The Regents of the University of California. Reprinted by permission of the University of California Press.

Altogether unexpected things came to the surface and were discussed in connection with these names. Each of these great figures from our classical philosophical tradition was completely transformed and seemed to proclaim a direct, compelling truth that was perfectly fused with the thought of its resolute interpreter. The distance separating our historical consciousness from the tradition seemed to be nonexistent. The calm and confident aloofness with which the neo-Kantian "history of philosophical problems" was accustomed to deal with the tradition, and the whole of contemporary thought that came from the academic rostum, now suddenly seemed to be mere child's play.

In actual fact, the break with tradition that took place in Heidegger's thought represented just as much an incomparable renewal of the tradition. Only gradually did the younger students come to see both how much appropriation of the tradition was present in the tradition, as well as how profound the criticism was in the appropriation. Two great classical figures of philosophical thought, however, have long occupied an ambiguous position in Heidegger's thought, standing out as much by their affinity with Heidegger as by their radical from him. These two thinkers are Plato and Hegel. From the very beginning, Plato was viewed in a critical light in Heidegger's work, in that Heidegger took over and transformed the Aristotelean criticism of the Idea of the Good and stressed especially the Aristotelean concept of analogy. Yet it was Plato who provided the motto for *Being and Time*. Only after World War II, with the decisive incorporation of Plato into the history of Being, was the ambiguity in regard to Plato removed. But Heidegger's thought has revolved around Hegel until the present day in ever new attempts at delineation. In contrast to the phenomenological craftsmanship that was all too quickly forgotten by the scholarship of the time, Hegel's dialectic of pure thought asserted itself with renewed power. Hence Hegel not only continually provoked Heidegger to self-defense, but he was also the one with whom Heidegger was associated in the eyes of all those who sought to defend themselves against the claim of Heidegger's thought. Would the new radicalism with which Heidegger stirred the oldest questions of philosophy to new life really overtake the final form of Western metaphysics and realize a new metaphysical possibility that Hegel had released? Or would the circle of the philosophy of reflection, which paralyzed all hopes of freedom and liberation, force Heidegger's thought too back into its orbit?

One can say that the development of Heidegger's late philosophy has scarcely encountered a critique anywhere that does not go back in the last analysis to Hegel's position. This observation is true in the sense of aligning Heidegger with Hegel's abortive speculative titanic revolution, as Gerhard Krüger[1] and countless others after him have argued. It is also valid in the positive Hegelianizing sense that Heidegger is not sufficiently aware of his own proximity to Hegel, and for this reason he does not really do justice to the radical position of speculative logic. The later criticism has occurred basically in two problem areas. One is Heidegger's assimilation of history into his own philosophical approach, a point that he seems to share with Hegel. The second is the hidden and unnoticed dialectic that attaches to all essentially Heideggerian assertions. If Hegel tried to penetrate the history of philosophy philosophically from the standpoint of absolute knowledge, that is, to raise it to a science, Heidegger's description of the history of Being (in particular, the history of the forgetfulness of Being) involved a similarly comprehensive claim. Indeed, there is in Heidegger nothing of that necessity of historical progress that is both the glory and bane of Hegelian philosophy. For Heidegger, rather, the history that is remembered and taken up into the absolute present in absolute knowing is precisely an advance sign of the radical forgetfulness of Being that has marked the history of Europe in the century after Hegel. But for Heidegger it is fate, not history (remembered and penetrable by understanding), that originated in the conception of Being in Greek metaphysics and that in modern science and technology carries the forgetfulness of Being to the extreme. Nevertheless, no matter how much it may belong to the temporal constitution of human beings to be exposed to the unpredictability of fate, this does not rule out the claim continually raised and legitimated in the course of Western history to think what is. And so Heidegger too appears to claim a genuinely historical self-consciousness for himself, indeed, even an eschatological self-consciousness.

The second critical motif proceeds from the indeterminateness and undeterminableness of what Heidegger calls "Being." This criticism tries by Hegelian means to explain the alleged tautology of

---

1. See Gerhard Krüger, "Martin Heidegger und der Humanismus," *Theologische Rundschau* 18 (1950): 148–178.

Being—that it is itself—as a disguised second immediacy that emerges from the total mediation of the immediate. Furthermore, are there not real dialectical antitheses at work whenever Heidegger explicates himself? For instance, we find the dialectical tension of thrownness and projection, of authenticity and inauthenticity, of "nothing" as the veil of Being, and finally, and most importantly, the way that truth and error, revealment and concealment revolve around one another in an inner tension [*Gegenwendigkeit*], which constitute the event of Being as the event of truth. Did not the mediation of Being and "nothing" in the truth of becoming—that is, in the truth of the concrete as Hegel undertook it—already mark out the conceptual framework within which alone the Heideggerian doctrine of the inner tension [*Gegenwendigkeit*] of truth can exist? Hegel, by his dialectical-speculative sharpening of the antithesis in understanding, overcame a thinking dominated by the understanding. Would it be possible to get beyond this achievement, so as to overcome the logic and language of metaphysics as a whole?

Access to our problem undoubtedly lies in the problem of "nothing" and its suppression by metaphysics, a theme Heidegger formulated in his inaugural address in Freiburg. In this perspective, the "nothing" of Parmenides and Plato, and also Aristotle's definition of the divine as *energia* and *dynamis* really constitutes a total vitiation of "nothing." God, as the infinite knowledge that has the being [*das Seiende*] from itself, is understood from the vantage point of privative experience of being human, such as in the experience of sleep, death, and forgetting, as the unlimited presence of everything present. But another motif seems to be at work in the history of metaphysical thinking alongside this vitiation of "nothing" that extends even into Hegel and Husserl. While Aristotelean metaphysics has culminated in the question, What is the Being of beings? it is the question placed by Leibniz and Schelling and then called the basic question of metaphysics by Heidegger, namely, "Why is there anything at all and not rather 'nothing?,'" which expressly continues the confrontation with the problem of "nothing." The analysis of the concept of *dynamis* in Plato, Plotinus, the tradition of negative theology, Nicolas of Cusa, and Liebniz, and all the way to Schelling—from whom Schopenhauer, Nietzsche, and the metaphysics of the will take their departure—all serve to show that the understanding of Being in terms of presence [*Präsenz*] is constantly threatened by the "nothing." In our own century, this situation is also found in Max Scheler's dualism of impulse and spirit and Ernst Bloch's philosophy of the not yet, as well as in such hermeneutical phenomena as the question, doubt, wonder, and so on. To this extent, Heidegger's approach has an intrinsic preparation in the subject matter of metaphysics itself.

In order to clarify the immanent necessity of the development within his own thought that led Heidegger to "the turn," and to show that it has nothing to do with a dialectical reversal, we must proceed from the fact that the transcendental-phenomenological conception of self in *Being and Time* is already essentially different from Husserl's conception of it. Husserl's constitutional analysis of the consciousness of time shows particularly well that the self-constitution of the primal presence (which Husserl could indeed designate as a kind of primal potentiality) is based entirely on the concept of constitutive accomplishment and is thus dependent on the Being of valid objectivity. The self-constitution of the transcendental ego, a problem that can be traced back to the fifth chapter of the *Logical Investigations,* stands wholly within the traditional understanding of Being, despite—indeed, precisely because of—the absolute historicity that forms the transcendental ground of all objectivities. Now it must be admitted that Heidegger's transcendental point of departure from the being that has its Being as an issue and the doctrine of the existentiells in *Being and Time* both carry with them a transcendental appearance, as though Heidegger's thoughts were, as Oskar Becker puts it,[2] simply the elaboration of further horizons of transcendental phenomenology that had not previously been secured and that had to do with the historicality of Dasein. In reality, however, Heidegger's undertaking means something quite different. Jaspers's formulation of the boundary situation certainly provided Heidegger with a starting point for explicating the finitude of existence in its basic significance. But this approach served as the preparation of the question of Being in a radically altered sense and was not the explication of a radical ontology in Husserl's sense. The concept of "fundamental ontology"—modelled after that of "fundamental theology"—also creates a difficulty. The mutual interconnection of authenticity and inauthenticity, of the revealment of and concealment of Dasein, which

---

2. See Oskar Becker, "Von der Hinfälligeit des Schönen und der Abendteuerlichkeit des Künstlers," published originally in the *Festschrift für Husserl* (1929), pp. 27–52.

appeared in *Being and Time* more in the sense of a rejection of an ethicistic, affect-oriented thinking, turned out increasingly to be the real nucleus of the "question of Being." According to Heidegger's formulation in *On the Essence of Truth,* ek-sistence and in-sistence are indeed still conceived from the point of view of human Dasein. But when he says that the truth of Being is the *un*truth, that is, the concealment of Being in "error," then the decisive change in the concept of "essence" which follows from the destruction of the Greek tradition of metaphysics can no longer be ignored. For Heidegger leaves behind him both the traditional concept of essence and that of the ground of essence.

What the interconnection of concealment and revealment means and what it has to do with the new concept of "essence" can be exhibited phenomenologically in Heidegger's own essential experience of thought in a number of ways. (1) In the Being of the implement that does not have its essence in its objective obstinacy, but in its being ready-to-hand, which allows us to concentrate on what is beyond the implement itself. (2) In the Being of the artwork, which holds its truth within itself in such a fashion that this truth is available in no other way but in the work. For the beholder or receiver, "essence" corresponds to tarrying alongside the work. (3) In the thing, as the one and only that stands in itself, "compelled to nothing," and contrasts in its irreplaceability with the concept of the object of consumption, as found industrial production. (4) And finally in the word. The "essence" of the word does not lie in being totally expressed, but rather in what is left unsaid, as we see in remaining speechless and remaining silent. The common structure of essence that is evident in all four of these experiences of thinking is a "Being-there" [*Dasein*] that encompasses Being-absent as well as Being-present. During his early years at Freiburg, Heidegger once said, "One cannot lose God as one loses his pocket knife." But in fact one cannot simply lose a pocket knife in such a fashion that it is no longer "there." When one has lost a long familiar implement such as a pocket knife, it demonstrates its existence [*Dasein*] by the fact that one continually misses it. Hölderlin's "Fehl der Götter" or Eliot's silence of the Chinese vase are not nonexistence, but "Being" in the thickest sense because they are silent. The gap that is left by what is missing is not a place remaining empty within what is present-to-hand; rather, it belongs to the being-there [*Dasein*] of that to which it is missing, and is "presencing" [*an-wesend*] in it. Hence "essence" is concretized, and we can demonstrate how what is present is at the same time the covering over of presence.

Problems that necessarily eluded transcendental inquiry and appeared as mere peripheral phenomena become comprehensible when we proceed from such experiences. In the first place, this holds for "nature." Becker's postulation of a paraontology is justified here insofar as nature is no longer only "a limiting case of the Being of a possible inner-worldly being." But Becker himself has never recognized that his counterconcept of paraexistence, which is concerned with such essential phenomena as mathematical and dream existence, is a dialectical construction. Becker himself synthesized it with its opposite and thus marked out a third position, without noticing how this position corresponds to the Heideggerian teachings after the "turn."

A second large complex of problems that comes into a new light in the context of Heidegger's later thought is that of the Thou and the We. We are familiar with this problem complex from Husserl's ongoing discussion of the problem of intersubjectivity; in *Being and Time* it is interpreted in terms of the world of concern. What constitutes the mode of being of essence is now considered from the point of view of the dialogue, that is, in terms of our capacity to listen to each other *in concreto,* for instance, when we perceive what governs a conversation or whenever we notice its absence in a tortured conversation. But above all, the inscrutable problem of life and corporeality presents itself in a new way. The concept of the living being [*Lebe-Wesen*], which Heidegger emphasized in his "Letter on Humanism," raises new questions, especially the question of its correspondence to the nature of human beings [*Menschen-Wesen*] and the nature of language [*Sprach-Wesen*]. But behind this line of questioning stands the question of the Being of the self, which was easy enough to define in terms of German idealism's concept of reflection. It becomes puzzling, however, the moment we no longer proceed from the self or self-consciousness, or—as in *Being and Time*—from human Dasein, but rather from essence. The fact that Being presences [*anwest*] in a "clearing," and that in this fashion thinking human beings are the placeholder of Being, points to a primordial interconnection of Being and human beings. The tool, the work of art, thing, the word— in all of these, the relation to human beings stands forth clearly in essence itself. But in what sense? Scarcely in the sense that the Being of the human self thereby acquires its definition. The example of language has already shown us that. As Heidegger says, language speaks *us,* insofar as we do not really preside over it and control it, although, of course, no one disputes the fact that it is we who speak it. And Heidegger's assertion here is not without meaning.

If we want to raise the question of the "self" in Heidegger, we will have first to consider and reject Neo-Platonic modes of thought. For a cosmic drama consisting in the emanation out of the One and the return into it, with the self designated as the pivot of the return, lies beyond what is possible here. Or one could consider what Heidegger understands by "insistence" as the way to a solution. What Heidegger called the "in-sistence" of Dasein and what he called errancy are certainly to be conceived from the point of view of the forgetfulness of Being. But is this forgetfulness the sole mode of coming to presence? Will this render intelligible the place-holding character of human *Dasein?* Can the concept of coming to presence and the "there" be maintained in exclusive relation to human Dasein, if we take the growth of plants and the living being into consideration? In his *On the Essence of Truth,* Heidegger still conceived of "insistence" from the point of view of the being that first "raised its head" [i.e., human beings]. But does not in-sistence have to be taken in a broader sense? And hence "ek-sistence" too? Certainly the confinement of the living being in its environment, discussed in the "Letter on Humanism," means that it is not open for Being as is man, who is aware of his possibility of not being. But have we not learned from Heidegger that the real Being of the living being is not its own individual being-there, but rather the genus? And is the genus not "there" for the living being, even if not in the same way that Being is present for human beings in the in-sistence of the forgetfulness of Being? Does it not compose a part of the Being of the genus that its members "know" themselves, as the profound expression of the Lutheran Bible puts it? Indeed, as knowing, are they not concealed from themselves but yet in such fashion that knowing passes over into it? Is it not also characteristic of in-sistence that the animal intends only itself [*conservatio sui*] and yet precisely in this way provides for the reproduction of its kind?

Similarly, we could ask about the growth of vegetation: Is it only a coming to presence for human beings? Does not every form of life as such have a tendency to secure itself in its Being, indeed to persist in it? Is it not precisely its finitude that it wants to tarry in this manner? And does it not hold for human beings as well that the Dasein in him, as Heidegger called it, is not to be thought of at all as a kind of highest self-possession that allows him to step outside the circuit of life like a god? Isn't our entire doctrine of human beings distorted rather than put in order by modern metaphysical subjectivism, in that we consider the essence of human beings to be society (ζῷον πολιτικον [social animal])? Is it not just this belief that declares the inner tension that is Being itself? And does it not mean that it is senseless to pit "nature" against "Being?"

Within this context, the continuing difficulty is that of avoiding the language of metaphysics, which conceives of all these matters in terms of the "power of reflection." But what do we mean when we speak of the "language of metaphysics?" It is illuminating that the experience of "essence" is not that of manipulating thinking. If we keep this distinction in mind, we can see that the concept of "recollection" has something natural about it. It is true that recollection itself is something and that in it history has its reality, not that history is simply remembered through it. But what takes place in "recollection?" Is it really tenable to expect something like a reversal in it— like the abruptness of fate? Whatever the case may be, the important thing in the phenomenon of recollection, it seems to me, is that something is secured and preserved in the "there," so that it can never not be, as long as recollection remains alive. Yet recollection is not something that clutches tenaciously at what is vanishing; the nonexistence of what disappears is not at all concealed or obstinately disputed by it. Rather, something like consent takes place in it (of which Rilke's *Duino Elegies* tells us something). There is nothing of what we have called insistence in it.

Conversely, what we may call fascination arises through the constructive capacity and technological power of insistence, that is, of human forgetfulness of Being. There is essentially no limit to the experience of Being, which, since Nietzsche, we call nihilism. But if this fascination proceeds from such a constantly intensifying obstinacy, does it not find its own ultimate end in itself, precisely by virtue of the fact that the constantly new becomes something left behind, and that this happens *without* a special event intervening or a reversal taking place? Does not the natural weight of things remain perceptible and make itself felt the more monotonously the noise of the constantly new may sound forth? To be sure, Hegel's idea of knowledge, concealed as absolute self-transparency, has something fantastic about it if it is supposed to restore complete at-homeness in Being. But could not a restoration of at-homeness come about in the sense that the process of making-oneself-at-home in the world has never ceased to take place, and has never ceased to be the better reality that is not deafened by the madness of technology? Does this restoration not occur when the illusory character of the technocracy, the paralyzing sameness of everything human beings can make, becomes perceptible, and human beings are released again into the really astonishing character of their own finite Being? This freedom is certainly not gained in the sense of an absolute transparency, or a being-at-home that is no longer endangered. But just as the thinking of what cannot be preconceived [*das Denken des Unvordenklichen*] preserves what is its own, for example, the homeland, what cannot be preconceived regarding our finitude is reunited with itself in the constant process of the coming to language of our Dasein. In the up and down movement, in coming into Being and passing away, it is "there."

Is this the old metaphysics? Is it the language of metaphysics alone that achieves this continual coming-to-language of our Being-in-the-world? Certainly it is the language of metaphysics, but further behind it is the language of the Indo-Germanic peoples, which makes such thinking capable of being formulated. But can a language—or a family of languages—ever properly be called the language of metaphysical thinking, just because metaphysics was thought, or what would be more, anticipated in it? Is not language always the language of the homeland and the process of becoming-at-home in the world? And does this fact not mean that language knows no restrictions and never breaks down, because it holds infinite possibilities of utterance in readiness? It seems to me that the hermeneutical dimension enters here and demonstrates its inner infinity in the speaking that takes place in the dialogue. To be sure, the technical language [*Schulsprache*] of philosophy is preformed by the grammatical structure of the Greek language, and its usages in Graeco-Latin times established ontological implications whose prejudiced character Heidegger uncovered. But we must ask: Are the universality of objectifying reason and the eidetic structure of linguistic meanings really bound to these particular historically developed interpretations of *subjectum* and *species* and *actus* that the West has produced? Or do they hold true for all languages? It cannot be denied that there are certain structural aspects of the Greek language and a grammatical self-consciousness, particularly in Latin, that fix in a definite direction of interpretation the hierarchy of genus and species, the relation of substance and accident, the structure of predication and the verb as an action word. But is there no rising above such a preschematizing of thought? For instance, if one contrasts the Western predicative judgment with the Eastern figurative expression, which acquires its expressive power from the reciprocal reflection of what is meant and what is said, are these two not in truth only different modes of utterance within one and the same universal, namely, within the essence of language and reason? Do concept and judgment not remain embedded within the life of meaning of the language we speak and in which we know how to say what it is we mean?[3] And conversely, cannot the connotative aspect of such Oriental reflective expressions always be drawn into the hermeneutical movement that creates common understanding, just as the expression of the work of art can? Language always arises within such a movement. Can anyone really contend that there has ever been language in any other sense than in the fulfilling of such a movement? Hegel's doctrine of the speculative proposition too seems to me to have its place here, and always takes up into itself its own sharpening into the dialectic of contradiction. For in speaking, there always remains the possibility of cancelling the objectifying tendency of language, just as Hegel cancels the logic of understanding, Heidegger the language of metaphysics, the Orientals the diversity of realms of Being, and the poet everything given. But to cancel [*aufheben*] means to take up and use.

---

3. Certainly Derrida would not agree with this rhetorical question. Rather, he would see in it a lack of radicality that refers back to "metaphysics"—and this includes Heidegger. In his eyes Nietzsche is the one who truly can be credited with overcoming metaphysical thought, and consequently he subordinates language to "*ecriture*" (see *l'Ecriture et la différance*). [Regarding the contrast between hermeneutics and this poststructuralistic following of Nietzsche, see my newer works in the *Ges. Werke*, volume 2, pages 330–360 and pages 361–372.]

CHAPTER EIGHT

PLATO (1976)

What we learned from Heidegger was above all the pervasive unity of the metaphysics originated by the Greeks and its continued validity under the subtly altered conditions of modern thought. The Aristotelean question concerning a primary science, which Aristotle himself expressly designates as the science to be sought for, initiated the tradition of Western thought. In this tradition the question of the Being of beings was posed in terms of the highest and most eminent of beings, namely, the divine. If Heidegger understood his own endeavor as a preparation for posing the question of Being anew, then this assumed that the traditional metaphysics, since its beginning with Aristotle, had lost all explicit awareness of the questionableness of the sense of Being. This was a challenge to the self-understanding of a metaphysics which would not recognize itself in its own consequences: in the radical nominalism of the modern age, and in the transformation of the modern concept of science into an all-embracing technology. The main concern of *Sein und Zeit* was to urge just such a recognition by metaphysics and its secondary formations. At the same time Heidegger's destruction of metaphysics gave rise to the question of the beginnings of Greek thought, beginnings which preceded the development of the metaphysical

From *The Question of Being*, trans. and ed. Mervyn Sprung (University Park and London: Pennsylvania State University Press, 1978), pp. 45–53. Copyright 1978 by the Pennsylvania State University. Reproduced by permission of the publisher.

question. It is well known that in this respect Heidegger, like Nietzsche, placed special emphasis on the origins of Greek thought. For Heidegger, Anaximander, Heraclitus, and Parmenides were not a preliminary phase of the metaphysical inquiry, but witnesses to the essential openness of the beginning—where *aletheia* (unconcealedness, truth) had as yet nothing of the correctness of a statement, indeed not even of the mere revealedness of a being.

But what of Plato in this matter? Did his thinking not stand in between the early thinkers and the scholastic form of metaphysics—a metaphysics which assumed its initial form in the teachings of Aristotle? How can his place be determined? Heidegger's questioning back to a point before the question of metaphysics was posed, i.e., to the Being of beings, was certainly not meant to be a return to a mythical pre-age, nor was a presumptuous criticism of metaphysics from a superior standpoint intended. Heidegger never wanted to "overcome" metaphysics as an aberration of thought. He understood metaphysics as the historical course of the West, determining its destiny. Here destiny is that which has overtaken us and which has irrevocably determined our own position and all possible ways into the future. There is no historical rue. And Heidegger most certainly attempted to find the way of his own questioning within the history of metaphysics and its internal tensions, and not apart from it.

Aristotle was in many respects not only his opponent but also his ally. It was especially Aristotle's repudiation of Plato's idea of a universal good, based on the concept of analogy, and Aristotle's penetration of the nature of *physis,* particularly Book VI of the *Nicomachean Ethics* and Book II of the *Physics,* which Heidegger interpreted in a fruitful way. It is evident that it is precisely these two "positive" aspects of Aristotle's thought which are the most important documentations of Aristotle's criticism of Plato. In the first place, there is the severing of the question concerning the "Good," as something which human beings bring into the question concerning human *praxis,* from the theoretical posing of the question concerning Being. In the second place, there is the criticism of the Platonic theory of Forms. This finds its expression in the ontological primacy of motility in Aristotle's concept of *physis* [nature] and claims to overcome the orientation toward the Pythagorean mathematical forms. Both point at Plato, and in both respects Aristotle appears almost as a forerunner of Heideggerean thought. The doctrine of *phronesis* as practical knowledge stands opposed to all objectifying tendencies of science, and in the concept of *physis* and its ontological primacy there is at least a hint of a dimension of "givenness" [*Aufgehen*] which is superior to any subject-object opposition.

This was certainly Heidegger's own fruitful "recognition"; it would be ridiculous to speak of Aristotle's influence on Heidegger. In depicting the role which Franz Brentano's treatise on the various significances of being [*Seiende*] in Aristotle had played for him, Heidegger himself told us what Aristotle meant to him as an initial inspiration. Brentano's careful delineation of the variety of meanings which lie in Aristotle's concept of Being led Heidegger to be seized by the question of what might be concealed behind this disconnected variety. In every case, taking Aristotle as the point of departure carried with it the implication of a critical orientation towards Plato's theory of forms.

But then, upon opening *Sein und Zeit,* we find right on the first page the famous quotation from the *Sophist* concerning the question of Being, which has always been posed, always in vain. It is true that this quotation contains no detailed articulation of the way in which the question of Being is posed. Furthermore, the overcoming of the Eleatic concept of Being which commences with the *Sophist* points in an entirely different direction from that of the question concerning the hidden unity of the various meanings of Being which had aroused the young Heidegger. There is still another passage in the *Sophist* which Heidegger does not quote, although he refers to it, and which actually, even though only in a merely formal way, implies the continuing predicament concerning Being. This predicament was the same in the fourth century before Christ as it is in our twentieth century.

The stranger from Elea expounds the two basic modes of manifestation of beings as motion and rest. These are two mutually exclusive modes of Being, but they appear to exhaust completely the possibilities of the manifestation of Being. If one does not wish to conceive of the state of rest, one must conceive of motion, and vice-versa. Where should one look if one does not wish to catch sight of one or the other but of "Being?" There appears to be no possibility whatsoever of open questioning. It is clearly not the intention of the Eleatic stranger to understand Being as the universal genus which differentiates itself into these two aspects of Being. What Plato has in mind, rather, is that in speaking about Being a differentiation is implicit which does not distinguish different realism of Being but rather suggests an inner structuredness of Being itself. Selfness or identity as well as otherness or difference are essential to all discourse about Being. These two aspects, far from being mutually exclusive, are rather mutually determining. Whatever is identical with itself is thereby different from anything else. Insofar as it is what it is, it is not everything else. Being and Non-being are inextricably intertwined. Indeed, it appears to be precisely the mark of a philosopher as against the sham logic of the sophist that it is the togetherness of Being (the affirmation) and Non-being (the negation) which constitutes the nature of beings.

Now it is precisely at this point that the later Heidegger takes up the question: the determinate nature of beings, whose relationship to Being constitutes the entire truth of Being, preceded and precluded any posing of the question concerning the meaning of Being. Heidegger, in fact, describes the history of metaphysics as the growing forgetfulness of the question concerning Being. The revealedness of beings—the self-manifestation of the *eidos* in its unchangeable form—amounts to the abandonment of the question concerning the meaning of Being. What manifests itself as *eidos,* i.e., as an unchangeable determinateness showing the "What-of-Being" [*Was-Sein*], understands "Being" implicitly as a continuous presence [*Gegenwart*], and this determines as well the meaning of uncon-cealedness, that is, truth, and establishes the criterion of right and wrong for every assertion about beings. The claim "Theatetus can fly" is false because people are incapable of flight. In this way, through his reinterpretation of the Eleatic doctrine of Being as the dialectic of Being and Non-being, Plato grounds the meaning of "knowledge" in the *logos* which allows assertions about the beingness of beings, that is, about the What-of-Being. In so doing, Plato predetermines the way the question will be put in the Aristotelian doctrine of τί ἦν εἶναι [the essence, that which something is], the core of his metaphysics. In this sense the distortion of the question of Being begins with Plato, and the criticism which Aristotle brings against the Platonic doctrine of forms does not change the fact that the science of Being which Aristotle sought remains within this prior determination and does not attempt to question behind it.

It is not appropriate to develop at this point the problematic of modern philosophy to which Heidegger's critical return to Greek metaphysics is a response. It will suffice to recall the way Heidegger defined the task of "destroying" the basic concepts of modern philosophy, especially the concepts "subjectivity" and "consciousness." Above all, the impressive way in which Husserl, in inexhaustible variations, attempted to determine the constitution of self-consciousness as temporal consciousness was a determining factor—in an antithetical way—in Heidegger's own way of taking up the problem of the temporal structure of *Dasein*. Certainly, Heidegger's familiarity with the Greek philosophical heritage stood him in good stead in critically distancing himself from Husserl's Neo-Kantian, idealistic programming of phenomenology. In any case, it is a crass simplification to interpret Heidegger's accentuation of history and the historical as merely a thematic turn which separates him from Husserl's thinking. Not only the controversy between Husserl and Dilthey but especially the unpublished second volume of the *Ideas,* with which Heidegger was naturally quite familiar, are evidence against any doubt of Husserl's concern with the question of history and the historical. Indeed, they confirm the attempt to accommodate Heidegger's *Sein und Zeit* within the Husserlian phenomenology, as in Oskar Becker's unlucky attempt in the Husserl *Festschrift* of 1928. There is no doubt that it was clear to Husserl from the beginning that the "mortal danger" of skepticism, which he took historical relativism to be, could not be averted without clarifying the constitution of the historical structure of human social life.

Nevertheless, what Heidegger undertook in *Sein und Zeit* was not only a deepening of the foundations of a transcendental phenomenology, it was also a preparation for a radical change which would bring the collapse of the entire concept of the constitution of all conceivable meanings in the transcendental ego, and above all of the concept of the self-constitution of the ego itself. In analyzing the temporal nature of the stream of consciousness, Husserl conceived of the self-manifestation of the stream, that is, the nonmediated presence, as the ultimate factor in the ego to which we can descend. He did not regard the structure of iteration, which becomes evident in the self-constitution of the ego, in any way as an *aporia,* but claimed it as a positive description. That meant, basically, he did not go beyond the Hegelian ideal of the perfect self-transparency of absolute knowledge.

Heidegger does not merely set the unpredictability of existence off against this ideal, as the Young Hegelians and Kierkegaard had already done in a variety of ways. That is not what is truly novel about his endeavor. If it were, he would have remained in fact dialectically dependent, caught in a Hegelianizing anti-Hegelianism. (It is odd to note that Adorno, in his "negative dialectic," never realized how close he comes to Heidegger, if one only sees Heidegger in light of his critique of Hegel.) The truth is that Heidegger, as a student of early Greek thought and as one who also entered into dialogue with it, posed the problem of facticity in a more radical and original sense. Because metaphysics in its beginnings attempted to question the unconcealedness of beings through the *logos* and its presence and preservation in thought and speech, the authentic dimension of the temporality and historicality of Being fell into a deep and lengthy shadow.

Heidegger, on the other hand, questioned behind the beginnings of metaphysics and sought to open a dimension in which, as with "historicism," historicality would no longer serve as a limiting hinderance to truth and the objectivity of knowledge. Nor can this be understood as a *coup de main* which attempts to solve the problem of historical relativism by radicalizing it. It seems to me to be significant that the later Heidegger, in his self-interpretation, no longer takes the problem of historicism seriously (see *"Mein Weg in die Phänomenologie"*). Historicality is for Heidegger the ontological structure of the "temporalizing" of *Dasein* in self-projection and thrownness, in the clearing and withdrawal of Being. It is concerned with a realm which lies behind all questioning concerning beings. It is possible to recognize, as Heidegger does, this dimension of the question of Being in its beginnings in the riddle of Anaximander, in the monumental singleness of Parmenides's truth and in Heraclitus's "one and only wise man." But one can raise the contrary question of whether the founders of metaphysical thinking themselves did not give evidence of this dimension and whether, in the *logos* of the Platonic dialectic of in Aristotle's of *nous,* which perceives essence and determines it as what it is, the realm in which all questioning and speech find their field of activity [*Spielraum*] does not become visible. Does the initial question of metaphysics concerning the "what" of beings really obstruct the question of Being completely, as without a doubt do the modes of speech developed in the sciences which logic makes into its analytical theme?

Heidegger, as it is well known, saw in Plato's doctrine of forms the first step in the transformation of truth from unconcealedness to the appropriateness and correctness of statements. That this is one-sided he himself later conceded, but his self-correction amounts merely to saying that Plato was not the first, rather *"aletheia"* was experienced right away and only as *orthotes,* as the correctness of statements (Heidegger, *"Zur Sache des Denkens,"* p. 78). I would like to raise the question, contrary to this, whether Plato himself did not attempt to think the realm of unconcealedness, at least in the Idea of the Good, and not merely because of certain complications and internal difficulties in the doctrine of forms; but rather whether from the very beginning he had not questioned behind this doctrine and thereby *aletheia* as correctness. It seems to me that something can be said for this.

Of course, one cannot read Plato's works through the eyes of the Aristotelean critique. This critique aims relentlessly at the refutation of the *chorismos* [separation or split] of the ideas, a point to which Aristotle always returns and which he developed into the essential difference between Socrates's definitional questions and Plato (*Met.* M 4). In fact, this thesis of Aristotle's suffers from a weakness which was made into an accusation, especially by Hegel and the Marburg Neo-Kantians, that Plato himself in his dialectical dialogues of the later period dealt with the *chorismos* in a radical way and critically rejected it. The genuine depth of the Platonic dialectic is constituted precisely by its claim to be able show the way out of this dilemma of the *chorismos* and participation by lessening the importance of the separation between what partakes and that in which it partakes.

That this is not merely a later development of Platonic thinking becomes clear, in my view, if one considers the exceptional role which the Idea of the Good played in Plato's works from early on. Because the Idea of the Good does not fit easily into the scheme of Aristotle's critique of *chorismos* and in fact, as could be shown, is only hesitantly and cautiously included in Aristotle's general critique of the Ideas, the critique of the Idea of the Good is carried out from a practical point of view. The theoretical problem remains, however, that it is not merely chance equivocations which permit calling very different things "good," but that this conceals a genuine problem which Aristotle attempted to solve in his doctrine of *analogia entis* [analogy of Being]. But let us turn to Plato himself.

Initially we encounter the question concerning the Good itself as the constant negative instance on which the collocutors understanding of *areté* [virtue] comes to grief. The underlying idea of knowledge, which is modeled on craft skill and whose meaning is the mastery of practical situations, proves to be inapplicable in the case of the Idea of the Good. It is obviously more than mere literary art when Plato's statements about the Good in itself have a tendency to withdraw in a peculiar way into a realm beyond. In the *Republic* the special position of the Idea of the Good in contrast to the *areté* concepts of definite content is insisted on so that it is only by means of a sense analogy, that of the sun, that the Good is spoken of. It is decisive that the sun functions as the *bringer* of light and that it is light which makes the visible world visible to the seer. It is significant that the Idea of the Good, conforming to the frequently used analogy, is, so to speak, only indirectly visible. Within the whole of the thought of the *Republic* that means that the constitution of the soul, the state and—in the *Timaeus*—the world is grounded in the One, that is, in the Good, even as the sun is the ground of light that binds together everything. The Good is that which bestows unity rather than that which is itself a One. It is, after all, beyond all Being.

There can be no doubt that this Super-Being should not be thought of after the manner of neo-Platonism as the source of a cosmic drama, nor is it the goal of a withdrawal and mystical union. It is true, however, that this One which is the Good, is not, as the *Philebus* shows, comprehensible in any way as one but only as a trinity of measure, appropriateness, and "truth" as most suitably befits the nature of the beautiful. "Is" the Good anywhere at all if not in the form [*Gestalt*] of the beautiful? And does that not mean that it is not an existent particular, but is to be thought of as the unconcealedness of emergence into the field of vision (τὸ ἐλτρανέστατον [stepping out into visibility], *Phaedrus* 250d).

Even Aristotle's interpretation of Plato takes account of this singular position of the Good in an indirect way. As was mentioned earlier, Aristotle, in the context of practical philosophy, denied the Idea of the Good any relevance at all and, on the other hand, carries out his criticism of the doctrine of Forms without regard for the Idea of the Good. But he sees the theoretical problem of the unity of the Good so closely related to the problem of the unity of Being that one is justified in distinguishing his ways of thinking, those of analogy and attribution, from his general approach to Plato's doctrine of Forms. It can be shown from Aristotle's own work that he could indeed distinguish between the acceptance of the Forms in general and their logical and ontological inadequacies which he pointed out, on one hand, and the principle of this acceptance, on the other— which forms the topic of Book VI of the *Metaphysics*. In Aristotle's terms, that is, the Good—and Being likewise—is not one Form among many but a beginning, an *arché*. It is not entirely clear if "the Good itself" is the one which as *arché*, together with twoness, forms the basis of all determinations of the Forms, or whether perhaps the One is itself prior to this twoness of One and indefinite plurality. One thing, however, is definite: The One is as little a number as the Idea of the Good is a Form in the sense of the *eidos* that Aristotle criticized as a vacuous duplication of the world.

The Idea of the Good is no longer spoken of in the later Plato when the central question of the dialectic, that is, the *logos ousias* [concept of essence], becomes thematic. That is even true of the *Philebus,* where the theme is explicitly the Good, admittedly the Good in the life of human beings. Here, however, the criterion of the Good, which, as we saw, was defined in the form [*Gestalt*] of the beautiful, cannot be left undiscussed. In the *Philebus* the funda- mental discussion of the four categories is conducted without espe- cially distinguishing the Idea of the Good. And in the *Sophist* and *Parmenides* the discussion of the Platonic dialectic appears to be far beyond the doctrine of Forms, and, indeed, these dialogues have been understood as the renunciation of the doctrine of the Forms. The doctrine of the *logos* of Being which is developed in these dialectical dialogues is, in any case, as little subject to Aristotle's *chorismos*-criticism as is the Idea of the Good. "Dogmatic Platonism," which Aristotle's criticism belabors, has no basis in these dialogues. On the contrary, the schema of the *dihairesis* which Plato presents as his dialectical method in these dialogues has been for some time understood as a successful resolution of the *methexis* problem (Natorp, N. Hartmann, J. Stenzel), which invalidates Aristotle's criticism. It is even more noteworthy that the possibility of dialec- tic in the sense of *dihairesis* [the analyzing or dissecting of concepts] cannot itself be justified by the dihairetic method. This doctrine of the highest categories is intended to explain how the disjunction and synthesis of what belongs together is possible at all. But this is presupposed in any discussion of the Many or One. The participa- tion of the Many in the One, on which level it could always come up as a problem, has as a separation *(chorismos)* and as overcoming of this separation a common basis in Being itself: It is Being and Non-being.

In this context the question of *pseudos* [error] arises and plays a constantly disconcerting role. One may understand the problem to mean roughly that, if thinking is distinguishing, one is capable of distinguishing falsely. As the Platonic analogy has it: Mistaking the joints when carving the sacrificial animals, one proves that one is not master of the true dialectic and so, after the manner of the sophist, one becomes prone to misconceptions of the *logos*. It remains unclear, however, how these misconceptions are possible if one understands the Being of the *eidos* as *parusia*, as pure contemporariness. So the question concerning *pseudos* becomes hopelessly complicated in the *Theatetus*. Neither the analogy of the wax tablet nor that with the dovecote advance the argument a single step: What could that be, in the case of *pseudos*, that could be meant with the "presence" of the false? What is *there* when a statement is false? A dove of falseness?

One can say that the *Sophist* attempts to advance this question toward a positive solution by means of the proof that Non-being "is" and is indissolubly conjoined with Being, as difference is with unity. If, however, Non-being means nothing but the difference which, along with identity, forms the basis of all differentiating speech, then it is indeed understandable how true speech is possible but not how *pseudos*, falseness, and illusion are possible. The coexistence of the other (the different) with the identical is far from explaining the existence of something as what it is not, but explains it merely as what it is, that is to say, this and nothing else. The mere criticism of the Eleatic concept of Being does not suffice to genuinely invalidate its basic assumption, the thinking of Being as presence in *logos*. Even if difference is a kind of visibility, the *eidos* of Non-being, then the question of *pseudos* remains a puzzle. Insofar as the existence [*Dasein*] of the "not" turns out to be the *eidos* of otherness, especially then the nothingness of *pseudos* conceals itself.

At most one can go along with Plato so far as to recognize a fundamental limitation in the way that "nothing" presents itself. Insofar as otherness turns up only when it is entertwined with sameness, that is, only with reference to something identifiable as the Non-being of everything else, are we thinking beings caught up in the unending discourse. Not only is it infinite regress in which all differentiation is lost; since a differentiation sameness is always

implied, an infinite indeterminacy is present with every single differentiation, an indeterminacy which the Pythagoreans called the *apeiron*
[the endless or infinite]: everything else forces its way through in
accompaniment. In this regard the "not" itself lies in "presence"
[*Anwesen*]. This is virtually the formulation found in the *Sophist* (258e),
the Non-being consists in the contra-position to Being. As the nature of the other and respectively the otherness, it is distributed at
the one time in a reciprocal relationship to beings. Only in this
distribution is it encountered and only thusly is it Non-being. It
seems entirely nonsensical to think of the totality of all differences as
being "there" [*als "da" zu denken*]—including the total presentness of
Non-being. The "not" of otherness is more than mere difference, it
is a genuine "not" of Being. It was the fundamental "not" in Being
that I think Plato had in view in the lecture "Concerning the Good,"
where he seems to have posited the indeterminable twoness alongside the determining one. But if one accepts the "not" of otherness
and difference, the nothingness of error truly becomes harmless, and
the concealment which began with the eleatic suppression of the
"nothing" [*des Nichts*] is perpetrated. One might bear in mind as well
that, in the production of the world according to the *Timaeus,* sameness
and difference function as cosmological factors and constitute knowledge and opinion, of course, *alethes doxa* [true opinion]. An ontological foundation for *pseudos doxa* [false opinion] is lacking.

Here we have assuredly reached the point where Heidegger
discerned the limits of the concept of *aletheia,* that is to say, the
beginning of the distortion of the question of Being.

One can, however, put the matter the other way around. As
we become aware that the ontological question concerning *pseudos* is
never really solved in Platonic thought, we are forced towards a
dimension in which Non-being does not mean mere difference and
Being mere identifiability, but a dimension in which the One is more
original, is prior to such a differentiation and at the same time makes
it possible. The grand one-sidedness of the Parmenidean insistence
on Being in which there is no "not," no negation, brought the abyss
of the "nothing" to light. The Platonic recognition of the "not" in
Being made the "not" of the other to Being harmless, but in so doing
the nothingness of "not" was brought to consciousness in an indirect
way. The suppression of the "nothing" through its interpretation as
difference occurs in a discussion whose context demands the inevi-

table recognition and ontological engrossment in the nothingness of the "not." For only after one has understood not only difference but also semblance [*Schein*] does one know who the sophist is. Semblance is not difference from Being, but rather its "appearance" [*Anschein*]. To me this does not seem to deny that Plato was aware of the deeper ontological problem which existed here and which was tied up with the possibility of sophistry. Neither difference, nor incorrect distinctions, nor willful confusion or even the false statements of a liar approach the phenomenon of sophistry whose enlightenment Plato was trying to bring about. Still, the most fitting analogy to the sophist is the con man—a mendacious human being through and through, completely devoid of any sense of truth. The sophist is not put into the class of ignorant imitators in the Platonic dialogue without thinking. But even that is not unambiguous enough. But there is one final distinction which conjures up the whole of the power of nothingness—a distinction made between two types of ignorant imitators. The distinction is between two kinds of imitators: there are those who really believe that they have knowledge, even though they do not; and then there are those imitators who secretly are aware of their lack of knowledge, but are compelled by fear and concern about losing their superiority to conceal this ignorance by veiling themselves in the false spell of their speech. And yet there is another distinction. There are two forms of such speech, both of which have something eerie about them precisely because the speaker feels his own emptiness. Plato calls them the "feigning imitators." On one hand there is the demagogue who lives off of applause (such as in the *Gorgias* where the rhetoric is characterized as flattery), and on the other hand there is the sophist, who must remain victorious and have the last word in discussions and arguments. Neither are liars, they are hollow figures of speech.

It is by way of this detour that the recognition of "nothing" is first shown by the "strangers" at the end with reference to the illusoriness and nullity of sophistry. Certainly it remains subliminal that *pseudos* is not simply error, but that it includes the eeriness of semblance within it. In Aristotle's theory of *aletheia* and *pseudos,* as it is given in Book IX of the *Metaphysics* (chapter 10), there are absolutely no traces of this to be found.

One must look back beyond Parmenides or forward beyond Hegel if one wishes to think the true affiliation of the nothingness of semblance with Being and wants to do away with notion that it is merely being disconcerted by error. It was Heidegger who attempted to take the step backward and in so doing took a step forward as well, a step which would allow modern civilization to realize the limits of Greek thought, of *aletheia* and its formative power. Thinking should not be allowed to traverse this limit.

CHAPTER NINE

THE TRUTH OF THE
WORK OF ART (1960)

When we look back today on the time between the two world wars, we can see that this pause within the turbulent events of our century represents a period of extraordinary creativity. Omens of what was to come could be seen even before the catastrophe of World War I, particularly in painting and architecture. But for the most part, the general awareness of the time was transformed only by the terrible shock that the slaughters of World War I brought to the cultural consciousness and to the faith in progress of the liberal era. In the philosophy of the day, this transformation of general sensibilities was marked by the fact that with one blow the dominant philosophy that had grown up in the second half of the nineteenth century in renewal of Kant's critical idealism was rendered untenable. "The collapse of German idealism," as Paul Ernst called it in a popular book of the time,[a] was placed in a world-historical context by Oswald Spengler's *The Decline of the West*. The forces that carried out the critique of this dominant Neo-Kantian philosophy had two powerful precursors: Friedrich Nietzsche's critique of Platonism and Christendom, and Søren Kierkegaard's brilliant attack on the

Reflexionsphilosophie of speculative idealism. Two new philosophical catchwords confronted the neo-Kantian preoccupation with methodology. One was the *irrationality of life,* and of historical life in particular. In connection with this notion, one could refer to Nietzsche and Bergson, but also to the great historian of philosophy, Wilhelm Dilthey. The other catchword was *Existenz,* a term that rang forth from the works of Søren Kierkegaard, the Danish philosopher of the first part of the nineteenth century, whose influence was only beginning to be felt in Germany as a result of the Diedrichs translation. Just as Kierkegaard had criticized Hegel as the philosopher of reflection who had forgotten existence, so now the complacent system-building of neo-Kantian methodologism, which had placed philosophy entirely in the service of establishing scientific cognition, came under critical attack. And just as Kierkegaard—a Christian thinker—had stepped forward to oppose the philosophy of idealism, so now the radical self-criticism of the so-called dialectical theology opened the new epoch.

Among the forces that gave philosophical expression to the general critique of liberal culture-piety and the prevailing academic philosophy was the revolutionary genius of the young Heidegger. Heidegger's appearance as a young teacher at Freiburg University in the years just after World War I created a profound sensation. The extraordinarily forceful and profound language that resounded from the rostrum in Freiburg already betrayed the emergence of an original philosophical power. Heidegger's magnum opus, *Being and Time,* grew out of his fruitful and intense encounter with contemporary Protestant theology during his appointment at Marburg in 1923. Published in 1927, this book effectively communicated to a wide public something of the new spirit that had engulfed philosophy as a result of the convulsions of World War I. The common theme that captured the imagination of the time was called existential philosophy. The contemporary reader of Heidegger's first systematic work was seized by the vehemence of its passionate protest against the secured cultural world of the older generation and the leveling of all individual forms of life by industrial society, with its ever stronger uniformities and its techniques of communication and public relations that manipulated everything. Heidegger contrasted the concept of the authenticity of Dasein, which is aware of its finitude and resolutely accepts it, with the "they," "idle chatter," and "curiosity," as fallen and inauthentic forms of Dasein. The existential seriousness with which he brought the age-old riddle of death to the center of philosophical concern, and the force with which his challenge to the real "choice" of existence smashed the illusory world of education and culture, disrupted well-preserved academic tranquility. And yet his was not the voice of a reckless stranger to the academic world— not the voice of a bold and lonely thinker in the style of Kierkegaard or Nietzsche—but of a pupil of the most distinguished and conscientious philosophical school that existed in the German universities of the time. Heidegger was a pupil of Edmund Husserl, who pursued tenaciously the goal of establishing philosophy as a rigorous science. Heidegger's new philosophical effort also joined in the battle cry of phenomenology, "To the things themselves." The thing he aimed at, however, was the most concealed question of philosophy, one that for the most part had been forgotten: What is Being? In order to learn how to ask this question, Heidegger proceeded to define the Being of human Dasein in an ontologically positive way, instead of understanding it as "merely finite," that is, in terms of an infinite and always existing Being [seiende Sein], as previous metaphysics had done. The ontological priority that the Being of human Dasein acquired for Heidegger defined his philosophy as "fundamental ontology." Heidegger called the ontological determinations of finite human Dasein determinations of existence "existentiells." With methodical precision, he contrasted these basic concepts with the categories of the present-at-hand that had dominated previous metaphysics. When Heidegger raised once again the ancient question of the meaning of Being, he did not want to lose sight of the fact that human Dasein does not have its real Being in determinable presence-at-hand, but rather in the motility of the care with which it is concerned about its own future and its own Being. Human Dasein is distinguished by the fact that it understands itself in terms of its Being. In order not to lose sight of the finitude and temporality of human Dasein, which cannot ignore the question of the meaning of its Being, Heidegger defined the question of the meaning of Being within the horizon of time. The present-at-hand, which science knows through its observations and calculations, and the eternal, which is beyond everything human, must both be understood in terms of the central ontological certainty of human temporality. This was Heidegger's new approach, but his goal of thinking Being as time remained so veiled that *Being and Time* was promptly designated as a "hermeneutical phenomenology," primarily because self-understanding still represented the real foundation of the inquiry. Seen in terms of this foundation, the understanding of Being that held sway in traditional metaphysics turns out to be a corrupted form of the primordial understanding of Being that is manifested in human Dasein. Being is not simply pure presence or actual presence-at-hand. It is finite, historical Dasein that "is" in the real sense. Then the ready-to-hand has its place within Dasein's projection of a world, and only subsequently does the merely present-at-hand receive its place.

But various forms of Being that are neither historical nor simply present-at-hand have no proper place within the framework provided by the hermeneutical phenomenon of self-understanding: the timelessness of mathematical facts, which are not simply observable entities present-at-hand; the timelessness of nature, whose ever-repeating patterns hold sway even in us and determine us in the form of the unconscious; and finally the timelessness of the rainbow or art, which spans all historical distances. All of these seem to designate the limits of the possibility of hermeneutical interpretation that Heidegger's new approach opened up. The unconscious, the number, the dream, the sway of nature, the miracle of art—all these seemed to exist only on the periphery of Dasein, which knows itself historically and understands itself in terms of itself. They seem to be comprehensible only as limiting concepts.[1]

It was a surprise, therefore, in 1936, when Heidegger dealt with the origin of the work of art in several addresses. This work had begun to have a profound influence long before it was first published in 1950, when it became accessible to the general public as the first essay in *Holzwege*.[b] For it had long been the case that Heidegger's lectures and addresses had everywhere aroused intense interest. Copies and reports of them were widely disseminated, and they quickly made him the focus of the very "idle chatter" that he had characterized so acrimoniously in *Being and Time*. In fact, his addresses on the origin of the work of art caused a philosophical sensation.

---

1. More than anyone else it was Oskar Becker, a student of Husserl and Heidegger, who doubted the universality of historicality in reference to this type of phenomena. See *Dasein und Dawesen* (Pfullingen, 1963).

It was not merely that Heidegger now brought art into the basic hermeneutical approach of the self-understanding of humans in their historicality, nor even that these addresses understood art to be the act that founds whole historical worlds (as it is understood in the poetic faith of Hölderlin and George). Rather, the real sensation caused by Heidegger's new experiment had to do with the startling new conceptuality that boldly emerged in connection with this topic. For here, the talk was of the "world" and the "earth." From the very beginning, the concept of the *world* had been one of Heidegger's major hermeneutical concepts. As the referential totality of Dasein's projection, "world" constituted the horizon that was preliminary to all projections of Dasein's concern. Heidegger had himself sketched the history of this concept of the world, and in particular, had called attention to and historically legitimated the difference between the anthropological meaning of this concept in the New Testament (which was the meaning he used himself) and the concept of the totality of the present-at-hand. The new and startling thing was that this concept of the world now found a counterconcept in the *"earth."* As a whole in which human self-interpretation takes place, the concept of the world could be raised to intuitive clarity out of the self-interpretation of human Dasein, but the concept of the earth sounded a mythical and gnostic note that at best might have its true home in the world of poetry. At that time Heidegger had devoted himself to Hölderlin's poetry with passionate intensity, and it is clearly from this source that he brought the concept of the earth into his own philosophy. But with what justification? How could Dasein, being-in-the-world, which understands itself out of its own Being, be related ontologically to a concept like the "earth"—this new and radical starting point for all transcendental inquiry? To answer this question we must return to Heidegger's earlier work.

Heidegger's new approach in *Being and Time* was certainly not simply a repetition of the spiritualistic metaphysics of German idealism. Human Dasein's understanding of itself out of its own Being is not the self-knowledge of Hegel's absolute spirit. It is not a self-projection. Rather, it knows that it is not master of itself and its own Dasein, but comes upon itself in the midst of beings and has to take itself over as it finds itself. It is a "thrown-projection." In one of the most brilliant phenomenological analyses of *Being and Time,* Heidegger analyzed this limit experience of *Dasein,* which comes up upon itself in the midst of beings, as "disposition" [*Befindlichkeit*], and he attributed to disposition or mood [*Stimmung*] the real disclosure of Being-in-the-world. What is come upon in disposition represents the extreme limit beyond which the historical self-understanding of human Dasein could not advance. There was no way to get from this hermeneutical limiting concept of disposition or moodfulness to a concept such as the earth. What justification is there for this concept? What warrant does it have? The important insight that Heidegger's "The Origin of the Work of Art" opened up is that "earth" is a necessary determination of the Being of the work of art.

If we are to see the fundamental significance of the question of the nature of the work of art and how this question is connected with the basic problems of philosophy, we must gain some insight into the prejudices that are present in the concept of a philosophical aesthetics. In the last analysis, we need to overcome the concept of aesthetics itself. It is well known that aesthetics is the youngest of the philosophical disciplines. Only with the explicit restriction of Enlightenment rationalism in the eighteenth century was the autonomous right of sensuous knowledge asserted and with it the relative independence of the judgment of taste from the understanding and its concepts. Like the name of the discipline itself, the systematic autonomy of aesthetics dates from the aesthetics of Alexander Baumgarten. Then in his third critique—the *Critique of Aesthetic Judgment*—Kant established the problem of aesthetics in its systematic significance. In the subjective universality of the aesthetic judgment of taste, he discovered the powerful and legitimate claim to independence that the aesthetic judgment can make over against the claims of the understanding and morality. The taste of the observer can no more be comprehended as the application of concepts, norms, or rules than the genius of the artist can. What sets the beautiful apart cannot be exhibited as a determinate, knowable property of an object; rather it manifests itself in a subjective factor: the intensification of the *Lebensgefühl* [life feeling] through the harmonious correspondence of imagination and understanding. What we experience in beauty—in nature as well as in art—is the total animation and free interplay of all our spiritual powers. The judgment of taste is not knowledge, yet it is not arbitrary. It involves a claim to universality that can establish the autonomy of the aesthetic realm. We must acknowledge that this justification of the autonomy of art was a great achievement in the age of the Enlightenment, with the insistence on the sanctity of rules and moral orthodoxy. This is particularly the case at just that point in German history when the classical period of German literature, with its center in Weimar, was seeking to establish itself as an aesthetic state. These efforts found their conceptual justification in Kant's philosophy.

Basing aesthetics on the subjectivity of the mind's powers was, however, the beginning of a dangerous process of subjectification. For Kant himself, to be sure, the determining factor was still the mysterious congruity that existed between the beauty of nature and the subjectivity of the subject. In the same way, he understood the creative genius who transcends all rules in creating the miracle of the work of art to be a favorite of nature. But this position presupposes the self-evident validity of the natural order that has its ultimate foundation in the theological idea of the creation. With the disappearance of this context, the grounding of aesthetics led inevitably to a radical subjectification in further development of the doctrine of the freedom of the genius from rules. No longer derived from the comprehensive whole of the order of Being, art comes to be contrasted with actuality and with the raw prose of life. The illuminating power of poesy succeeds in reconciling idea and actuality only within its own aesthetic realm. This is the idealistic aesthetics to which Schiller first gave expression and that culminated in Hegel's remarkable aesthetics. Even in Hegel, however, the theory of the work of art still stood within a universal ontological horizon. To the extent that the work of art succeeds at all in balancing and reconciling the finite and the infinite, it is the tangible indication of an ultimate truth that philosophy must finally grasp in conceptual form. Just as nature, for idealism, is not merely the object of the calculating science of the modern age, but rather the reign of a great, creative world power that raises itself to its perfection in self-conscious spirit, so the work of art too, in the view of these speculative thinkers, is an objectification of spirit. Art is not the perfected concept of spirit, but rather its manifestation on the level of the sense intuition of the world. In the literal sense of the word, art is an intuition of the world [*Welt-Anschauung*].

If we wish to determine the point of departure for Heidegger's meditation on the nature of the work of art, we must keep clearly in mind that the idealistic aesthetics that had ascribed a special significance to the work of art as the organon of a nonconceptual understanding of absolute truth had long since been eclipsed by

Neo-Kantian philosophy. This dominant philosophical movement had renewed the Kantian foundation of scientific cognition without regaining the metaphysical horizon that lay at the basis of Kant's own description of aesthetic judgment, namely, a teleological order of Being. Consequently, the Neo-Kantian conception of aesthetic problems was burdened with peculiar prejudices. The exposition of the theme in Heidegger's essay clearly reflects this state of affairs. It begins with the question of how the work of art is differentiated from the thing. The work of art is also a thing, and only by way of its Being as a thing does it have the capacity to refer to something else, for instance, to function symbolically, or to give us an allegorical understanding. But this is to describe the mode of Being of the work of art from the point of view of an ontological model that assumes the systematic *priority of scientific cognition*. What really "is" is thing-like in character; it is a fact, something given to the senses and developed by the natural sciences in the direction of objective cognition. The significance and value of the thing, however, are secondary forms of comprehension that have a mere subjective validity and belong neither to the original givenness itself nor to the objective truth acquired from it. The Neo-Kantians assumed that the thing alone is objective and able to support such values. For aesthetics, this assumption would have to mean that even the work of art possesses a thing-like character as its most prominent feature. This thing-like character functions as a substructure upon which the real aesthetic form rises as a superstructure. Nicolai Hartmann still describes the structure of the aesthetic object in this fashion.

Heidegger refers to this ontological prejudice when he inquires into the thing-character of the *thing*. He distinguishes three ways of comprehending the thing that have been developed in the tradition: it is the bearer of properties; it is the unity of a manifold of perceptions; and it is matter to which form has been imparted. The third of these forms of comprehension, in particular—the thing as form and matter—seems to be the most illuminating, for it follows the model of production by which a thing is manufactured to serve our purposes. Heidegger calls such things "implements." Viewed theologically, from the standpoint of this model, things in their entirety appear as manufactured items, that is, as creations of God. From the perspective of human beings, they appear as implements that have lost their implement-character. Things are mere things, that is, they are present without reference to serving a purpose. Now Heidegger shows that this concept of being-present-at-hand, which corresponds to the observing and calculating procedures of modern science, permits us to think neither the thing-like character of the thing nor the implement-character of the implement. In order to focus attention on the implement-character of the implement, therefore, he refers to an artistic representation—a painting by Van Gogh depicting a peasant's shoes. The implement itself is perceived in this work of art—not a being that can be made to serve some purpose or other, but something whose very Being consists in having served and in still serving the person to whom it belongs. What emerges from the painter's work and is vividly depicted in it is not an incidental pair of peasant's shoes; rather the true essence of the implement comes forth as it is. The whole world of rural life is in these shoes. Thus, it is the work of art which is able to bring forth the truth of this entity. The emergence of truth that occurs in the work of art can be conceived from the work alone, and not at all in terms of its substructure as a thing.

These observations raise the question of what a *work* is that truth can emerge from it in this way. In contrast to the customary procedure of starting with the thing-character and object-character of the work of art, Heidegger contends that a work of art is characterized precisely by the fact that it is *not* an object, but rather stands in itself. By standing-in-itself it not only belongs to its world; its world is present in it. The work of art opens up its own world. Something is an object only when it no longer fits into the fabric of its world because the world it belongs to has disintegrated. Hence a work of art is an object when it becomes an item of commercial transaction, for then it is worldless and homeless.

The characterization of the work of art as standing-in-itself and opening up a world with which Heidegger begins his study consciously avoids going back to the concept of genius that is found in classical aesthetics. In his effort to understand the ontological structure of the work independently of the subjectivity of the creator or beholder, Heidegger now uses "earth" as a counterconcept alongside the concept of the "world," to which the work belongs and which it erects and opens up. "Earth" is a counterconcept to world insofar as it exemplifies self-sheltering and closing-off as opposed to self-opening. Clearly, both self-opening and self-closing-off are present in the work of art. A work of art does not "mean" something or function as

a sign that refers to a meaning; rather, it presents itself in its own
Being, so that the beholder must tarry by it. It is so very much
present itself that the ingredients out of which it is composed—
stone, color, tone, word—only come into a real existence of their
own within the work of art itself. As long as something is mere stuff
awaiting its rendering, it is not really present, that is, it has not come
forth into a genuine presence. It only comes forth when it is used,
when it is bound into the work. The tones that constitute a musical
masterwork are tones in a more real sense than all other sounds or
tones. The colors of a painting are colors in a more genuine sense
than even nature's wealth of colors. The temple column manifests
the stone-like character of its Being more genuinely in rising upward
and supporting the temple roof than it did as an unhewn block of
stone. But what comes forth in this way in the work is precisely its
being closed-off and closing-itself-off—what Heidegger calls the Being of the earth. The earth, in truth, is not stuff, but that out of
which everything comes forth and into which everything disappears.

At this point, *form* [*Form*] and *matter* [*Stoff*], as reflective concepts, prove to be inadequate. If we can say that a world "rises" in a
great work of art, then the arising of this world is at the same time its
entrance into a reposing form [*Gestalt*]. When the form [*Gestalt*]
stands there it has found its earthly existence. From this the work of
art acquires its own peculiar repose. It does not first have its real
Being in an experiencing ego, which asserts, means, or exhibits something and whose assertions, opinions, or demonstrations would be its
"meaning." Its Being does not consist in its becoming an experience,
Rather, by virtue of its own existence it is an event, a thrust that
overthrows everything previously given and conventional, a thrust in
which a world never there before opens itself up. But this thrust
takes place in the work of art itself in such a fashion that at the same
time it is sustained in an abiding [*ins Bleiben geborgen*]. That which
arises and sustains itself in this way constitutes the structure of the
work in its tension. It is this tension that Heidegger designates as the
conflict between the world and the earth. In all of this, Heidegger
not only gives a description of the mode of Being of the work of art
that avoids the prejudices of traditional aesthetics and the modern
subjectivitistic thinking, he also avoids simply renewing the speculative aesthetics that defined the work of art as the sensuous manifestation of the Idea. To be sure, the Hegelian definition beauty shares

with Heidegger's own effort the fundamental transcendence of the antithesis between subject and object, I and object, and does not describe the Being of the work of art in terms of the subjectivity of the subject. Nevertheless, Hegel's description of the Being of the work of art moves in this direction, for it is the sensuous manifestation of the Idea, conceived by self-conscious thought, that constitutes the work of art. In thinking the Idea, therefore, the entire truth of the sensuous appearance would be cancelled [*aufgehoben*]. It acquires its real form [*Gestalt*] in the concept. When Heidegger speaks of the conflict between world and earth and describes the work of art as the thrust through which a truth occurs, this truth is not taken up and perfected in the truth of the philosophical concept. A unique manifestation of truth occurs in the work of art. The reference to the work of art in which truth comes forth should indicate clearly that for Heidegger it is meaningful to speak of an event of truth. Hence Heidegger's essay does not restrict itself to giving a more suitable description of the Being of the work of art. Rather, his analysis supports his central philosophical concern to conceive Being itself as an event of truth.

The objection is often made that the basic concepts of Heidegger's later work cannot be verified. What Heidegger intends, for example, when he speaks of Being in the verbal sense of the word, of the event of Being, the clearing of Being, the revealment of Being, and the forgetfulness of Being, cannot be fulfilled by an intentional act of our subjectivity. The concepts that dominate Heidegger's later philosophical works are clearly closed to subjective demonstration, just as Hegel's dialectical process is closed to what Hegel called representational thinking. Heidegger's concepts are the object of a criticism similar to Marx's criticism of Hegel's dialectic in the sense that they too are called "mythological."

The fundamental significance of the essay on the work of art, it seems to me, is that it provides us with an indication of the later Heidegger's real concern. No one can ignore the fact that in the work of art, in which a world arises, not only is something meaningful given to experience that was not known before, but also something new comes into existence with the work of art itself. It is not simply the laying bare of a truth, it is itself an event. This offers us an opportunity to pursue one step further Heidegger's critique of western metaphysics and its culmination in the subjectivism of the modern age. It is well known that Heidegger renders *aletheia,* the Greek word for truth, as *unconcealedness.* But this strong emphasis on the privative sense of *aletheia* not only means that knowledge of the truth tears truth out of the realm of the unknown or concealedness in error by an act of theft (*privatio* means "robbery"). This is not the only reason why truth is not open and obvious and accessible as a matter of course, though it is certainly true and the Greeks obviously wanted to express it as such when they designated beings as they are as unconcealed. They knew how every piece of knowledge is threatened by error and falsehood, and that everything depends on avoiding error and gaining the right representation of beings as they are. If knowledge depends on our leaving error behind us, then truth is the pure unconcealedness of beings. This is what Greek thought had in view, and in this way it was already treading the path that modern science would eventually follow to the end, namely, to bring about the correctness of knowledge by which beings are preserved in their unconcealedness.

In opposition to all this, Heidegger holds that unconcealedness is not simply the character of beings insofar as they are correctly known. In a more primordial sense, unconcealedness "occurs," and this occurrence is what first makes it possible for beings to be unconcealed and correctly known. The concealedness that corresponds to such primordial unconcealedness is not error, but rather belongs originally to Being itself. Nature, which loves to conceal itself (Heraclitus), is thus characterized not only with respect to its possibility of being known, but rather with respect to its Being. It is not only the emergence into the light but just as much the sheltering itself in the dark. It is not only the unfolding of the blossom in the sun, but just as much its rooting of itself in the depths of the earth. Heidegger speaks of the "clearing of Being," which first represents the realm in which beings are known as disclosed in their unconcealedness. This coming forth of beings into the "there" [*da*] of their Dasein obviously presupposes a realm of openness in which such a "there" can occur. And yet it is just as obvious that this realm does not exist without beings manifest in themselves in it, that is, without there being an open place [*Offenes*] that openness occupies. This relation is unquestionably peculiar. And yet even more remarkable is the fact that only in the "there" of this self-manifestation of beings does the concealedness of Being first present itself. To be sure, correct knowledge is made possible by the openness of the there. The beings that come forth out of unconcealedness present themselves for that which preserves them. Nevertheless, it is not an arbitrary act of revealing, an act of theft, by which something is torn out of concealedness. Rather, this is all made possible only by the fact that revealment and concealedness are an event of Being itself. To understand this fact helps us in our understanding of the nature of the work of art. There is clearly a tension between the emergence and the sheltering that constitute the Being of the work itself. It is the power of this tension that constitutes the form-niveau of a work of art and produces the brilliance by which it outshines everything else. Its truth is not constituted simply by its laying bare its meaning, but rather by the unfathomableness and depth of its meaning. Thus by its very nature the work of art is a conflict between world and earth, emergence and sheltering.

But precisely what is exhibited in the work of art ought to constitute the essence of Being itself. The conflict between revealment and concealment is not the truth of the work of art alone, but the truth of every being, for as unconcealedness, truth is always such an *opposition of revealment and concealment.* The two belong necessarily together. This obviously means that truth is not simply the mere presence of a being, so that it stands, as it were, over against its correct representation. Such a concept of being unconcealed would presuppose the subjectivity of the Dasein that represents beings. But beings are not correctly defined in their Being if they are defined merely as objects of possible representation. Rather, it belongs just as much to their Being that they withhold themselves. As unconcealed, truth has in itself an inner tension and ambiguity. Being contains something like a "hostility to its own presence," as Heidegger says. What Heidegger means can be confirmed by everyone: the existing thing does not simply offer us a recognizable and familiar surface contour; it also has an inner depth of self-sufficiency that Heidegger calls its "standing-in-itself." The complete unconcealedness of all beings, their total objectification (by means of a representation that conceives things in their perfect state) would negate this standing-in-itself of beings and lead to a total leveling of them. A complete objectification of this kind would no longer represent beings that stand in their own Being. Rather, it would represent nothing more than our opportunity for using beings, and what would be manifest would be the will that seizes upon and dominates things. In the work of art, we experience an absolute opposition to this will-to-control, not in the sense of a rigid resistance to the presumption of our will, which is bent on utilizing things, but in the sense of the superior and intensive power of a Being reposing in itself. Hence the closedness and withdrawnness of the work of art is the guarantee of the universal thesis of Heidegger's philosophy, namely, that beings hold themselves back by coming forward into the openness of presence. The standing-in-itself of the work betokens at the same time the standing-in-itself of beings in general.

This analysis of the work of art opens up perspectives that point us farther along the path of Heidegger's thought. Only by way of the work of art were the implement-character of the implement and, in the last analysis, the thingness of the thing able to manifest themselves. All-calculating modern science brings about the loss of things, dissolving their character of standing-in-themselves, which "can be forced to do nothing," into the calculated elements of its projects and alterations, but the work of art represents an instance that guards against the universal loss of things. As Rilke poetically illuminates the innocence of the thing in the midst of the general disappearance of thingness by showing it to the angel,[c] so the thinker contemplates the same loss of thingness while recognizing at the same time that this very thingness is preserved in the work of art. Preservation, however, presupposes that what is preserved still truly exists. Hence the very truth of the thing is implied if this truth is still capable of coming forth in the work of art. Heidegger's essay, "What Is a Thing?" thus represents a necessary advance on the path of his thought.[d] The thing, which formerly did not even achieve the implement-status of being-present-to-hand, but was merely present-at-hand for observation and investigation, is now recognized in its "whole" Being [*in seinem "heilen" Sein*] as precisely what cannot be put to use.

From this vantage point, we can recognize yet a farther step on this path. Heidegger asserts that the essence of art is the process of poeticizing. What he means is that the nature of art does not consist in transforming something that is already formed or in copying something that is already in Being. Rather, art is the projection by which something new comes forth as true. The essence of the event of truth that is present in the work of art is that "it opens up an open place." In the ordinary and more restricted sense of the word, however, poetry is distinguished by the intrinsically linguistic character that differentiates it from all other modes of art. If the real project and the genuine artistic element in every art—even in architecture and in the plastic arts—can be called "poetic," then the project that occurs in an actual poem is bound to a course that is already marked out and cannot be projected anew simply from out of itself, the course already prepared is language. The poet is so dependent upon the language he inherits and uses that the language of his poetic work of art can only reach those who command the same language. In a certain sense, then, the "poetry" that Heidegger takes to symbolize the projective character of all artistic creation is less the project of building and shaping out of stone or color or tones than it is their secondary forms. In fact, the process of poeticizing is divided into two phases: into the project that has already occurred where a language holds sway, and another project that allows the new poetic creation to come forth from the first project. But the primacy of language is not simply a unique trait of the poetic work of art; rather, it seems to be characteristic of the very thing-being of things themselves. The work of language is the most primordial poetry of Being. The thinking that conceives all art as poetry and that discloses that the work of art is language is itself still on the way to language.

CHAPTER TEN

MARTIN HEIDEGGER—
85 YEARS (1974)

That Martin Heidegger is celebrating his eighty-fifth birth-day must be a true surprise for some of the younger generation. The thinking of this man has been a part of our general consciousness for so many decades, and in spite of all the changes in the constellations, he has remained indisputably a presence throughout all of the fluc-tuations in our century. Periods in which Heidegger looms large and periods in which he is but a distant figure come and go, as is the case for the truly great stars that determine epochs. It was during the period directly following World War I when the effects of this young assistant to Husserl began to be felt in Freiburg. Even then a unique aura radiated from him.

The effect that he had on academia increased drastically dur-ing the five years that he taught in Marburg, suddenly bursting forth into the public sphere in 1927 with *Being and Time*. In one fell swoop he was world famous [... *der Weltruhm war da*].

In our times, in a Europe provincialized since 1914 where usually only the natural sciences have been able to call forth rash international echos—names like Einstein, Planck, and Heisenberg come to mind—and where at best some theologians such as Karl Barth were carried beyond national barriers by the church, this world-wide fame of the young Heidegger was completely unique. And after the fall of the Third Reich, when Heidegger was not allowed to continue as a professor at Freiburg due to his initial commitment to Hitler, a true international pilgrimage to Todtnauberg began, where Heidegger spent the greatest part of the year in his cottage, an extremely modest little house nestled in the Black Forest.

The 1950s represented another high point of Heidegger's presence, even though he was seldom active anymore as a teacher. I can remember how he came to Heidelberg for a lecture on Hölderlin during this period, and what a technical problem it was to control to some degree the life-threatening crowd in the large lecture hall at the New University. And it was like that every time this man made an appearance in public.

Then, with the frenzied development of the economy and technical knowhow, of prosperity and comfort, new, sober ways of thinking emerged among the academic youth. Technology and the Marxist critique of ideology became the decisive intellectual forces, and Heidegger disappeared from the "idle talk," which he had once characterized so negatively—up until his most recent appearance in our day. He is gradually being rediscovered by a new generation of students as if he were a forgotten classic.

What is the secret of this enduring presence? He certainly never lacked opponents; he still has them today. In the 1920s he had to work against the resistance of innumerable forms of academic self-righteousness. He was not thought of too highly in the ten years from 1935 to 1945, and the whole of public opinion in the period from after the war up to this day has been no less harsh. The destruction of reason (Lukacs), the jargon of authenticity (Adorno), the abandoning of rational thinking for a pseudo-poetic mythology, his quixotic battle against logic, the flight from time into "Being"—one could lengthen this list of attacks and accusations considerably. But in spite of this, when the Klostermann Press announces the planned release of a seventy-volume publication of his collected works, they can be sure that everyone is listening. Even the eye of someone who knows nothing of Heidegger can scarcely continue to wander when it comes across a photograph of this solitary old man—a man who peers into himself, listens to himself, and reflects beyond himself. When people claim to be "against" Heidegger—or even "for" him—then they make fools of themselves. One cannot circumvent thinking so easily.

Why is this so? How did it come to be? I can remember exactly how I first heard his name. It was in Munich in 1921. In one of Moritz Geiger's seminars a student gave a most strange and passionate speech using rather unusual expressions. Later, when I asked Geiger what that was all about, he said very casually, "Oh that. He has been Heideggerized."[a] And was I not also Heideggerized soon thereafter? It was scarcely a year later that my teacher, Paul Natorp, gave me a forty-page manuscript from Heidegger to read, an introduction to some Aristotle interpretations. For me this was like being hit by a charge of electricity. I had experienced something like this when, as an 18-year-old, I first came across some verses by Stefan George (whose name was completely unknown to me). The understanding that I brought to Heidegger's analysis of the "hermeneutical situation" at that time was certainly insufficient for a philosophical interpretation of Aristotle. But, first of all, that Aristotle was brought into focus via a discussion of the young Luther, of Gabriel Biel and Petrus Lombardus, of Augustine and of St. Paul, and then second that a highly unusual language was spoken there, that the talk was of the "in-order-to," of the "upon-which," of the "grasping-in-advance" [*Vorgriff*] and "grasping-through" [*Durchgriffs*]—such remains in my memory still today—it grasped through. This was not simply a scholarly activity or a comforting solution to a historical problem. All of Aristotle was imposed upon us, and my eyes were opened as I received my first instruction in Freiburg.

Yes, that was it—my eyes were opened. Today people like to say of Heidegger that his thought lacks conceptual precision and is couched in a vague, poetic language. And it is definitely true that Heidegger's language was just as far from the strange "almost English" that has become the style in philosophy today as it was from the mathematical symbolism and the games with categories and modalities that I used to play in Marburg. When Heidegger lectured, one could see the things in front of one, as if they were physically graspable. The same could be said of Husserl, although there it was a more tame version and was restricted to the more basic area of phenomenology. Even his terminology was not the most phenomenologically productive aspect of his language. It is no coincidence that the young Heidegger preferred over all of Husserl's other works his sixth logical investigation, in which Husserl developed the concept of the "categorical intuition" [*Anschauung*]. Today, this doctrine is often considered unsatisfactory, and there is a tendency to replace it with modern logic. But his praxis—like Heidegger's—cannot be so easily refuted. This was an encounter with a living language in philosophizing, a language that cannot be replaced with the technical precision of logical means.

In the Fall of 1923, Heidegger left for Marburg as a young professor. As a farewell gesture, he invited a large number of friends, colleagues, and students up to his place in the Black Forest for a summer celebration. That evening, an immense log was set on fire up on a hill, and Heidegger delivered a talk that impressed all of us. It began with the words, "Being alert with the fire of the night"—and his next words were, "The Greeks . . ." Certainly, the romanticism of the youth movement was swaying along with his words, but this was more than just that. It was the determination of a thinker who saw the present and the past, the future and the Greeks as a totality.

Heidegger's arrival in Marburg cannot be overdramatized, although he personally would not have been interested in causing a sensation. Certainly his appearance in the lecture hall was accompanied a bit by the self-assurance of one who knew that he is going to have an effect, but the essence [das Eigentliche] of his person and teachings consisted in the way he completely immersed himself in his work and in the way this radiated from him. Lectures suddenly became something completely new. They were no longer the teaching apparatus of a professor who put all of his own energy into research and publications.

The great monologues from texts lost their precedence with Heidegger. What he offered was much more: It was the complete supply of all of the power—and what ingenious power—of a revolutionary thinker who would literally startle himself with his own ever more radical questions and who was so filled with the passion of thought that it was carried over into the auditorium, unable to be stopped by anything. Who could forget the bitterly angry polemics with which Heidegger caricatured the cultural and educational affairs [Betrieb] of the day, the "madness in the vicinity," the "they," the "idle talk," "all of this without a derogatory meaning"—and this as well! Who could forget the sarcasm used when he discussed his colleagues and contemporaries? How could anyone following him then forget the breathtaking storm of questions that he developed early on in the semester, only to completely entangle himself in the second or third question—but then to roll these deep, dark clouds of sentences together at the end of the semester, from which lightening flashed, leaving us half stunned.

After Nicoli Hartmann heard one of Heidegger's lectures for the first (and only) time—the first one that Heidegger gave in Marburg—he said to me that he had not seen such a dramatic and energetic entrance since Hermann Cohen. These two were very much antipodes: the cool, reserved Baltic, who came across like a bourgeous seignior; and the dark-eyed, small, rustic man of the mountains, whose temperament always cut through any restrained discipline. I saw them once as they met each other on the steps of Marburg University. Hartmann was going to his lecture, dressed as usual in striped pants, a black jacket, and a white, old fashioned tie; Heidegger was on his way out in a ski suit. Hartmann stopped for a minute and asked, "Are you going to lecture like that?" There was a special reason for Heidegger's satisfied laughter. Namely, he was giving a lecture on skiing that evening, which was to serve as an introduction to a then new course on dry skiing. The way he began the lecture was pure Heidegger: "One can learn to ski only on the slopes and for the slopes." The typical knock-out punch; it dealt a heavy blow to fashionable expectations, but simultaneously provided an opening for new expectations. "I will take anyone who can make a respectable stem turn with me on every ski trip."

Heidegger, a skier from his childhood, certainly had an athletic side, and it had infected the Heidegger school. We were the second-best volleyball team in Marburg—we always made it to the finals—and Heidegger joined the exercise team year-round—even if he was not as superior to us in this as he was in everything else.

Naturally, he did not always run around in a ski suit, but he was also never to be seen in a black jacket. He had his own suit—we called it his *existential suit*. It had been designed by the painter Otto Ubbelohde and belonged to a new sort of men's clothing that vaguely resembled a farmer's garb. In this clothing Heidegger certainly did have something of the unassuming splendor of a farmer dressed for Sunday.

Heidegger began his day quite early, and early in the morning, he gave us a dose of Aristotle four times each week. Those were memorable interpretations, not only because of their power to illustrate relevantly, but also because of the philosophical perspective that they opened up. In Heidegger's lectures we were confronted with matters [*Sachen*] in such a way that we no longer knew if the matters [*Sachen*] he was speaking of were his or Aristotle's. It was a profound hermeneutical truth that we began to understand then and that I was later to defend and justify theoretically.

We were a very proud, small group, and we let our pride in our teacher and his work habits go to our heads—and to consider now what was going on in the second and third ranks of the Heideggereans, with those whose academic talent was limited or who had not yet progressed very far along in their education. Heidegger affected them like an intoxicant. This storm grew to such proportions and Heidegger's radical, entangling questions were on the lips of so many imitators that the scene began to take on the character of a burlesque. I admit, I would have not liked to have been a colleague of Heidegger's then. Students who had cribbed from the master perfectly "how he hacked and spit" began to show up everywhere. These young people disrupted a few seminars with these "radical questions," but it was more that their involvement with these questions hid their own idleness. When they uttered their dark, Heideggerized German, some professors must have been reminded of the scene that Aristophanes described in his comedy, where the Attic youth were kicked over their traces by the teachings of Socrates and the Sophists. But one could certainly not blame Socrates then because his students got carried away or hold it against him that not every follower was freed by his teachings to pursue his own serious work—and one cannot now hold this against Heidegger. But it is still a curious turn of events that Heidegger, the one who had coined the expression *liberating solicitude,* in spite of this liberation—no, precisely because of this liberation—could not impede the loss of so many people's freedom. Moths fly toward light.

We noticed this when Heidegger was writing *Being and Time.* Occasional observations were expounded upon in advance. One day, in a seminar on Schelling, he read this sentence to us: "The *Angst* of life itself drives human beings out of the center." Then he said, "Tell me a single sentence from Hegel that compares to this sentence in profundity!" It is well known that the initial effect of *Being and Time*—especially on theology—was to make an existential appeal to our impending death [*zum Vorlaufen zum Tode*]; it was a call to authenticity. One hears more Kierkegaard in this than Aristotle. But already in the book on Kant, which appeared in 1929, the talk was no longer of the Dasein of a human being but suddenly of the "the Da-sein in a human being." The question concerning Being and its "Da," which Heidegger had gleaned from the Greek *aletheia* (unconcealedness), could no longer be missed. This was no revival of Aristotle. Rather, this was a thinker who had been preceded not only by Hegel but also by Nietzsche, and who reflected back upon the beginning, upon Heraclitus and Parmenides, because the neverending interplay between disclosing [*Entbergung*] and concealment [*Verbergung*] and the secret of language, in which both idle talk and the "sheltering" [*Bergung*] of truth occurred, had unfolded before him.

Heidegger first realized this when he returned home to Freiburg and the Black Forest and began "to feel the energy of his old stomping ground" as he had put it in a letter to me. "It all came to me in a rush." He named this thought-experience the "turn" [*Kehre*]—not in the theological sense of a conversion [*Bekehrung*], but rather in the sense of the word as he knew in his dialect. A turn is a bend in a way [*Weg*] as it moves up a mountain. Here one does not turn around; rather, the way itself turns in the opposite direction—to ascend. To where? No one can easily say. The fact that Heidegger named one of the most important collections of his later works *Holzwege*[b] is significant. These are ways that ultimately lead nowhere, but nevertheless, they encourage one to climb into a heretofore uncharted area—or they force one to turn around. But, in any case, one is still in the heights.

I know nothing from personal experience of Heidegger's Freiburg period, the period beginning in the year 1933. Yet, it was visible from a distance that Heidegger pursued the passion of thinking with a new enthusiasm after his political interlude and that his thinking led into new, impassable areas. An essay dealing with some of the key words in Hölderlin's poetry appeared, oddly enough, in the journal *The Internal Reich*. It sounded like Heidegger had shrouded his thinking in Hölderlin's poetic words on the divine and divinities.

Then, one day in 1936, we drove to Frankfurt to hear Heidegger's three-hour lecture "The Origin of the Work of Art." "A Landscape Devoid of People" was the title of the commentary by Sternberger in the *Frankfurter Zeitung*. The challenging austerity of this thoughtful excursion must have been strange to this newspaper correspondent, a friend of the panorama of the human hustle and bustle. And it was, in fact, quite unusual to hear talk of the earth and the heavens, and of a struggle between the two—as if these were concepts of thought that one could deal with in the same way that the metaphysical tradition had dealt with the concepts of matter and form. Were these metaphors? Concepts? Expressions of thought?

Perhaps the proclamation of a neoheathenistic mythology? Nietzsche's
Zarathustra, the teacher of the eternal return of the same, seemed to
be Heidegger's new model, and during this period Heidegger did in
fact devote himself to an intensive explication of Nietzsche. His
labor culminated in a two-volume work—the true counterpart to
Being and Time.

But this was not Nietzsche, and it had nothing to do with
religious eccentricity. Even if there were occasional eschatological
overtones and even if the talk—as if from an oracle—was of "the
god" who "presumably, could suddenly appear," this was an extrapo-
lation of philosophical thought and not the words of a prophet. It
was a difficult struggle for a philosophical language that would be
capable of reaching back beyond Hegel and Nietzsche to retrieve the
oldest beginnings of Greek thinking. Up in his cottage one day during the war, I remember how Heidegger began to read an essay on
Nietzsche that he had been working on. He stopped suddenly,
pounded on the table so hard that the tea cups rattled, and exclaimed
with frustration and doubt, "This is Chinese!" Heidegger had run
into a linguistic impasse; he was experiencing a deficiency in language, as happens only to those who have something to say. It required all of his power to hold out under this deficiency and to let
nothing offered by the traditional ontotheological metaphysics and
its conceptualizations distract him from his question concerning Being. And it was this dogged energy of his thought that permeated the
whole atmosphere when he delivered a lecture—be it "Building,
Dwelling, and Thinking" in the great hall of the Darmstädter dialogues, the lecture on the "thing" [*das Ding*], which danced to a
puzzling roundelay, or the explication of a poem by Trakl or of a later
Hölderlin text, often taking place in the all too distinguished
Bühlerhöhe sanitarium. Once even Ortega y Gasset followed him
there, drawn by this prospector of language and thought.

Later, he immersed himself completely into the structure of
academic life once again. He gave a talk on "Hegel and the Greeks"
in a regular work conference of the Heidelberger Akadamie der
Wissenschaften. He delivered a long, difficult lecture called "Identity
and Difference" as part of a ceremony celebrating the anniversary of
the Freiburg University. On one such occasion he also held a seminar, just like in the old days, with his then-aging students. The seminar was on a single sentence from Hegel: "The truth of Being is the
essence." This was really the old Heidegger: Spellbound with his

own questions and thought, gingerly testing the ground out in front to see if it was solid, annoyed when others could not find the place he had sought out as a hold, and unable to help except by prodding us with his own thoughtful interjections. Often I was able to get him together with my own circle of students in Heidelberg. Sometimes a discussion would ensue, i.e., one would be taken along on a journey of thought, unable to deviate from the way. *Only those who go along know that there is a way.*

Today the majority think of things differently. They no longer want to go along; rather, they want to know in advance where they are going—or they are of the opinion that they have a better idea of where one should go. Their only interest in Heidegger is in categorizing him—for example as belonging to the crisis of late capitalism. They see him as fleeing from time into Being or into an irrational intuitionalism, neglecting modern logic. Perhaps the moderns are mistaken insofar as they neither would have anything to classify nor would they even know that there was anything to overcome critically if this thinking was not simply there [*da*]. In reflecting less upon this thinking than the thought of contemporaries, these moderns are effectively closed themselves off to all reflection about this thinking. But there are two points that no one can deny. First, no one prior to Heidegger had done the kind of retrospection necessary to show the link between Greek thought and its founding of science and establishment of metaphysics, on the one hand, and the turn in the course of human history towards today's technological civilization and the ensuing struggle for control of the earth, on the other. And second, no one had dared to tread far enough out onto the shaky ground of unconventional concepts to allow human experiences of other cultures, especially of Asian cultures, to emerge from afar and show themselves for the first time as experiences that could possibly be our own.

The poet Paul Celan was one of the many pilgrims who journeyed to Todtnauberg, and his encounter with Heidegger resulted in a poem. This is really something to consider: After being persecuted as a Jew, this poet—he lived in Paris rather than Germany, but he was a German poet—anxiously ventured this visit. He must have been greeted both by the eyebrights of the little rustic estate, complete with the flowing stream (with "the starred die [*der Sternwürfel*] atop"), and by this little rustic man with the flashing eyes. He entered his name in the house register like so many before, a line of hope that he held in his heart. He walked over the soft meadows with the thinker, both individuals, standing alone like the flowers ("orchis and orchis"). Only later, during the drive home, did it become clear what Heidegger, then still crude, had muttered to him—he began to understand. He understood the risk of this way of thinking, one that others ("the person") can listen in on without being able to understand; he understood the risk of treading on shaky ground—such as on a log pathway that one cannot follow to the end. The poem reads:

Todtnauberg

arnicas, eyebrights, the
drink from the well with the
starred die atop,

in the
cottage,

the line in the book
—whose names have been entered
before mine?—
the line in this book,
written with a hope, today,
harbored in the heart,
of a thinker's,
coming
word

fields in the forest, unleveled,
orchis and orchis, standing alone,

crude, later, with the drive,
clear,

he who drives us, the person,
who listens along with,
the half-
traversed log
pathway in the moor

damp,
much.

CHAPTER ELEVEN

THE WAY IN
THE TURN (1979)

In a certain sense, the philosophical work of Martin Heidegger already belongs to history. That is, for a long time now it has gone beyond the first and second wave of its effect and has taken a firm place among the classics of philosophical thought. This fact implies that each present age has to determine anew its position in relation to, or its attitude towards, his work. Someone who has himself participated as a contemporary in the development and dissemination of Heidegger's philosophical questioning will not only have to redetermine the place of Heidegger's thinking in recent philosophy, but also his own standpoint in relation to it. Also, he will not claim to judge the historical significance of Martin Heidegger, but, on the contrary, will strive to continue to participate in the movement of thought initiated by Heidegger's questions.

After all, it is safe to say that the position developed by Heidegger has to be determined under two totally different aspects:

From Hans-Georg Gadamer, "Heidegger's Paths," trans. C. Kayser and G. Stack, in *Philosophic Exchange*, 2, no. 5 (Summer 1979). Copyright 1979 by the Center for Philosophic Exchange. Reprinted by permission of the Center for Philosophic Exchange. As in the other reprinted chapters, revisions have been made to bring the translation of some of Gadamer's technical terms in line with my translation and to accommodate revisions in the German text Gadamer made.

(1) under the aspect of role in the academic philosophy of this century (especially within the German scene) and (2) under the aspect of his impact on, and significance within, the general consciousness of our epoch. His rank is principally determined by the fact that these two aspects can no more be separated from each other in his case than in the case of other great classical thinkers such as Kant, Hegel or Nietzsche.

Within the academic philosophy of our century, Heidegger's thinking may be classified, in terms of his own admission, as part of the phenomenological movement. And, whoever is familiar with the development of Husserl's phenomenology to which Heidegger is referring also knows that this means, at the same time, a kind of placement in relation to the then prevailing Neo-Kantianism. These orientations must not be understood in a narrow sense of philosophical schools. For, in regard to both orientations, Heidegger's thought presents itself in a decidedly critical profile.

For years Heidegger was assistant to, and later on a young colleague of the founder of the phenomenological school. And, doubtlessly, he learned much from the masterful art of description in which Edmund Husserl excelled. His first great effort in the realm of thought, *Sein und Zeit* [*Being and Time*], introduced itself in theme and language (and even through the place of its publication) as a phenomenological work. The expression "phenomenology"—in the manner in which Husserl used it—contained a polemical allusion to all theoretical constructions of thought that originated from within the constraints of an inaccessible system. Husserl's power of phenomenological intuition had proven itself precisely in the reflection and criticism of all of the constructivistic biases of contemporary thought. This was especially the case in his famous criticism of psychologism and naturalism. One will also have to admit that Husserl's carefulness in description was coupled with a genuine methodological consciousness. The phenomena that he brought to recognition were not a naive set of "givens," but correlates to his analysis of the intentionalities of consciousness. Only by going back to the intentional acts themselves could the concept of the intentional object—i.e., the phenomenon or that which was meant as such—be secured.

As Heidegger named and elucidated the concept of phenomenology in the introduction of his own first work, it could almost be read as a simple variation on Husserl's methodological program. Yet, in spite of this, a new accent was heard by virtue of the fact that Heidegger, in a paradoxical emphasis, did not introduce the concept of phenomenology from the direction of its "givenness," but rather, from its "ungivenness," its hiddenness.

Although Heidegger, in this first presentation of his thought, avoided an overt critique of Husserl's phenomenological program (something he had attempted to formulate for some time in his lectures), the critical distinction between his and Husserl's phenomenological point of departure could not be overlooked in the development of *Being and Time*. It proved not to have been in vain that Heidegger (in section seven of *Being and Time*) had understood the idea of phenomenology in terms of the hiddenness of the phenomenon and as a discovery that had to be wrested from hiddenness.

By means of his idea of phenomenology, Heidegger did not only intend to display the customary certainty of the descriptive method's victory in which the phenomenologist felt his superiority to the theoretical constructions of contemporary philosophy. Rather, the hiddenness that was dealt with here was, so to speak, more deeply rooted. Even the classic analysis of thing-perception that Husserl had developed as a gem of his phenomenological art of description to the finest possible subtlety could still be accused, taken as a whole, of hiding a prejudice. That, indeed, was Heidegger's first accomplishment: he turned the pragmatic or functional context in which perceptions and perceptual judgments meet against the Husserl's descriptive structure. What he elaborated in the conception of "ready-to-hand" [*Zuhandenheit*] was not, in truth, a higher dimension in the wide thematic field of Husserl's investigation of intentionality. To the contrary, the simple perception that apprehends something as presence-at-hand [*Vorhandenes*] and makes it present proved to be an abstraction based upon a dogmatic prejudice—the prejudice that what is presence-at-hand [*Vorhandenheit*] must receive its ultimate proof through pure presence to consciousness. The young Heidegger had already dealt with the logic of impersonal judgments as a student of Heinrich Rickert, and here he may have followed a dark impulse that was now raised to the level of theoretical clarity. The result of his dissertation, namely, that the shout of "fire!" resisted the logical transformation into a predicative judgment and could only be coerced into a logical scheme, may have been felt by the later Heidegger as a confirmation of his first intuition: at the base of all logic lies an ontological restriction.

In the meantime, by reinterpreting the metaphysics and ethics of Aristotle in a new and ingenious way, Heidegger had acquired the intellectual tools that allowed him to expose the ontological prejudices that continued to permeate his own thinking, as well as that of Husserl and Neo-Kantianism. These ontological principles were operative in the then current concept of consciousness and especially in the fundamental role of the concept of transcendental subjectivity. The recognition that subjectivity was a transformation of substantiality and a final ontological derivation of Aristotle's concepts of Being and essence gave such impact to Heidegger's pragmatically toned critique of Husserl's analysis of perception that it toppled all perspectives and especially the very foundations of Husserl's program. In speaking of *"Dasein"* Heidegger did not only replace the concepts of subjectivity, self-awareness and the transcendental ego by a new word of striking force; by elevating the time-horizon of human existence, an existence that knows itself to be finite (i.e., is certain of its end), to the rank of a philosophical concept, he transcended the understanding of Being that was the basis of Greek metaphysics. The leading concepts of the modern philosophy of consciousness, subject and object, as well as their identity in speculative thinking, proved themselves to be dogmatic constructions as well.

However, it was not the case that the phenomenological conscientiousness of Husserl did not endeavor to break the dogmatism of the traditional concept of consciousness. That was precisely the point of the concept of intentionality—that consciousness was always "consciousness *of* something." Also, the evidence-postulate of complete apodicticity that could be met only by the *ego cogito* [I think] did not represent for Husserl a passport to freedom. Rather, he dissolved, in a lifelong, continually refined analytical process, the basic Kantian concept of the transcendental unity of apperception into a constitutional analysis of internal time-consciousness, and he worked out, more and more carefully, the process-character of the self-constitution in the "I think." With the same insistence Husserl pursued—under the rubric of "intersubjectivity"—the aporia of the constitution of the *alter ego* [the other I], of the "we," and of the monadic universe. This is especially the case in his unfolding of the problematic of the life-world [*Lebenswelt*] in his studies concerning the "crisis" [*Krisis*], for these showed that he wanted to meet every challenge that could be raised from the standpoint of the problematic of history. It should be noted, however, that Husserl's analyses pertaining to the problem of the life-world were considered as countermoves to Heidegger's critical insistence on the historicality of *Dasein*.

It remains a peculiar fact that Husserl's critical defense in his *Krisisabhandlung* was simultaneously directed against Heidegger and Scheler, even though they did not belong together at this particular point. Scheler never questioned the eidetic dimension as such from the perspective of historicality, as Heidegger did in a fundamental ontology construed as a hermeneutics of facticity. Rather, Scheler tried to ground phenomenology in metaphysics. It is not "spirit" or *Geist* that experiences "reality." Rather, it is "urge" or "drive" or, more precisely, *Gefühlsdrang:* the striving or impulse towards the satisfaction of felt needs. The unactualized essence-look of "spirit" itself must break forth from the reality of the striving itself. Phenomenology has no ground in itself. Indeed, for Husserl, this was a turning away from the assumption that philosophy ought to be an exact science insofar as the science of actuality cannot be exact by virtue of its very nature. The "crisis-treatise" is primarily concerned with the clarification of such "misunderstandings." At any rate, Husserl considered it a fact that both Scheler and Heidegger simply had not understood the inevitability of the transcendental reduction and of the ultimate foundation for the apodictic certainty of the *cogito*.

We may illustrate the disparity in regard to the emerging problematic by pointing out that Heidegger considered Husserl's mode of inquiry into the ontological prejudices upon which the metaphysical tradition rested hopelessly entangled. When, towards the end of the 1950s, Heidegger got together with some of my own students in Heidelberg and participated in a seminar which I was giving on the subject of Husserl's analysis of time-consciousness, he asked us what Husserl's analysis had to do with *Being and Time*. Every answer that was given to him was rejected; it had "nothing" to do with it!

That was certainly said on the basis of the decisiveness by which the later Heidegger had freed himself from the transcendental mode of questioning; a freedom that had not yet been truly achieved even in *Being and Time*. All the same, one will have to admit, when looking back with Heidegger on his own development, that his starting point with "Being-in-the-World" and the explication of the question of Being along the lines of this allegedly "transcendental" analysis of *Dasein* truly pointed in a completely different direction. An analysis of time-consciousness such as Husserl's no longer satisfied Heidegger, even though Husserl's progress beyond Brentano consisted precisely in the fact that he recognized the temporality [*Zeitlichkeit*] of time-consciousness itself. In addition, Husserl turned against a theory of time-consciousness that conceived of the past and the becoming past only under the perspective of memory and, in so doing, conceived of it as something brought back to the present.

This step leading beyond Brentano is expressed in the concept of "retention": a holding fast that is an original function of the presently perceiving consciousness. However, Heidegger's problem was much more radical. *Being and Time* was not at all, as Oskar Becker interpreted it at the time, a mere elaboration of a problem on a higher level within Husserl's phenomenological program. This "piece of philosophical anthropology" that was contained in *Being and Time* (*Sein und Zeit,* first edition, p. 17) was subordinated to a much more far reaching question concerning the nature of Being. This "Being" Heidegger oriented along something he called "Being as a whole" and, later on, he always insisted that this "Being" could not be clearly read from *Dasein* as the "place of understanding of Being" (p. 11, footnote b in Vol. 2 of the *Collected Works*).

In the Marburg lecture of the summer of 1928 (vol. 26, *Collected Works*) the following presupposition is asserted: that "a possible totality of all beings is already there." Only then can there be Being in understanding (p. 199). *Dasein* is admittedly exemplary, however, not as a case of Being that has been marked by our thinking but, rather, as the being "that is in the manner of being its 'there' [*da*]." Even the later term, *Lichtung* or "clearing" already appears here. However, it is still characterized by an anthropological turn towards the characteristics of the elucidated disclosedness of *Dasein,* but with the ontological sense of "protruding into the openness of the 'there': 'ek-sistence' [*Ek-sistenz*]" (*Sein und Zeit,* p. 177, footnote c). Even the term "the turn" (which later became a key word) can be found already in 1928. It is used to refer to "ontology itself expressly turned back into the metaphysical ontic in which it is always standing." Here, too, Heidegger is still thinking in terms of human existence or *Dasein* insofar as the latent change that the fundamental ontology undergoes as the analytic of *Dasein* (when considered as a "temporal analysis") is called "the turn."

Heidegger's later marginal notes in his cottage copy give a totally new interpretation to the exemplary function of human existence (*Sein und Zeit,* p. 9, footnote c). Human existence is "exemplary" in the sense of the "happening" of Being that accompanies it. That, naturally, is a clear change in interpretation. But even such altered interpretations (for that is surely what they are) have their truth. They bring to light Heidegger's unclear intention. For the rekindling of the question of Being it was the "there" of human existence, the *Da* of *Dasein,* that was of essential importance, not so much the priority of the Being of *Dasein.*

There are similar questions of interpretation in regard to other critical points in Husserl's program. Thus, in Heidegger's chapter concerning *Mitsein* or "being with" (section 26 of *Being and Time*) this analysis is completely defined in terms of the critical delimitation against Husserl's problematic of intersubjectivity. Indeed, the dominant ontological prejudice governing his thought is no less recognizable in Husserl's treatment of the problem of intersubjectivity than it is in his description of the allegedly "pure" perception. There, only a higher level "transcendental intuition" is supposed to animate the pure thing-perception in the *alter* ego! Obviously, Heidegger adopts a polemical orientation towards Husserl when, in contrast to such an account, he speaks of "being with" or *Mitsein* as an a priori condition of all being-with other *Dasein* [*Mitdasein*] and when he expressly makes the claim of an equal originality, a claim with which he frequently counters Husserl's idea of a "last foundation" (cf. p. 131). The *Mitsein* is not added later as a supplement to *Dasein.* Rather, *Dasein* is always at the same time *Mitsein,* regardless of whether others join in being there or not, regardless of whether they can do without me or whether I "need" no one.

When Heidegger designates *Dasein* and *Mitsein* as modi of Being-in-the-World and denotes Care [*Sorge*] as the basic constitution of "Being-in-the-World, he still follows, in the structure of his argument, the mode of thinking in terms of a transcendental proof that Husserl shared with the Neo-Kantians. In reality, however, he was not merely aiming, in his transcendental analytic of human existence, at a concretization of transcendental consciousness, that is, substituting factical, human *Dasein* for the fantastically stylized transcendental ego. Indirectly, that was already made apparent by the fact that he phenomenologically orients the question of the "who?" of *Dasein* towards the "everydayness" [*Alltäglichkeit*] of existence, which is bound to a "circumspective concern" for the world, for what is "ready-to-hand" and "together" [*Miteinander*]. In this "fallenness" the true phenomenon of the "there" is constantly hidden, as is true "I myself." It is the "they" [*das Man*] that is no one and has been no one that is encountered first and foremost by *Dasein*. This is not only to be understood polemically in the sense of a cultural criticism of the century of anonymous responsibility. Rather, behind it was the critical motive that questioned the concept of consciousness itself. But this required a unique preparation that was peculiar enough in itself: to make visible, behind this fallenness in the world of circumspective concern and "solicitude" others [*Fürsorgen*], the authenticity of *Dasein*, the "there" veiled by "the nothing," and to accomplish this through the anticipation of death.

It is true that Heidegger always emphasized that the "everydayness" of existence that understands itself as circumspective concern and "solicitude" belongs as much to *Dasein* as the highest peak of the moment in which the mineness [*Jemeinigkeit*] of *Dasein* reveals itself through the mineness of dying and in which the original character of temporality (in contrast to the inauthenticity of the vulgar understanding of time and of eternity as well) reveals itself as finite temporality. However, even at this level in the development of his thinking, Heidegger reflected on the question of if a mere reversal of fundamental relationships might be sufficient or whether there was not even in a temporal interpretation of Being as such already a misinterpretation in hiding: "Already the basic act of constitution of ontology, that is, of philosophy, the objectification of Being, that is, the projection of Being to the horizon of its comprehensibility, is given to uncertainty. . . ." (vol. 24, p. 459).

Here the entire problematic of the objectification of Being can be felt, the problematic that led him to "the turn." In the same place from which the above quotation was taken, Heidegger says that the horizon of comprehensibility could be reduced insofar as objectification—which is connected with such thematization—"is contrary to the everyday relations to beings." "The project itself necessarily becomes an ontic one. . . ." These statements from the lecture in 1927 give a new dramatic accent to an assertion found in *Being and*

Time (*Sein und Zeit,* p. 233) that sounds more like a rhetorical question there: ". . . it even becomes questionable . . . whether a genuine ontological interpretation of *Dasein* is not bound to fail precisely because of the manner of Being of this thematic being itself."
Then that was more of a rhetorical question. But, in retrospect—which is only now possible—there is a question that has been occupying me since the appearance of *Being and Time,* a question that assumes greater urgency for me: Was the introduction of the problem of death into the train of thought of *Being and Time* truly cogent and commensurate with the actual subject matter? In his formal argument, Heidegger claims that the ontological interpretation of "Being-in-the-World" as "Care" (and, consequently, as temporality) would have to show explicitly "the potentiality-for-being-whole" of *Dasein* if it wants to attain self-certainty. But this *Dasein* becomes limited because of its finitude, its Being-towards-an-end, that happens in death. Thus, reflection of death is called for. Is this really convincing? Is it not much more convincing that it is in the structure of *Sorge* or "Care" as such and in its temporal interpretation that finiteness is already contained? Does not *Dasein,* in projecting itself towards the future, continuously experience "the past" as the passage of time itself? Insofar as *Dasein* is continuously involved in its anticipation of death (for this is what Heidegger really means and not that with this anticipation the "whole" or totality of *Dasein* comes into view), it is the experience of time as such that confronts us with the essential finiteness that governs us as a whole.

It may be noted, after all, that Heidegger proceeded precisely along this way and never again placed the problematic of death at the center of his thought. In his cottage copy Heidegger leaves these passages intact, and the way of his thinking ultimately led him from the ecstatic horizon of *Dasein* and the instant into the structural analysis of the dimensionality of time. (See *Being and Time.*)

And the later marginal notes of *Being and Time* point in the same direction. There, the expression "the place of the understanding of Being" [*Stätte des Seinsverständnisses*] (*Sein und Zeit,* p. 11, footnote b) is especially instructive. With this expression Heidegger obviously wants to mediate between the older point of departure from *Dasein* (in which its Being is at stake) and the new movement of thought of the "there" [*Da*] in which *das Sein* or Being forms a clearing. In the word place [*Stätte*] this latter emphasis comes to the fore: it is the scene of an event and not primarily the site of an activity by *Dasein.*

The entire structure of the argument in *Being and Time* seems to be dominated by a twofold motivation that is not completely balanced. On the one hand, there is the ontological denotation of the "disclosedness" of *Dasein* that is the basis and premise of all other ontic phenomena in relation to the activity of *Dasein* and of the inner tension between the inauthenticity and authenticity of *Dasein.* On the other hand, the exposure of the authenticity of *Dasein* in contrast to its inherent inauthenticity is at stake in Heidegger's thinking. However, not in the sense of the existential appeal along the lines of Jaspers, but with the purpose of delineating true temporality and the time-horizon of Being in its universal range. Both of these motives combine in the aprioristic fundamental thought with which Heidegger equipped the transcendental question of Being at that time.

At any rate, there can be no doubt that by sacrificing the transcendental understanding of the self and by sacrificing the horizon of understanding Heidegger's thinking lost the sense of urgency that made it appear similar to the so-called "philosophy of existence" of his contemporaries. Certainly, Heidegger had already emphasized in *Being and Time* that the tendency to fallenness of *Dasein,* its absorption in the circumspective concern of the world, is not a mere error or lack, but that it is just as original as the authenticity of *Dasein* and is an essential part of it. Certainly, the magic phrase, "the ontological difference," with which Heidegger worked in his Marburg period, did not only have the obvious meaning of a differentiation between Being and beings that constitutes the essence of metaphysics. Rather, it also aimed at something that could be called the difference in Being itself, a difference that finds its reflective expression in a struggle and resolution [*Austrag*] within metaphysics.

During his Marburg years, even before the publication of *Being and Time,* Heidegger did not intend that the ontological difference (a formula he constantly used) be understood as if this differentiation between Being and beings was one made by ourselves in our thinking. And certainly Heidegger, from the very beginning, was aware of the fact that the aprioristic scheme of Neo-Kantianism and Husserl's separation of essence and fact were insufficient for a convincing delineation of the scientific-theoretical specificity of philosophy against the aprioristic basic concepts of the positive sciences.

The paradoxical formula of a "hermeneutics of facticity" is an eloquent expression of this, as is the reversion of an existential analytic in existence.

Heidegger was fully justified in opposing the understanding of *Being and Time* as a "dead-end street." By recognizing the question of Being in general, it led into the open. And yet it was like an opening into a new realm when Heidegger used the surprising phrase, "the *Dasein* in human beings," in his next publication, *Kant and the Problem of Metaphysics*. Where this was to lead could not yet be seen in the Kant book. Even before 1940, in marginal notes in a copy of his Kant book that he had sent to me as a replacement for the one I had lost, Heidegger criticized himself in the following way: "relapsed totally into the standpoint of the transcendental question." The idea of a finite metaphysics that he developed there (and which he tried to support by means of Kant) ultimately held onto the thought of a transcendental foundation that was the same as that presented in his Freiburg inaugural lecture. That is certainly neither coincidental nor a mere half-heartedness in Heidegger's thinking. On the contrary, it reflects the serious problem concerning the means by which the radical impulse of thought that was directed towards the destruction of the conceptuality of metaphysics could be reconciled with the idea of philosophy as a strict science. At that time, Heidegger still accepted this idea—to the growing disappointment of Jaspers, as the latter's recently published *Notizen über Heidegger* indicate. That is the reason for his "transcendental" self-interpretation in *Being and Time*. The transcendental philosophy could still understand itself as a science even if it rejected all hitherto existing metaphysics as dogmatic. In doing so, it was able to offer the sciences as such an argument by which it could see itself confirmed as the true heir of metaphysics. This was still completely true for Husserl's program; for Heidegger, it becomes problematic.

Being and Time fused, in a remarkably magnificent simplification, the understanding of Being in metaphysics (i.e., in Greek thought) with the concept of scientific objectivity that is the foundation of the self-understanding of the positive sciences in modern times. Both were construed as "present-at-hand," and it was the claim of *Being and Time* to demonstrate the derivative character of this understanding of Being. But this means to show that the Being of *Dasein* gains, not in spite of, but because of, its finiteness and historicality, its authentic character, from which such derivative modes of Being as present-at-hand or objectivity could be understood in the first place. Such an enterprise was destructive for the configuration of thought in classical metaphysics. When Heidegger, on the basis of *Being and Time,* asked the question "What Is Metaphysics?" this question, too, was more a case of a questioning metaphysics itself than a revival of it or a re-founding of metaphysics on a deeper basis.

It is well-known that Heidegger's way of thinking during the 1930s and the early 1940s was not manifested by means of publications, but more in the form of academic teaching or by appearing in special lectures. The literary public first learned, in a comprehensive way, about what Heidegger called "the turn" when the "Letter on Humanism" was published in 1946. Only in the following years were the steps Heidegger had taken during the 1930s delineated more clearly by the publication of *Holzwege.* Everyone immediately noticed that here the framework of scientific institutions and the self-understanding of philosophy as scientific philosophy was transgressed. The addition of the vocabulary of the poet Hölderlin as well as Heidegger's strangely powerful reflections were not necessary in order to see a rekindling of the question of Being. The question that *Being and Time* had aimed at had burst open, as a result of the original impulse, the frameworks of science and metaphysics.

Certainly, there were also new themes that Heidegger's thinking began to focus upon: the work of art, the thing and language; obviously, these were issues for thought for which the metaphysical tradition had no commensurate concepts. The essay on "The Origin of the Work of Art" developed, with the greatest urgency, the conceptual inadequacy of so-called aesthetics. And, with the problem of the "thing," a new challenge was set for the process of thinking for which neither philosophy nor science had any means available for dealing with it. For long ago the experience of the "thing" had lost its legitimacy for the scientific thinking of the modern age.

What are "things" in an age of industrial production and general mobility? In reality, the concept of the "thing" had lost its philosophical birthright a long time ago, that is, since the beginning of modern natural science and the paradigmatic function of mechanics for this science. Within the realm of philosophy, too, the concept of "thing" had been replaced, characteristically, by the concepts of the object and the percept [*Gegenstand*]. But, in the meantime, it was not

only a change in the form of science and in the conceptual understanding of the world, but a change in the appearance of the world
itself which no longer left a place for the "thing." Even if one
allowed the work of art a continued existence in a kind of protective
area of cultural awareness, in a kind of *musée imaginaire,* the disappearance of thing was an irresistible process that no regressive or
progressive thinking could ignore.

Thus, it was by no means an expansion into new areas (nor
even a resounding of the old tones of cultural criticism) that forced
Heidegger to direct the question of Being precisely and primarily
toward the form of life [*Lebensform*] that today we call the age of
technology. In doing so, he had no intention of confusing romantic
conjurations of a fading and paling past with the task of thinking
"what is." Heidegger was quite serious when, in *Being and Time,* he
granted the inauthenticity of *Dasein* its essential right in relation to
the authenticity of *Dasein,* even if it did sound like a self-repudiation
of his passion for cultural critiques. Now, in contrast to that, the
"thinking-to-the-end" of the modern age, the escalation of the technical world-project to an all-determining fate of human beings formed
the one, uniform level of experience from which Heidegger's question of Being received its orientation. The oft-quoted "forgetfulness
of Being," with which Heidegger had originally characterized metaphysics, proved to be the fate of the entire age. Under the sign of
positive science and its translation into technology, the "forgetfulness
of Being" is carried towards its radical completion. For technology
allows nothing else beyond itself to be noticed that might have a
more authentic Being in the reservation of "the sacred." Thus, a new
pointedness is found in Heidegger's thinking insofar as he attempted
to think in the total concealedness and absence of Being, the presence of this absence: that is, Being itself. However, this in itself was
not a mode of calculating thinking. It would be misunderstood if one
endeavored to calculate, from Heidegger's point of departure, the
possibilities that may or may not be realized in the future of
humanity.

There can be no calculative thinking at all that is thinking
about thinking as if it were disposable or calculable. Here Heidegger
is very close to Goethe when he said, "My son, I did it very cleverly, I
never thought about the thinking." Heidegger's thinking is not thinking about thinking either. What Heidegger thought about technology

and about the turn is not in actuality thinking about technology or the turn, but it is a standing in Being itself, which elicits thinking that follows from its own inner necessity. He calls this "essential" thinking and also talks about "thinking beyond" [*Hinausdenken*] or "thinking against" [*Entgegendenken*]. This is not thinking in the sense of seizing or grasping something; rather, this is something like "a projection" of Being into our thinking, even if only in the radical form of the total absence of Being.

It is not necessary to stress that such thinking-endeavors cannot use terms and concepts with which one can size up, grasp and overpower objects. Consequently, such a form of thinking gets entangled in an extreme lack of language insofar as the thinking and speaking that is being attempted here does not achieve anything, nor does it possess a store of ensured terms for an object. Even the utterances with which Heidegger attempts to oppose this calculating thinking that considers future possibilities retain something of the awkward prejudgment that accompanies conceptualizations. Certainly, it is true that all fore-seeing that hopes for something new, different and saving does not include real calculations or even pre-calculations. And when Heidegger refers to the arrival of Being and then adds, "very suddenly, presumably!" (VuA, 180), or when he says, in that famous interview, "Only a god can save us," these phrases are more rejections designed to repudiate the calculating intent to know about and to dominate the future than real statements. Being cannot be ascertained or thought as something that can be grasped, as something accessible to us. This is why such utterances are in no way predictions. They are not at all real statements of his thinking nor of the thinking of "what is." For such statements it also holds true that, to use Heidegger's language, the project contained in them becomes itself necessarily an ontic one.

How, then, can such counter-thinking come about? There is no need to speculate about this; on the contrary, the essays presented by Heidegger can be questioned. There is no doubt that in this sequence of relatively short works which in every case acquired the angle of their questioning from the criticism of metaphysical conceptualization and theory-formulation, the direction of his thinking is maintained with an almost monomanical insistence. However, the formation of a conceptual language commensurate with this angle of questioning and consistent with itself is hardly achieved.

When Heidegger looked back upon what he had achieved towards the end of his life, and when he planned a kind of introduction to the complete edition of his works that he prepared, he chose as its motto: "Ways, not works." Ways [*Wege*] are there to be walked upon, such that one can leave them behind and progress forward; they are not something static on which you can rest or to which you can refer. The language of the later Heidegger is a constant breaking up of habitual phrases, a charging of words with a new, elemental pressure that leads to explosive discharges. His language establishes nothing. Therefore all of the almost ritualistic repetition in the diction of the later Heidegger, as it is also frequently found among his disciples, is entirely inappropriate. However, his language is not exchangeable at will. Ultimately, it is as completely untranslatable as the words of a lyric poem, and it shares with the lyric poem the evocative power that proceeds from the complete unity and inseparability of the form of sound and the function of meaning.

And yet, it is not the language of poetry, for such language is always tuned to the poetic tone in which a poem is embedded. Heidegger's language, however, remains—even in the stammering search for the right word—the language of thought. A language that overtakes itself continuously, a dialectic answering to something pre-thought and preconceived.

Let us take an example. *"Nur was aus Welt gering, wird einmal Ding."* ["Only what smalls (or rounds) from the world, will ever become thing."] This sentence cannot even be translated into German! At the end of a long pathway of thought that opposed the undifferentiated equalizing of all things near and far with the true essence of the thing, the smallness [*das Geringe*] of the thing is understood, for a moment, as a process, a happening, an event that is expressed in the verb *geringen*. Although this verb does not exist in the German language, it alludes to *ringeln* ["curl"], *geringlet* ["curled"], and the rich field of meaning surrounding "ring," "circle," "encircle," and "around." In addition, it alludes to the total roundness of the world—the globe—from which the insignificance of the thing is wrested and in which it rounds itself. This mode of thinking follows the furrows that it makes in language. Language, however, is like a field from which a variety of seeds can come forth.

Here we are reminded of Heidegger's interpretation of the saying of Anaximander in which he finds the *"Weile"* [while] that is given to beings when it experiences its "genesis." Along these lines, the smallness [*das Geringe*] of the thing is something that *"aus Welt gering."* Certainly, *das Geringe* is used first as a noun derived from an adjective, but, by forming a noun from the adjective, *gering,* a collective totality of movement is evoked, just as is done by *"Gemenge, Geschiebe, and Getriebe."* Thus, Heidegger finally dares to change it completely into the imperfect tense of a verb. This is similar to *"Nichten," "Dingen"* and *"Sein"* [Being] that he spells *"Seyn."* The *"einmal"* or "ever" of the sentence in question underpins the past meaning of the artificial verb, *gering,* as does the rhymed answer *Ding.* In the neologism *"gering"* you can hear allusions to the following: *"gerinnt"* [coagulates], *"gerannt"* [coagulated], *"gelingt"* [succeeds], *"gelang"* [succeeded], but, in addition, *"geraten"* [to come off, to turn out] and *"geriet"* [came off] also belongs to the same semantic field. Thus, the final sentence of the essay on "the thing" summarizes the way that has been travelled and it means: only where world has curled itself around the round ring of a center, regardless of how small it might be, will a thing come to be in the end.

The question can be raised whether this coercion of language and this creation of words does what it is meant to do: that is, to communicate, to be communicative, to gather thinking into the word and to gather us in the word around something commonly thought. Neologisms (if, that is, they can be called that here—for, in actuality, they are additions of new semantic relations to already existing semantic units) require support, that is why poets who have the support of rhythm, melody and rhyme can get away with the most astonishing creations. Examples of German poets, in this regard, are Rilke and Paul Celan. Heidegger dared to do something similar in his very early thinking. One of the earliest creations of this type that I encountered when I had not yet met Heidegger, and when he had not yet published, a creation that demonstrated his new and daring treatment of language, was the phrase: *"es weltet"* [it is worlding]. That struck the target like a flash of lightning lighting a long yawning darkness; the darkness of the beginning, of the origin, of earliness. Even for this darkness he found a word (not a new one, but one from an entirely different area: the language used to describe the weather in northern Germany). When he said, as early as 1922, *"Leben ist diesig—es nebelt sich immer wieder ein"* [life is hazy, it always shrouds itself in fog], he meant that it surrounds itself with fog again and again and does not grant clarity and a clear view for very long.

The support that Heidegger is searching for in his thinking is not of the long-lasting quality that the word fused into a poem displays. Many of his props break down instantly. Here, I am reminded of *"Entfernung"* for *"Näherung."* However, within the ducts of his thought they provide their guiding epagogical service. Heidegger expresses it in the following way: "Thinking follows the furrows that it makes in language." And language, as I have said, is like a field from which the most diverse seeds can come forth.

Granted, these are images, metaphors, parables, means of speech that are props used in following a direction of thought, nothing that shall or can be kept forever; they just come forth as do words when you want to say something. And "saying" means "showing," keeping and communicating, but only for those who look around themselves.

That is why the untranslatability of this language is not a loss or even an objection to the kind of thinking that articulates itself in this manner. Wherever translation, i.e., the illusion of a free and unrestricted transposition of thought, fails, thinking breaks through. We do not know where thinking will lead us. Where we believe we know, we only believe that we think. For, then it would not be a "standing" under the challenge that strikes us and which we do not choose. Thinking challenges us, and we have to stand or fall. Standing, however, means to stand fast, to correspond, to answer—and not to play, in a calculating manner, with possibilities.

CHAPTER TWELVE

THE GREEKS (1979)

There are many aspects of a thinker of Martin Heidegger's stature that show his importance and illustrate the magnitude of his effect. There is the way he picked up the concept of existence as coined by Kierkegaard. There is his analysis of angst and of Being toward death, which had a particularly profound effect on the Protestant theology of the 1920s and which also influenced the first reception of Rilke. There is his "turn" in the 1930s to the German poet Hölderlin, from whom Heidegger gained an almost prophetic message. There is the splendid attempt and counterattempt at a coherent interpretation of Nietzsche, in which the will to power and the eternal return of the same were thought together for the first time. And, in particular during the period after World War II, there is his interpretation of occidental metaphysics with its culmination in the age of universal technology as the fate of the forgetfulness of Being—whereby one constantly has the feeling that some sort of secret theology of a concealed god is lurking in the background. One may want to haggle over details concerning Heidegger's interpretations. Or one may want to have absolutely nothing to do with Heidegger's overcoming of metaphysics, perhaps rejecting it as a secular presumptuousness or, precisely the opposite, as the last, yes, definitely the last, dying gasp of nihilism. But argue as one may, no one can deny that the challenge presented by Heidegger's daring thought to the European philosophy of the last fifty years is simply unparalleled. And in the face of the almost breathtaking effect of the

Heideggerean thought experiments, no one can deny the internal necessity of his way, even if it comes across to some as the wrong way leading into the fields of the ineffable.

Nonetheless, the diversity of these aspects found in Heidegger's works and effect, as well as the unity of the way that he has taken, is apparent in his relationship to the Greeks as it is nowhere else. Greek philosophy has certainly played a leading role in German thought since the days of German idealism, with regard to both history and historical problems. Hegel and Marx, Trendelenburg and Zeller, Nietzsche and Dilthey, Cohen and Natorp, Cassirer and Nicolai Hartmann make up an impressive list of witnesses, and the list could be easily lengthened if we also were to consider the great classical philologists of the Berlin school.

But with Heidegger something new began: There was a new nearness and a new critical inquiry concerning the Greek beginnings that directed his first independent steps and then accompanied him constantly up until his last years. Anyone who has read *Being and Time* can easily verify this—from near and from far. But to be aware of the extent to which Aristotle was present in Heidegger's thought in those early Marburg years, one must have sat in on Heidegger's lectures during that period. In the year 1922, just as I finished my doctorate, I came down with polio precisely at the time when I had wanted to go to Freiburg to study Aristotle with Heidegger. He comforted me then with the news that an extensive "phenomenological interpretation of Aristotle" would appear in the next volume of an annual: "The first part (about fifteen pages) deals with the *Ethica Nicomachea A, Metaphysica* A.1.2., and the *Physica* A.8; the second part (of about the same length) is concerned with the *Metaphysica* ZHΘ, *De Motu An, De Anima*. The third part will appear later. Since the annual will be published later, I will send you a separate copy." This publication never came to be. Only a copy of an introduction to it, an analysis of the hermeneutical situation in which Aristotle presented himself to us, became known to a few people. I became aware of it by way of Natorp. This bold and exciting manuscript became the basis for Heidegger's appointment to Marburg, and the appointment was the reason why the intended publication never came to be.

Heidegger was confronted with some new, immense tasks, and the series of Marburg lectures, which are now in the process of being published, is an impressive testimony to the way they were managed.

One can get only a preliminary idea from *Being and Time* and perhaps the lectures on logic given in 1925–26 (vol. 21 of the *Gesamtausgabe*, par. 13) of how much Heidegger's interpretations of Aristotle influenced the Marburg lectures. But anyone who heard Heidegger during the Marburg years has a much better idea of this. Aristotle was forced on us in such a way that we temporarily lost all distance from him—never realizing that Heidegger was not identifying himself with Aristotle, but was ultimately aiming at developing his own agenda against metaphysics. The primary value of these early interpretations of Aristotle lie in their ability to wipe away the scholastic overlay and serve as a model of a hermeneutical "fusion of horizons," which allowed Aristotle to come to language like a contemporary. Heidegger's lectures had their effect. I myself learned something really crucial about the "*dianoetic* [intellectual] virtues" from his textual and resolute interpretation of the sixth book of the *Nicomachean Ethics;* namely, that *phronesis* and its closely related *synesis* are nothing other than the hermeneutical virtues themselves. Here, in the critique of Plato that crystallizes the differentiation between *techne, epistime,* and *phronesis,* Heidegger took his first, decisive step away from "philosophy as a rigorous science." It was no less important that Heidegger was able to think the categories and concepts of *dynamis* and *energia* together, an affinity that is very apparent in the line of thought presented in Aristotle's *Metaphysics.* Bröcker worked out these Heideggerean ideas concerning the connection between *kinesis* and *logos,* and a few other works by other followers belong here as well. Heidegger himself made use of his old manuscripts when he gave the seminar on Aristotle's *Physics* B 1 in Freiburg in 1940, the text of which was first published in *Il Pensiero III* in 1958.

Beginning with the essay on Anaximander in *Holzwege,* all of Heidegger's later publications that have something to do with his relationship to the same degree. In the earlier studies this fusion was pushed almost to the point of identification. The treatise on Aristotle's *physis* attempted with radical determination to recreate this Aristotelian concept and to set it off against the modern attack on "nature" by contemporary science. It is obvious that Heidegger was making use of his earlier studies. Even though the treatise develops the Aristotelean concept of *physis* entirely in light of the beginnings of

Greek thought and stands resolutely opposed to the later reformulation of the concept of nature by Latin and contemporary thinking, it still cannot be classified as fitting squarely into the later theme of overcoming metaphysics.

But this should not be taken to mean that there was something like a break in Heidegger's philosophical development. In truth, this seems to me to be much more a question of perspective. The fact that Heidegger still made use of his earlier studies of Aristotle in 1940 and that these studies served as the basis of a work published in 1958 points much more to a continuity in his thinking through the so-called turn. His involvement with the Greeks was of fundamental importance to him; it distinguished him from all other phenomenologists from early on. (I went to Freiburg in 1923 not so much for Husserl's phenomenology as to learn about Heidegger's interpretations of Aristotle.) His orientation was influenced so strongly by the Greeks that, by comparison, the transcendental conception of a self in *Being and Time* had something provisionary about it.

In this respect, the famous "turn" was anything but a break in Heidegger's thinking. It was much more his running up against an inappropriate interpretation of self, one that had been prescribed by the strong influence of Husserl. Even the theme of overcoming metaphysics, which was only later expressed as a theme, must be thought of as a consequence of his orientation to the Greek beginnings.

The later Heidegger also saw Greek thinking as a whole as having something originative. Although the question concerning Being appeared even then always and always only as the question concerning the Being of beings, it had not yet been driven from the original experience of *da* and of *aletheia* by the "imposition of the Roman will" [*römische Willensstellung"*] (Dilthey) or by the contemporary "concern [*Sorge*] about a recognized knowledge" (Heidegger's lectures in Marburg in 1923).

What else could have been so helpful for the Heideggerean question, which attempted to break the logical immanence of the transcendental self-consciousness, but Greek thinking—thinking that covered the enormous questions of the beginning, of Being and "nothing," and of the One and the Many, and that was also capable of thinking *psyche, logos,* and *nous* without falling prey to the idols of self-knowledge and the methodological primacy of self-consciousness. The historical effort to think Greek and to wring the

Greek way of thinking from our own modern habits of thought served Heidegger's own interrogative impulse here in a peculiar way. He did not simply try to overcome the subject-object split by way of the phenomenological reduction of pure consciousness. Rather, he posed to the field of reduction of intentionality and to the research into the noetic-noematic correlation itself the question, What does "Being" mean?—be it the "Being" of consciousness, of ready-to-hand, of present-to-hand, of Dasein, or of time.

Thus, we have here a unique case. As an inquirer consumed by his own questions, Heidegger had been always searching for a interlocutor, and ultimately he was to invent some rather powerful partners. There was Nietzsche, for example; Heidegger traced out the metaphysical implications inherent in Nietzsche's thought and then faced these implications himself as his own greatest challenge. Or there was Hölderlin, the poet of poetry—who was no thinker of thought—who prodded Heidegger in his thinking and promised to propel his thinking out beyond the entanglements surrounding the concept of self-consciousness as found in German Idealism. But he had already found at the very beginning his true partners—the Greeks. They constantly demanded of him that he think them in an even more Greek way and, in so doing, demanded that he recapitulate questions he had posed to them. This thinker, who had gained a reputation for rendering coercive interpretations, often impatiently shoved history [das Historische] aside when he heard and rediscovered only himself in the texts—but here he could not be "historical" [historisch] enough when trying to rediscover himself.

Without a doubt, the beginnings of Greek thought are shrouded in darkness, and what Heidegger recognized in Anaximander, Heraclitus, and Parmenides was certainly himself. But these were, in fact, only collected remnants; they had not been preserved as texts, and they did not contain complete speeches or thoughts. Thus, Heidegger was using fragments when he attempted to erect his own building, fragments that he turned over and over again and assembled according to his own blueprint.

There are certainly some coercive acts in Heidegger's use of the pre-Socratic texts that I would not defend. For instance, he rips Anaximander's δ᾿ικην καὶ τισιν [just reparation and penance] apart, an expression that is more or less a set phrase. In the case of Parmenides's verses, he ignored the fact that τ᾿αυτά [the same] can be used only as a predicate. And it goes on. But all in all one has to say that our ability to understand pre-Socratic quotes is no different than Plato and Socrates's, especially with respect to the words of Heraclitus. On one occasion Socrates made the famous comment that a Delic diver was needed to understand his fragments. But what Heidegger did understand was excellent. . . . Methodically, he went about it the right way, inasmuch as he used the Aristotelean text as a springboard for his inquiry into the pre-Socratic beginnings. The single extant text that includes everything was in fact that of Aristotle. Only the thought-event of the Platonic dialogues—the first philosophical text that we still have—remained inaccessible to this impatient questioner in spite of all of the momentum behind his appropriations.

Like coming out of a hot spring—that is what Heidegger loved to call it when he would immerse himself in Aristotle's shapeless studio papers—these originative experiences of Greek thought rose up out of the consistent analyses of Aristotle and came into Heidegger's view, challenging him with their simplicity and otherness. To think what it must have meant for this young man who had been educated in scholastic Aristotelianism when he developed an ear for the language of these beginnings. In *aletheia* he saw not so much the unconcealedness and unhiddenness of speaking, but first and foremost the being itself that showed itself in its true Being, like pure, unadulterated gold. That was thought in a Greek way. Thus, it was with true enthusiasm that Heidegger defended the distinguished position of truth [*Wahrsein*] in Aristotle's *Metaphysics* (Θ 10) as the completion of the whole train of thought found in the central books of that text. And this was certainly not done from the perspective of the philosophy of identity found in German Idealism, the perspective that must have made this chapter so attractive to the Hegelians; rather, this was done from a perspective that had been brushed by an echo of the experience of Being, which allowed him to think it <Being or, possibly, truth> within the horizon of time. One could learn directly from Plato and Aristotle that Being is presentness [*Anwesenheit*] and that that which is always present [*das immer Anwesende*] is most of all beings.[a] But beyond that Heidegger made the ingenious observation that "always," ἀεί, had nothing to do with *aeternitas* [eternity], but must be thought along the lines of the currentness [*Jeweiligkeit*] of that which is present. This can be drawn from the usage of the language: ὁ ἀεὶ βασιλεύων[b] refers to the king who is currently governing. (We also say in German, *"wer immer König ist!"*.)[c] It is well known that the later Heidegger recognized specifically that the Greeks themselves did not think of this experience of Being as *aletheia;* rather, they understood *aletheia* more along the lines of a correspondence between Being and appearance, between *usia* and *phantasia* (Met. Δ 23) (the "false" things as well as the "false" talk, see *Zur Sache des Denkens,* p. 77). But that does not change the fact that the experience of Being itself, which articulates itself in statement, cannot be measured by the statement or thought in which it presents itself. The late Heidegger speaks of the event or of the clearing that made the presentness of beings possible in the first place. This was certainly not thought in a Greek way, but it did sketch out something unthought in Greek thinking. To a great extent this was true of the Aristotelean analysis of *physis,* inasmuch as the question concerning Being was approached in this analysis within the horizon of time. This treatise occupies more or less a central position in Heidegger's incessant efforts to think with the Greeks and to think back beyond them in a more originary way. The *Gesamtausgabe* has made a couple of volumes available that deal with the lectures given in Freiburg ("Heraklit," vol. 55; "Parmenides," vol. 54).

To think the Greeks more Greeklike—does this challenge not lead to some hopeless hermeneutical difficulties, especially if attempted with one of Aristotle's pedagogic texts, such as his lectures on physics? Certainly this text no longer belongs to the groping attempts of earlier times at converting the Homeric verse and a mystical vocabulary into conceptual language. It may well be possible to divine something left unthought in these pre-Socratic quotes, but the use of arguments and speeches had been introduced into the disciplines of logic and dialectics after the pre-Socratic period, and a new pedagogic school came into being—something to which the Aristotelean text itself attests. Can it be justified historically, or is it even possible at all to think back behind the use of pedagogy in Aristotle's texts? Does this not degenerate into an artificial archaism, like that which we come across with some of Heidegger's risky endeavors with the German language?

Well, it is certainly correct that in both cases Heidegger consciously used force in an attempt to break the preunderstanding of words, a preunderstanding that seems so natural to us. But in

Aristotle's case is this way so far off? When Heidegger translates *arche* not as principle, but as beginning, control, departure, and having at one's disposal [*Verfügung*], there is a some justification for that inasmuch as the issue at hand here is the terminological introduction of the word by Aristotle himself. No terminological fixation can ever completely sever the semantic ties of a word found in common use. And the famous catalogue of concepts in *Metaphysics* shows how very aware Aristotle was of this himself. In fact, one finds in the very first chapter of Aristotle's own linguistic analysis an analysis of not only the various meanings of *beginning* but also of the special meaning of the word as "control" and "execution of an office." We learn from this that "principle" is not simply a point of departure (of Being, becoming, and especially of knowledge) that one leaves; rather, it is contemporary through it all [*ein durch alles Gegenwartiges*]. A being of nature, which has the beginning of *kinesis* in itself, does not only initiate such movements from within itself (without being prodded); rather it "can" [*"kann"*] do it. But this includes the possibility that it may remain at rest, which means that it controls its movement. Thus, the animal has its own type of propulsion, and the plant has its "beginning" in itself that allows it to maintain its life. Therefore it must be granted the status of *anima vegetativa*. The Being of a being of nature is its "motility" [*Bewegtheit*]. This includes movement as well as being at rest.

It is similar in other cases, such as when Aristotle makes a specific terminological use of a common word or when, by combining morphemes, he invents a new word like *energeia* or *entelecheia*. Such new formations of words are then capable of pulling known words over into the ontological sphere; this happens in the case of the word *dynamis,* the "ability" [*"Können"*], which Aristotle defines in a general sense as *"arche kineseoos"* [the beginning of movement]. Heidegger renders it "suitability" [*Eignung*], but he even finds this dangerous because "we are not thinking Greek enough and do not understand the suitability for . . . as the way of coming forth into view in which the suitability fulfills itself by still holding back and within itself."

This certainly sounds a bit Chinese, but that is because his explication includes a whole series of other translations that Heidegger had already put forth with *physis, logos,* and *eidos.* In these cases Heidegger is correct. Again it is unmistakable that the new Aristotelean concept *"dynamis"* simply cannot be understood as "possibility"; rather the familiar meaning of the word *dynamis,* namely, ability, speaks with it. An ability is motility, which always includes a holding-within-itself. In Aristotle's terminological usage this gains an ontological meaning.

The case with *physis* as coming forth, as "arising" or "coming up" [*Aufgang*] is similar. We speak of seeds coming up, and we find a reference to this at the very beginning of Aristotle's linguistic analysis (Δ 4). Obviously Aristotle still heard such a close association between "coming up" and the word *physis* that he would most gladly have pronounced it with a drawn out upsilon. The same is true for *eidos.* Here, too, it cannot be denied that the power of the word *eidos,* with its resonance of "sight <of>" [*Anblick*] and "appearance" [*Aus-Sehen*], is not exhausted by the logical reference to the species, but rather "sight" speaks again even in Aristotle (as in Plato, see the *Sophist,* 253c3, d5). Thus, in the *Physics* we have "η στέρησις ε᾽ῖδος πως ᾽εστιν [the withdrawal is somehow an *eidos*/form]."[1]

One could go on endlessly like this in an effort to show that thinking more Greek-like is not so much thinking differently as it is thinking-with-an-other—a way of thinking which withdraws from our thinking because our thinking is completely fixated on objectivity, on overcoming the resistant character [*Widerständlichkeit*] of the object in a percipient certainty of ourselves. With a reference to only two words, which Aristotle transformed into concepts and which seem to have moved into the perspectives of our thinking with irresistible force, a semantic contribution can be brought to light which works to justify Heidegger's acts of violence.

One of these words is *metabole.* It is rightly translated by us as "<a sudden> change" [*Umschlag*], and it is actually used in Greek not only for the weather but also for the ups and downs of human fate. With Aristotle the word obtains a terminological status. It ex-

---

1. *Physis*, 193b–d19. The Greek phrase ε᾽ῖδός πως means "somehow," an *eidos.* Heidegger's translation is somewhat unfortunate. Incidentally, one senses some legitimate resistance when Heidegger speaks of the "ε᾽ῖδος προαιρετον" [preferred *eidos*/form] with reference to the case of *techne* (p. 141)—as if the eidos is "chosen" in the way that Hercules chose virtue at the crossroads, instead of the given purpose of the affair determining our intentions. This is also apparently the reason why Plato assumed there were "ideas" of the artificial things and named them paradeigmata" [example or model]. This is one case where Heidegger did not think Greek enough.

presses the formal structure of *kinesis,* which is found in all types of movement. This is surprising for us because, according to this, spatial movement seems to lose its essential continuity and sounds like a pure change or alteration of place. For us a sudden change is the opposite of such a movement. The word implies to us first and foremost the loss of settledness. When we say that the weather suddenly changes, we do not mean that the bad weather has ceased but rather that the beautiful weather has come to an end. That is more or less self-evident in Greek thinking as well, Parmenides is so settled on the settledness of Being that he almost reduced it to empty names when "humans hold as true and ascertain γίγνεσθαί τε καὶ ὀλλσθαι, εἶναί τε καὶ οὐχί, καὶ τόπον ἀλλασσειν διά τε Χροα φανον ἀμείβειν."[2, d] Obviously, a complaint about the unreliability and unsettledness of Being is to be found lurking behind this phrase. When we speak of a movement of place or alteration, we think not of a sudden change, but primarily of a transition of one into another. So what does it imply that Aristotelean thinking characterizes all types of movement with the structure of sudden change, of abruptness? Here Heidegger seems to be right about the Greeks when he stresses "that in a sudden change something appears that was concealed and absent until now."

This certainly does not contradict the experience of a sudden change that alters that which was constant—a notion that Eleatic thinking had revolted against—but the sudden change in such an experience is obviously a positive experience of Being and does not simply imply a loss of Being. This is what distinguishes it conceptually in Aristotle's *Physis.* That in which a sudden change takes place is thought of as Being. This is an opening that leads back behind the constant Being of Parmenides into the deep dimensions of its origins, which Parmenides himself did not reflect upon, and this is what still rings through in Aristotle's terminological coinage of *metabole* [changing, shifting, reshaping]. That natural beings have within them-

---

2. Fr. B, 40ff. (The fragment number refers to the collection by Hermann Diels, *Die Fragmente der Vorsokratiker* [Weidmannsche Verlagsbuchhandlung, 1951] p. 238.) The text of Parmenides's poem leaves no room for doubt. If the color is called "radiant" (φανόν), then that means that Parmenides's keeping its "passing" in view. (In German we also have the ambiguous phrase, "Die Farbe ist vergangen" [the color is gone].)

selves an arche for sudden change is a positive ontological distinction, not a diminution of "Being." The other pre-Aristotelean uses of *metabole* concur with this. The site in which the sudden change occurs is always mentioned. Therefore, we reach the compelling conclusion that everything depends upon what comes out of this, that is, what this sudden change leads to. The complete confirmation of this is found in the structure of unrestricted emerging [*Entstehens*]. There we really have the sudden change from "nothing" into Being, which Aristotle formally characterized as the sudden change κα᾽ τ αντιφασιν [according to its opposite]. Thus, movement does in fact have, to quote Heidegger, "as a way of Being, the character of coming forth into the presencing [*Anwesung*]."

Finally, and perhaps, the most surprising is the word *morphe* [form or shape]. With this we hear so clearly the potter's shaping hand as it works the malleable material that, without giving it a second thought, we understand Aristotle's remark "καὶ τὸ ε᾽ ιδος το κατα τον λόγον" [and its *eidos* (form) according to the *logos* (concept or reason)] from our own perspective by way of a reference to *techne*. And in fact Aristotle himself immediately introduces this analogy with *techne*. *Physis* is self-creating. Then along comes Heidegger, who teaches that even for Aristotle creating is not simply producing. If for Aristotle *morphe* is more *physis* than *hyle* [raw material or matter], then there is only the appearance of an analogy to *techne*.

In truth, it is much more the genesis, the unrestricted emerging, that makes the *morphe*-character of *physis* visible: "Furthermore, from one human being emerges another human being, but a bedstead does not give rise to another bedstead" (Aristotle's *Physics*, 1936b). Thus, Heidegger is justified in interpreting the process of technical production in the following way: *morphe* is even in this case "the mustering into appearance" so that "the suitability of those suited visibly and completely steps out." Also, in the case of *techne* the concern is not so much with producing as with emerging and creating—such as the natural process of self-emerging, like of a corn seed, for example, which we stick into the earth.

This way of conceptually coining the term *morphe* actually is supported somewhat by the natural usage of the word. Even Aristotle uses the word almost exclusively for living beings that render their own forms. The verb μορφόω [I form or shape] comes on the scene for the first time fairly late. The earliest use of the word *morphe* can

be found in the *Odyssey,* where it is used to describe a natural formation and well-formedness, and all later customary linguistic usage
corresponds to this. *Morphe* is that to which something strives for
completion, it is the "as what" that something presents itself, the "as
what" that something emerges. The appearance of a technical interpretive structure is obviously false.[3]

   But enough of this discussion of semantic voices that accompany the Aristotelean concepts. The lesson it teaches us is clear
enough. That we generally restrict the realm of meaning of the Greek
terms used by Aristotle to their terminological function is not so
much a consequence of the linguistic distance that separates us from
the naturally spoken Greek; rather, it is a consequence of the effec-
tive-historical determinedness of our preunderstanding, which has
been heavily influenced by the Roman-Latin and then more recent
instrumentalistic translations of the Aristotelean world of concepts.
We have become completely incapable of thinking of our fine German word *Ursache* <cause, reason, or motive> as *die Sache* <thing,
matter, or affair>, which it actually means, the *causa,* the *cosa.* We are
able see in it its function only as that which causes [*das Verursachende*]
or brings about [*das Bewirkende*]. It seems completely artificial and
scholastic for us to speak of Aristotle's four causes [*Ursachen*]; only
the *causa motrix* seems to us to be correctly called a *cause*—or we
might be willing to include the frowned upon final cause, but certainly not form and matter. They are simply not forms of "causality."

   It reverberates with false echos when we try to think Greek.
Erudition or historical learning certainly allow us to sense the otherness, but we are simply unable to think anything that does not correspond to something already found in our own thinking. The
conceptual words of philosophy become estranged from themselves
because they have nothing to say about beings; rather they enter into
the compulsion of thought. This is what Heidegger called the *language of metaphysics.* It was first articulated in Aristotle's thinking, and
it now controls our whole world of concepts. Heidegger's violent
rememberances against this control are not merely the result of a
refined historical conceptualization and learned historical sense—as

---

3. In contrast, things are different with the term *hyle.* This is undoubtedly a "technical" expression. But this is precisely because *hyle* is not "Being" in a true sense,
whereas *morphe* is.

if the past gave itself away to anyone. His thinking was certainly not called into the arena by a mere historical <*historisches*> interest in the "original" Greek thinking. As a man of our century—a century in which the beginning letters of the words "History" and "Historicality" have been capitalized with the largest upper-case letters—and filled with an awareness of the inappropriateness of the traditional philosophical concepts for the understanding of Christian faith, Heidegger was never satisfied with the traditional understanding of metaphysics. The return to the originative Aristotle gifted him with a genuine clue. That *"physis"* constitutes the character of Being of this or that being, a being that can never be denied its ontological valence, does not mean that only natural beings possess such an ontological valence; but it does mean that Being must be thought so that that which is found in motility [*das in Bewegtheit Befindliche*] must be recognized as being. Physics is not metaphysics. However, the highest being, the divine, is itself to be thought as the highest "motility." This can be learned from the conceptual connections between "movement" and the guiding concepts *"energeia"* and *"entelecheia."* Our thinking has become receptive to Heidegger's insight, because it has been so strongly influenced by the talk of an end to metaphysics and to the emergence of the a priori character of the "positive" age. Nietzsche's metaphysics of value presents us with this most extreme end. At the peak of modernity, where Being is dispersed into becoming and into the eternal return of the same, questions could be posed by Nietzsche that forced their way back behind metaphysics. And this is especially true of Heidegger. He recognized in metaphysics the fate of our world, a fate that is being fulfilled by the control of the world through science—and by the collapse toward which we are rushing. But then the question concerning the beginning is no longer a historical question, but rather a question posed to fate itself. Is "Being" still being kept for us? That the answers given, which are ultimately our fate and history, could free us to pose the question anew—to which they wanted to be the answers—this constitutes our way of philosophizing.

It is rather surprising that one of Aristotle's late text, the *Physics,* could be of some help in this regard. Indeed, Aristotle attempted here—against the Pythagorean thinking of Plato—to renew an older way of thinking in which Being is thought as motility instead of a constant numerical harmony. But it is still astonishing to see what appears from behind the superficial contradiction between *physis* and *techne* when we learn to read with Heidegger. Certainly these are only receding echos, but by comparison our understanding of nature and spirit, of space and movement, of malleable matter, and of the eternally unchanging form seems so very superficial. We are better able to think what "is" when we learn to think of Being as the arising [*als den Aufgang*], as that which creates itself and puts itself forth at any one time as a being—but as something that is more than that framed in its appearance. Being is not only a showing-of-itself; it is also a self-retaining, and that can be seen clearly with reference to motility. What we have to consider if we want to overcome the blindness of our own action and its destruction of the world is sketched out in this initial understanding of *physis*. Heidegger quotes the words of Heraclitus where he says that nature is accustomed to concealing itself, and he correctly recognizes that the challenge does not lie in penetrating nature and breaking its resistance; rather, the challenge is precisely to accept nature as it is in itself and however much of itself it displays. Certainly this thinking is no longer Greek; not only is *physis* thought of in this way, but Being—and Being first and foremost—is also thought of as *aletheia,* as the clearing, as that which comes on the scene prior to all appearing beings and yet remains concealed behind them. But Heidegger's bold thought experiments have nevertheless taught us to think the Greeks more Greeklike.

CHAPTER THIRTEEN

THE HISTORY OF
PHILOSOPHY (1981)

Within the German philosophical tradition, the history of philosophy has been considered an essential part of theoretical philosophy itself since Schleiermacher and Hegel. It is therefore essential that we keep this in mind when considering the topic "Heidegger and the History of Philosophy," which means that the question to be posed should take the following form: Which aspects of the basic orientation that has held sway over German philosophy since Hegel can be found in Heidegger's thinking? The background that frames this question is clear; it was created by the emergence of a historical consciousness. The legacy of German Romanticism is such that, since its advent, the problem of history has affected not only historical research in general but even the orientation of theoretical philosophy as well. Prior to the age of Romanticism there was no history of philosophy in the fundamental sense that we are using the term here. What did exist was simply a chronicling erudition, one that was certainly dominated by definite, dogmatic presuppositions but that did not serve the function of establishing philosophical foundations. Of course, the situation with Aristotle's famous doxography was quite different; he had built it into his pedagogical lectures with very definite pedagogical intentions—different until this later became a completely distinct branch of scholarly work in ancient pedagogy [*Schulwissenschaft*]. The Hegelian program of a history of philosophy was itself philosophy in the fullest sense, a special section within the philosophy of history that, for its part, attempted to place even reason in history. Indeed, Hegel virtually named the history of philosophy the heart [*das Innerste*] of world history. However, the more substantial claim of the Hegelian history of philosophy, that is, to have discovered the necessity inherent in the sequence of formations of philosophical thought and, thus, to have exposed the role played by reason in the development of the history of thought, could not withstand the critique of the historical school for very long. A good example of such a critique can be found in the orientation of Wilhelm Dilthey, who can virtually be regarded as *the* thinker of the historical school. In spite of all of his openness to Hegel's genius—an openness that grew with age—he was always in essence a cautious follower of Schleiermacher. To bring teleology into the investigation of the history of thought was not his affair; he saw himself as adhering to a purely historical method. This was to lead to the development of the so-called history of problems [*Problemgeschichte*] by the Neo-Kantians, which was the only way to philosophically investigate the history of philosophy at that time; it dominated the scene at the beginning of this century. Even if one could not find some type of necessity underlying the progression of the different designs of the systems of thought, one could still attempt to uncover a type of progression within history, thereby raising the treatment of fundamental philosophical problems to the level of a philosophical standard. This was more or less the way that the influential textbook by Wilhelm Windelband, *The History of Philosophy,* was constructed. It was in no way devoid of a historical dimension, but in the final analysis it was based upon the assumption of a constancy of problems from which, depending upon the changing historical constellation, varying answers followed. In a like manner, the Marburg Neo-Kantians pursued the history of philosophy as the history of problems.

As Heidegger began to make his contemplative way, the tide had just begun to turn against the history of problems. At that time, that is, the period during and following World War I, the criticism of the systematic unity of the Neo-Kantian conceptual system was emerging, and it also cast doubts on the philosophical legitimation of the history of problems. The disintegration of the transcendental framework of the Neo-Kantian philosophy, a framework that alone was capable of preserving the legacy of idealism, forced the collapse of the history of problems, for it derived its problems from this legacy. This movement away from the history of problems was mirrored in Heidegger's efforts as well. At that time he was attempting to move the systematic, transcendental conception of philosophy espoused by his admired teacher Husserl, the founder of phenomenology, in the direction of the historical reflection found in Dilthey's thought. His efforts produced a type of synthesis between Dilthey's problematic of historicality and the scientific problematic of Husserl's basic transcendental orientation. Therefore, in *Being and Time* we encounter the astonishing combination of a dedication to Husserl and a tribute to Dilthey—astonishing inasmuch as Husserl's proclamation of phenomenology in *Philosophy as a Rigorous Science* contains a quasi-dramatic criticism of Dilthey and the concept of *Weltanschauung.* When we raise questions concerning Heidegger's actual intentions and what led him away from Husserl toward a region proximate to the problem of historicality, then it becomes quite clear—especially now—that he was engrossed not so much with the then contemporary difficulty with historical relativism as with his own interest in the Christian legacy. Now that we know more about Heidegger's first lectures and initial thought experiments of the early 1920s, it is clear that his critique of the official Roman Catholic theology of his time pushed him closer and closer to the question of how an appropriate interpretation of the Christian faith could be possible or, to put it in another way, how could one ward off the infiltration of the foreign Greek philosophy—which forms the foundation of both the Neo-Scholasticism of the twentieth century and the classical Scholasticism of the Middle Ages—into the Christian message? <There were several formative elements at work then.> There was [*Da war*] the inspiration he took from the young Luther; there was his admiring emulation of Augustinian thought and especially his engrossment in the eschatological mood fundamental [*Grundstimmung*] to St. Paul's Epistles. All of this led him to view metaphysics as a type of misunderstanding of the original temporality and historicality experienced in the Christian claim of faith.

The introduction Heidegger wrote for his planned *Aristotles-Interpretationen*[1] gives a clear testimony to this. The key word that Heidegger used then when approaching the tradition of metaphysics

---

1. This text has not yet been published, but it can be obtained in a publishable form, and I have been familiar with it since 1923.

was *destruction*—destruction above all of the highly conceptual character of the more recent philosophy and especially of the sheaf of concepts associated with the ontologically indemonstrable notion of consciousness, the *res cogitans* of Descartes. So, Heidegger began with Aristotle, the first and most distinguished subject in the history of philosophy. The form that all of his dealings with the history of philosophy was to take was already sketched out in his early approach to Aristotle's thought—approached simultaneously with critical intentions and an interest in phenomenological renewal, this was destruction and construction in one. Even then he followed the basic tenant of Plato's *Sophist,* that is, that one should strengthen the position of one's opponent. This was an Aristotle that had become curiously more up-to-date. Heidegger preferred his ethics and rhetoric—in short, disciplines of the Aristotelian pedagogical program that were presented as being clearly detached from questions concerning the principles of theoretical philosophy. Above all, the criticism that he encountered there of the Idea of the Good, the highest principle of the Platonic doctrine, seemed to address his own primary concern, namely, the issue of temporal-historical existence and the criticism of transcendental philosophy. His interpretation of *phronesis* as a ἄλλο εἶδος γνωσεως, another type of knowing, was actually a sort of confirmation <of the validity> of his own theoretical and existential interest. This extended to theoretical philosophy and metaphysics as well, inasmuch as Heidegger already had the "famous analogy," as he often called it, in view—although in those years it was not yet thought out in a sufficiently self-conscious way. This was the basis within Aristotle's *Metaphysics* from which Heidegger was able to put into question in a like manner the systematic derivation of all value from any one principle, be it Husserl's transcendental ego or Plato's idea of the Good. Because of this interest, the publication the *Opus Tripartitum* by Meister Eckhart in 1923 must have been an inspiration to him. Also, when the tractate *"De Nominum Analogia"* by Cajetan fell into his hands, it became the subject of a thorough study that spilled over into his classes.

    Meanwhile, as he became increasingly engrossed in his own counterproject [*Gegenentwurf*] to Husserl's transcendental phenomenology, a project that first came to light with the completion of *Being and Time,* the figure of Aristotelian metaphysics came to represent unambiguously the point of origin of all opposing positions against which Heidegger sought to develop his own thought experiments. Thus, the concept of metaphysics slowly developed into a "code name"; that is, into a word that referred to the conglomerate of opposing tendencies against which Heidegger was developing his own question concerning the meaning of Being and the essence of time, a question motivated by his Christian inspiration. Yet, his famous inaugural lecture entitled "What Is Metaphysics?" stood in an ambiguous relationship to metaphysics inasmuch as the concept of metaphysics was used, or at least it seemed to have been used, in a positive sense. Later, when he began to formulate anew his own thought project in complete detachment from Husserl's model—and this is what we refer to as Heidegger's *turn*—metaphysics and its eminent representatives were to function only as the backdrop against which he critically set off his own philosophical intentions. From then on metaphysics no longer appeared as the question concerning Being; rather, it was portrayed as the actual, fateful obscuring of the question of Being, as the very history of the forgetfulness of Being that began with Greek thinking and continues through more recent thought up to the fully developed world-view and belief structures inherent in calculative and technical thinking, that is, up to today. From then on the <various> stages of the advancing forgetfulness of Being and the contributions of the eminent thinkers of the past were forcibly arranged in a fixed historical order, and this obligated Heidegger to delineate his project from Hegel's analogous attempt at a history of philosophy. Indeed, Heidegger always insisted that he never claimed in his own confrontation with the forgetfulness of Being and the language of metaphysics that there was a necessary progression from one stage of thought to the next. But inasmuch as he attempted to describe metaphysics from the perspective of his question concerning Being as a uniform instantion of the forgetfulness of Being, indeed, of a forgetfulness of Being continually on the rise, then it was inevitable that his own project have something of the logically compulsive character that typified the construction into which Hegel's history of world thought had degenerated. Unlike Hegel's, his was certainly not a teleological construction beginning with the end; rather, it was a construction based on a beginning, a beginning that already held the fate of Being [*Seinsgeschick*] of metaphysics. But "necessity" was included, even if it existed only in the sense of ἐξ ʽυποθʼεσεως αναγκαιον [something necessary according to a hypothesis].

Thus, it is a good idea to examine how his general project deviates from that of Hegel's in order to orient ourselves to his relationship to the history of philosophy. The first thing one is struck with is the peculiar place that the beginning of Greek philosophy—Anaximander, Parmenides, and Heraclitus—inhabits in his thinking. This should not come as a surprise because we had found a similar privileging of this beginning in Nietzsche, whose radical critique of Christianity and Platonism had also singled out pre-Socratic thinking, the philosophy of the tragic age of the Greeks. In an approach frequently used, Heidegger attempted to work out this original situation as a sort of counterimage to the actual fateful way taken by occidental thought as presented in the history of metaphysics. In his studies of Anaximander he expounded, in a most original and surprising way, upon elements of his own thinking that dealt with the character of time and temporalization. The famous solitary extant fragment from Anaximander's teaching, which we usually understand as one of the first conceptions of the self-sustaining and self-regulating unity of Being—referred to in Aristotelean terms as *physis*—displayed to him the temporal character of Being whenever it is in the process of showing itself: It has the character of tarrying [*Weile*]. But, of course, more than all else it was the pedagogical poems of Parminedes and the puzzling aphorisms of Heraclitus that he endeavored to see in a new light. Both Heraclitus and Parmenides had served as key witnesses for German idealism, and correspondingly, they played an important role in the Neo-Kantian history of problems. Parmenides was the man who first brought the question concerning Being into a sort of identity relationship with the concept of thinking, or of consciousness (in Greek it was referred to as *noein*), and Heraclitus was the profound founder of the contradiction as a dialectical image of thought, behind which the truth of becoming, the Being of becoming, could be envisaged. Heidegger thus endeavored repeatedly to overcome the idealistic misconception of the beginnings of Greek philosophy, a misconception that saw its culmination in Hegel's metaphysics—and respectively in the Neo-Kantian transcendental philosophy, which had disregarded its own Hegelian tendencies. It must have been the far-reaching problematic of the concept of identity itself and its internal connections with the concept of difference, which played a central role not only in Hegel's *Logic* but in Hermann Cohen and Natorp's interpretations of Plato as well, that he found especially challenging. Heidegger attempted to completely rethink identity and difference from the vantage point of "Being," as ἀλήθεια, as the "resolution" [*der Austrag*], and ultimately as the "clearing" or the "event" of Being, and then to contrast this with the idealistic, metaphysical interpretation. At this point it could no longer remain concealed from him that even here, with these early Greek thinkers, Greek thinking was already on its way, so to speak, to its later development into metaphysics and idealism. Heidegger saw precisely this as the true fate of our occidental history, as the fate of Being: Being presents itself as the "essence" of beings, calling forth the calamity of Onto-Theology—which, in Aristotle, shows up as the question of metaphysics.

Heidegger's work with Heraclitus and his concept of *logos* was motivated by the same intentions. Today, in the newly published lecture, we can see the unbelievable intensity, force, and logical consistency present in Heidegger's attempts to utilize fully Heraclitus's aphorisms with reference to his own question concerning Being. One should not expect to find in Heidegger's treatment of these texts a new, historical insight that relates directly to Parmenides's pedagogical poems or Heraclitus's aphorisms. But Heidegger was able to disclose a primordial experience of Being (and of "nothing") lurking behind these works, and his impressive, archaizing interpretations opened up enough space for one to be able to read these texts—in their darkness and fragmentary shortness—against the grain of Hegel's conception of as "reason in the history" of thought.

If like Heidegger, one understands metaphysics as the fate of Being—fate that finally pushed Western humanity to the extreme of a complete forgetfulness of Being with the advent the technical— then all further steps taken within his confrontation with the history of philosophy will appear peculiarly predetermined. This shows up in Plato's case in the most astonishing way. Thanks to his interpretive powers, Heidegger was able to give a very impressive interpretation of Plato's *Sophist* during his formative years, an interpretation that eventually was to give rise to the motto for *Being and Time*. But in his first extensive treatment of Plato, that is, his essay "Plato's Doctrine of Truth," which was published together with the "Letter on Humanism" in Switzerland in 1947, Plato's concept of the "Idea" appeared from the outset under a foreboding auspice, one portending the subordination of ἀλήθεια to ορθότης of truth to correctness or mere commensurateness with a pregiven being. Seen in this way, Plato did take another step in the direction of the "forgetfulness of Being" that led to the stabilization of Onto-Theology or metaphysics. It is far from obvious that this is the only way to read Plato. In fact, as a result of this reading, all the aspects of the history of Platonism that had fascinated the young Heidegger, such as Augustine, Christian mysticism, and the *Sophist* itself, played no substantial role in his later thinking. Yet, it is conceivable that one could find precisely in Platonic philosophy one possible way to get back behind the question as formulated in Aristotelian and the post-Aristotelian metaphysics, so that the dimension of self-manifesting Being, the Being of *aletheia* that articulates itself in the *logos,* could be recognized in the dialectic of Ideas. But Heidegger no longer associated this perspective with Plato; he believed it to have been maintained only by the oldest of thinkers.

His later reception of Aristotle was similar in this respect. At least the peculiar and controversial chapter on the ᾿όν ὡς αληθές; that is, Being as true-Being (*Met.* Θ 10),[a] still played a decisive role in his Marburg lectures, where its portrayal is not without some contemplative sympathy. But with the formation of the world historical figure of metaphysics, even that side of Aristotle lost its luminous power. *Being and Time* shows how, proceeding either from an analysis of the concept of time or especially from his need to raise his own question concerning Being and play it off against this question as it was raised by metaphysics, he saw both the Aristotelian formulation of this question and the turn of the modern age—represented by Descartes—as representing a part of the history of the forgetfulness of Being. But one text in particular documents Heidegger's early ambivalent engagement with Aristotle: It is Heidegger's interpretation of Aristotle's *Physics* Chapter II, Book 1, a single interpretation made virtually unique by the power and intensity of his thought. This is a characteristic example of the ambiguity—but also of the productivity of this ambiguity—that accompanied the dialogue Heidegger attempted to have with metaphysics. More than all else, his exposé made the two-sidedness inherent in the concept of *physis* apparent. Of course, Heidegger argues in his interpretation that Aristotle's concept of *"physis"* represents the decisive step taken toward "metaphysics," but at the same time he recognized in this concept, in this "emergence" [*Aufgehen*] of beings, a preformation of his own concept of the "clearing" of Being and the "event." Next to appendixes to the texts on Nietzsche, Heidegger's treatise on this chapter of Aristotle's *Physics* remains his most mature and perspectivally rich examination of Greek thinking. In general, his way through the history of philosophy resembles the trail of a diviner. Suddenly the divining rod dips down, and the diviner makes a strike.

Here one is also reminded of Heidegger's occasional references to the intuitions [*Intuitionen*] of Leibniz—and he was especially drawn to Leibniz's bold language. Whereas attempting to regain the actual metaphysical dimension, a dimension that Leibniz had searched for in between the modern science of physics and the traditional figure of the Aristotelian metaphysics of substance—a dimension Whitehead also attempted to gain in his thought, as is well known—Heidegger came across the word *existiturire* in one of Leibniz's tractates. This was fascinating to him; the word was not *existere,* which traditionally means being present-at-hand, an object-for-a-judgment, or a being-represented. The linguistic form itself of this Latin neologism rings of the openness of movement of Being toward the future: *Existiturire* is like a thirst for Being. Naturally, given Heidegger's own philosophical intentions, this worked like a lure—an anticipation of Schelling.

If we keep our guiding question in mind, that is, how does Heidegger draw a sharp contrast between his own peculiar, negative teleology of the forgetfulness of Being and Hegel's teleological system of the history of philosophy, then Heidegger's examination of Kant must assume a central position for several reasons. For it had been Hegel's claim that, following Fichte's initial lead, he had developed transcendental philosophy to its fullest possible breadth, autonomy, and universality—and Neo-Kantianism took over this Hegelian agenda without being completely aware of its un-Kantian beginnings, and this applies to Husserl as well. In contradistinction to this, Heidegger's early turn to Kant—it was after all the first book that he saw published after *Being and Time*—was decisively anti-Hegelian in its conception. Heidegger was not concerned with realizing transcendental thought in the sense of extending this principle to universal proportions, which was the task first undertaken by Fichte in his *Wissenschaftslehre* and which was more recently the goal of Husserl's transcendental phenomenology. Rather, precisely the two-sided nature of the two sources of knowledge, precisely the restriction of reason to that which could be given in the intuition seemed to offer Heidegger a foundation for an alliance <with Kant>. Of course, his attempt to interpret Kant in light of a "finite metaphysics" was a highly violent deed, and he did not pursue it for very long. After his encounter with Cassirer in Davos and, more important, following his growing insight into the inappropriateness of this transcendental self-interpretation for his own thinking, Heidegger began to interpret Kant's philosophy as being more entangled in the history of the forgetfulness of Being, as shown by his later works on Kant.

Hegel had come into Heidegger's field of vision quite early. How could such a gifted Aristotelian like Heidegger not have picked up on the fascination that emanated from Hegel, this Neo-Aristotelian? We can also assume that a thinker like Hegel would have been especially appealing to Heidegger due to his dynamic and powerful language. In any case, Hegel's *Phenomenology of Spirit* as well as his *Logic* became the subject of one of Heidegger's analyses in the mid-1920s. It came as no surprise that he preferred Hegel's *Phenomenology of Spirit* over the *Logic*. Eventually he could sense, as can we, that the late Husserl's "genetic" phenomenology converged roughly with the earlier Hegelian project presented in the *Phenomenology of Spirit*. And his only published analysis of Hegel is dedicated to the "Introduction" to the *Phenomenology of Spirit;* this text, which offers a step-by-step commentary on the development of Hegel's thought, appears in *Holzwege*—and is perhaps truer to the title *Holzwege* than any other work in the volume. It is a renewed attempt to derive the fundamental principle of Absolute Idealism from the text of the "Introduction" to the *Phenomenology of Spirit*—an undertaking I believe would have been more suited to the later versions of Fichte's *Wissenschaftslehre*. But, be that as it may, it still documents the continuing challenge and great fascination that the Hegelian thesis of an universal history of metaphysics held for Heidegger. He emphasized repeatedly up to his death that he found the talk of a collapse of the Hegelian system and Hegelian idealism to be completely inappropriate. It was not the Hegelian philosophy that collapsed, but rather everything else that followed, including Nietzsche. This was a statement that he often repeated. And similarly, he never wanted his talk of an overcoming of metaphysics to be understood as if he meant that it was possible to proceed beyond Hegelian metaphysics or that one should pursue this endeavor for its own sake. As is well known, he often speaks of taking a step back [*von dem Schritt zurück*], which was to allow the space of *aletheia* or the clearing of Being to open itself up in thinking. Heidegger also saw in Hegel the final form of modern thinking, a thinking dominated by the notion of subjectivity. He was not blind to the efforts made by Hegel to overcome the narrowness of subjective idealism, as he called it, and to find an orientation that did justice to the "we," to the mutuality of objective reason and the objective spirit. But in Heidegger's eyes this effort was simply an anticipatory move that foundered when it came across the force of the Cartesian concepts and Cartesian method. He certainly must have recognized that Hegel was one of the masters at the conceptual trade. This could also be the reason why—in spite of his sympathy for Schelling—he always chose to examine the issue of overcoming or completing this Absolute Idealism with reference to Hegel.

Given this state of affairs, Hegel must have appeared to him to have been the last Greek, as he himself loved to say. It was Hegel who, as a type of consummator, risked extending the influence of the true, authentic Greek archconcept, that is, the *logos,* into the world of history. For this reason the recently published Heidegger lectures from 1930 NN 31, which deal with Hegel's *Phenomenology of Spirit,* are dedicated entirely to the task of contrasting the type of inquiry found in *Being and Time* with Hegel's Onto-Theology, which is oriented toward logic. By comparison, his interpretation of the Introduction (Hegel's theory of experience), which first emerged in 1942 and was published in *Holzwege,* was of a completely different composure. To speak with Heidegger, it was already "tacitly thought from the vantage point of an event" [*vom Ereignis her*].

By comparison, Schelling's profundity must have resembled more closely his own innermost philosophical motivations. I had already heard Heidegger read in a seminar on Schelling the following sentence from the *Freiheitsschrift,* "The *Angst* of life drives the creature from its center," and then he went on to add, "Gentlemen, show me a single sentence out of Hegel's work that has such depth." The later Schelling began to loom larger and larger behind Kierkegaard and, later, Nietzsche as well. He frequently delved into Schelling's *The Essence of Human Freedom* in his classes. In the end, he approved the publication of his interpretation <of Schelling>, but, of course, without concealing his opinion that Schelling was conceptually incapable of doing justice to the depth of his intuitions. Heidegger recognized in him his innermost problem, the problem of facticity, of the insoluble darkness of the foundation—in God as in everything that is real and not merely logical. This ruptured the boundaries of the Greek *logos*.

It was Nietzsche who figured in the final, magnificent, and ambiguous work that resulted from Heidegger's confrontation with the history of philosophy. Following two smaller works, the next two-volume opus was dedicated to Nietzsche. Of course, it was only after *Being and Time* that Nietzsche fully entered into Heidegger's horizon, and it is indicative of a complete misunderstanding to attribute to Heidegger a position sympathetic to Nietzsche. Also, Derrida's endeavor to trump Heidegger by way of Nietzsche is in no way drawing out the true consequences of Heidegger's approach. In Heidegger's eyes, the extreme measure of completely dissociating opinion from sense or meaning [*Sinn*], as Nietzsche does in his critique of consciousness, could still be understood as belonging within the framework of metaphysics—as its unessence. The self-willing will appeared as the last extreme of the subjective thinking of the modern age, and something that had always been understood as a mere paradox prior to Heidegger, that is, the coexistence of the doctrine of the will to power (or the doctrine of the overman) and the doctrine of the eternal return of the same, was united in Heidegger's thought—but as the most radical expression of the forgetfulness of Being that Heidegger was to encounter in the history of philosophy. The proliferation of notes on the subject that Heidegger added to the second volume of his work on Nietzsche proves just how concerned he was with situating Nietzsche in the history of the forgetfulness of Being; the notes show how interested Heidegger was in retreating from this path.

Yet, it remains undoubtedly true that Heidegger's overcoming of metaphysics was not intended to be a triumph over it. Later, he expressly called it *getting over* [*Verwindung*] metaphysics. That is to say, when one gets over an ache or an illness, the achiness and sick feeling remains there in its entirety—it is not so simply forgotten. Thus, he saw his own thinking as a continuing dialogue with metaphysics, which means that he was always speaking, to a greater or lesser extent, the language of metaphysics. He would have been completely locked within the language of metaphysics if he had not found, situated at its pinnacle, a new interlocutor within the history of metaphysics. This was Hegel's friend, the poet Friedrich Hölderlin.

Hölderlin brought to Heidegger's language a new, semi-poetic vocabulary. The parallels that exist between Hölderlin's mythical poetizing and Heidegger's "back to the origin" is truly astonishing, and in the final analysis it was the only unambiguous conversation in Heidegger's thoughtful dialogue with the past. All of his other important philosophical interlocutors, that is, Heraclitus, Parmenides, Aristotle, Hegel, and Nietzsche, maintained a peculiar ambiguity in his readings: In part they spoke for him, but in part they rejected him, inasmuch as they all worked together to prepare for the fate of the occidental forgetfulness of Being. One becomes aware with both Parmenides and Heraclitus that they searched for truth, the *"sophon,"* in the experience of Being and, yet, simultaneously pressed forward to learn about the variety of beings. In this way Being, as the Being of beings, becomes essence, and *aletheia* is no longer thought of as unconcealedness [*Unverborgenheit*], but rather as the Being of that which is unconcealed [*des Unverborgenen*]. And Aristotle's case is similar. Even if Heidegger does see in his <Aristotle's> revival, in the deepening of his concept of *physis,* and in his *analogia entis* [analogy of Being][b] a resurfacing of the illuminating experience of a beginning, in the end he interprets the multidimensionality of Aristotle's "first philosophy" as proceeding entirely in the direction of Onto-Theology.

Similarly, Heidegger consciously interpreted Hegel's philosophy as the completion of this Onto-Theology—in spite of all the affinities that exist between his own critique of the idealism of consciousness and Hegel's critique of subjective idealism. When all is said and done, we are forced to admit that Heidegger's thoughtful dealings with the history of philosophy are burdened with the violence of a thinker who was veritably driven by his own questions and a desire to rediscover himself everywhere. His destruction of metaphysics became a kind of struggle with the power of this tradition of thought. Ultimately, this was to manifest itself in an almost painful deficiency in language, one that drove this thinker, in spite of his powerful language, in the most extreme enigmas. This thoughtful way of metaphysical thinking is really the only one that has, in any fundamental way, left behind traces of a way [*eine Wegspur*] in language, in the languages with which we are familiar, that is, Greek, Latin, and the modern languages. Without these traces, even Heidegger, in his effort to question back behind the beginning of this way, would have been left speechless.

CHAPTER FOURTEEN

THE RELIGIOUS
DIMENSION (1981)

To raise the question concerning the religious dimension in Heidegger's thought is to present a challenge or at least to begin a paradoxical undertaking. One need only to think of Jean-Paul Sartre, who, as one of his admirers from a Nietzschean perspective, presented Heidegger as one of the representative atheistic thinkers of our epoch. In spite of this I would like to show that an understanding of Heidegger as an atheistic thinker can be based upon only a superficial appropriation of his philosophy.

Of course, it is a completely different question to ask whether the claims made on Heidegger by Christian theology are justified—even though half a century has already passed in which Christian theologians have been turning to Heidegger's thought. The question concerning Being, whose recapitulation became a task that Heidegger adopted as his in particular [*Heideggers eigenster Auftrag*], is not to be understood as a question concerning God, as Heidegger himself made unambiguously clear. Through the years, his orientation to the contemporary theology of both denominations became more and more critical. But one must ask, Does not the very existence of such a critique of theology itself show that *God*—whether revealed or concealed—was not an empty word to him? It is well known that Heidegger came from a Catholic family and had been raised in the

167

Catholic religion. He attended a high school in Konstanz that, although not entirely a Catholic school itself, was nevertheless located in an area where both Christian denominations—Catholic and Protestant—had a strong following. After graduating from high school, he went to stay with the Jesuits in Feldkirch (Vorarlberg) for a while, although he was to leave again shortly thereafter. Moreover, he belonged to the theological seminary in Freiburg for a few semesters.

Both Heidegger's religious involvement and his philosophical leanings were already very pronounced in his early youth. Even in the early years, his unchallenged religious affiliation was filled with a passionate interest in philosophy. His principal at the high school seminary in Konstanz—Groeber, who later became the bishop in Freiburg—quickly recognized his brilliant gift and his devotion to philosophy. Heidegger once related the story to me of how one of his teachers caught him reading Kant's *Critique of Pure Reason* under his desk—during a boring class, of course. This was surely a free ticket to a great intellectual future. After this episode, Groeber gave him a modern and scholarly, although not very profound, book on Aristotle to read. It was Franz Brentano's *Concerning the Multifarious Meanings of Being* [*Seiende*] *in Aristotle*. In a conscientious analysis, this study develops the variety of the meanings of Being in Aristotle's philosophy, but it remains mute before the question of how they are connected—and precisely this became an inspiration for the young Heidegger, something he talked about often. Aristotle's distinction between the different meanings of *Being* challenged one to inquire about their concealed unity, although certainly not in the sense of a systemization like what Cajetan and Suarez, the scholastics of the Counter-Reformation, tried to introduce into Aristoteleanism. But the fact that Being was not a genus, as in the scholastic doctrine of the *analogia entis* [analogue of Being], was a motif that often turned up from that time on—although not as metaphysical doctrine but as an expression of an open and pressing question that one had to learn to ask—What is this, this "Being?"

Heidegger's talent brought him quick success. Under Rickert he wrote his dissertation on the doctrine of judgment in psychologism, and his minors for his exams were—one would never guess!—mathematics and physics. He mentioned this work during a lecture in Marburg with the comment, "When I was still involved in child's play." He received the qualification to be a university lecturer at the age of 27, and became the assistant to Rickert's follower in Freiburg. Of course, this was Husserl, the founder of phenomenology, from whom Heidegger learned the ingenious technique of phenomenological description. Already in these early years as an assistant professor, Heidegger was an unusual success as a teacher, and he quickly developed an almost magical influence on those who were younger as well as those who were his age. Among those, Julius Ebbinghaus, Oskar Becker, Karl Löwith, and Walter Bröcker are now well-known names. Rumors about Heidegger reached me in Marburg, where I was preparing for my doctorate. Students were showing up from Freiburg and, even then in 1920–21, were talking less about Husserl than Heidegger and his exceedingly unconventional and profoundly revolutionary lectures. There he used the phrase *It is worlding* [*es weltet*], for example. Now we recognize that that was a magnificent anticipation of his later and latest thinking. At that time, one could not hear such things from a Neo-Kantian—or from Husserl. Where is the transcendental ego? What kind of word was that? Is there such a word at all? Ten years before the so-called turn, when Heidegger overcame his own transcendental conception of self and his dependence on Husserl, he had found here his first word, one that did not assume a subject or transcendental consciousness at all. *Worlding,* expressed like an early herald of the event of the "clearing."

We have learned in the interim a bit about this first phase of Heideggerean thought that occurred in Freiburg after World War I. Pöggeler has informed us about some aspects of it. Karl Lehmann reconstructed the importance of St. Paul to the young Heidegger in a superb essay. Also, Thomas Sheehan has recently been able to give a thorough account of Heidegger's course of lectures on "The Phenomenology of Religion" given in 1920, which was accessible to him via an older transcript.

From these sources one can see that the early Christian community's experience of time especially fascinated Heidegger, the eschatological instant that allows for neither measurements of nor "expectations" nor estimations concerning the amount of time that will pass before the return of Christ—for he will come "like a thief in the night" (First Epistle of St. Paul to the Thessalonians). Measured time, calculations about time and the whole background of Greek ontology, which governs our concept of time in philosophy and science, breaks down in the face of this experience. A private letter Heidegger wrote to Karl Löwith (one of his young students and friends) in 1921 shows that this was not merely a philosophical challenge; rather, this was one of the fundamental concerns of this young thinker. In this letter, Heidegger wrote that it would be "a fundamental mistake to measure me (hypothetically or not) against figures such as Nietzsche, Kierkegaard, . . . or any of the other creative philosophers. Such is not to be prohibited, but then it must be said that I am not a philosopher, and I am only deluding myself to believe that I could be something comparable." And then he wrote, "I am a Christian theologian!"

One is not going wrong if one recognizes here the deepest directive for Heidegger's way of thinking: He saw himself then as a Christian theologian. That is to say that all of his efforts to sort things out with himself and with his questions were motivated by a desire to free himself from the dominating theology in which he had been raised—so that he could be a Christian. He received from the distinguished teachers in the Freiburg Theology Department, as he later said himself, the qualifications needed for this "theological" task, and more than anyone else it was the young Luther who came to be of primary importance to him then. But the aforementioned course, "The Phenomenology of Religion," shows that he also turned back to the oldest documents of the New Testament, the Epistles of Paul, with a real affinity.

Two masters provided him with proper conceptual schooling. First of all, there was Husserl's phenomenological proficiency. It was characteristic that, as Husserl's assistant, Heidegger taught *not* the Neo-Kantian program found in the *Ideen* of 1913 but rather the *Logischen Untersuchungen*. These investigations had implications that extended far beyond Husserl's thinking—especially the sixth investigation, a new revision of which had just come onto the scene at that time. Here the question of what is meant by *is* gained an important place; what kind of "noetic" act is it in which the formal category of *is* is intended? The doctrine of the "categorical intuition"—and undoubtedly Husserl's masterful analysis of temporal consciousness as well (which Heidegger was to publish later)—challenged Heidegger: What a detailed and analytical craft—and what a deadend road, which was even farther removed from Heidegger's question concerning the Christian faith than from Augustine's famous despair concerning the possibility of understanding the puzzle of time.

It was *not* the "idealistic" explication of the *Ideas* that Heidegger found attractive. He may well have admired the consistency with which Husserl worked transcendental subjectivity into this topic, and it certainly made him immune to feeble attempts to break out to "reality," attempts made not only by the "Munich Phenomenology" but even by Scheler himself. But the principle of the transcendental ego appeared to him to be suspicious from early on. Thomas Sheehan related the story to me once of how Heidegger had shown him an offprint of Husserl's essay *Philosophy as a Rigorous Science* from 1910. There is a place therein where Husserl says that our method and our first principle must be "To the things themselves!"—and at this place the young Heidegger had written in the margin, "We want to take Husserl at his word." This certainly was intended polemically—instead of getting entangled in the doctrine of the transcendental reduction and in the search for an ultimate foundation in the *cogito,* Husserl should have followed his own principle of "To the things themselves!"

To gain the needed distance from Husserl's transcendental idealism without reverting back to the naiveté of a dogmatic realism, Heidegger turned to another greater master: Aristotle. Indeed, he could not expect to find here someone who would vouch for the credibility of his own questions—questions with a religious motivation—but returning from phenomenology to his early studies in Aristotle gave him the chance to discover a new Aristotle, one that showed a very different side than the one preferred by scholastic theology. Certainly, he could not deceive himself about the fact that the Greek concept of time was formed through Aristotle's *Physics* and that there was no way to proceed directly from the Greek conception to a conceptual explanation of the eschatological instant. But the proximity of Aristotle's thought to the factical Dasein in its concrete consummation in life and in its natural orientation to the world gave Heidegger some indirect help. Heidegger presented his studies of the Aristotelean ethics, physics, anthropology *(De Anima),* rhetoric, and naturally, owing to its central role, metaphysics in a series of lectures that he held in the following semesters. As he informed me in a letter in 1923, this was to become a voluminous publication in the *Jahrbuch für Philosophie und phänomenologische Forschung.* But that never came to pass; he assumed a position as professor in Marburg, and the appointment presented him with a new set of tasks.

However, Aristotle remained one of the focal points of his activities as a teacher.

How could Aristotle help him? Did he only serve as a contrast to the Christian experience of time and the fundamental role of historicity in the more modern thinking? Was he only a counterexample?

The contrary is true. Aristotle was like the key witness in the effort to get back "to the things themselves," and he testified indirectly against his own ontological biases, attacking with a notion that Heidegger was later to call *Being as present-at-hand*. Thus, he became a critical advisor for Heidegger's new questions. The phenomenological interpretations of Aristotle that Heidegger was then preparing for publication in Husserl's *Jahrbuch,* were not really concerned with the scholasticism that was so dear to philosophical theology, a theology that found its ultimate basis in the Aristotelian orientation to physics and in Aristotle's "moving God" of metaphysics. Rather, the proximity of Aristotle's "practical philosophy" and his *Rhetoric* to the concrete, factical consummation of Dasein interested Heidegger; the ways of "being true" [*Wahrsein*], of ἀληθεύειν, which are discussed in the sixth book of *Nicomachean Ethics,* appealed to Heidegger principally because they marked a site in these texts where the primacy of judgment, of logic, and of "science" in understanding the facticity of human life met up with a decisive limit. An ᾽άλλο γένος γνώσεως [another type of knowing] is given its due when the effort is geared not toward cognizing an object and obtaining objective knowledge but toward gaining as much clearness as possible about the factically living Dasein. That is why, next to his ethics, Aristotle's *Rhetoric* became important, because it deals with *pragmata* [ways of acting or deeds] and *pathemata* [impressions or sufferings]—and not with objects.

Moreover, Aristotle was to help the young Heidegger in another, astonishing way. The Aristotelean critique of Plato's Idea of the Good offered some substantial support for his "existential" critique of the transcendental concepts of the subject and object. Just as the Good is not a highest object or principle, but rather differentiates itself into a variety of ways of being encountered, "Being" is also present in all that is, even if in the final analysis there is an eminent being that ensures the presence [*Anwesenheit*] of all. It was the question concerning Being as such that Aristotle—and with him

Heidegger—was attempting to answer. With this in view and with reference to Aristotle's *Physics* and *Metaphysics,* Heidegger was able to show that Being in its motility, Being in its unconcealedness, are not so much areas of objects about which one can make statements; rather, every understanding of Being is founded on an understanding of motility, as all statements are founded on unconcealed presentness [*Anwesenheit*]—and thus ultimately on ᾽ όν ῾ως ἀληθες [the true-Being or a being as true, unconcealed]. This has nothing to do with realism as opposed to subjective idealism, nor is it a theory of knowledge; it describes rather the thing itself, which, due to its "Being-in-the-world," "knows" nothing of the "subject-object split."

But from behind this interest in the "nonscholastic" Aristotle appeared Heidegger's old question concerning Christian theology. Was there no more appropriate way for Christians to understand themselves than the ways offered by contemporary theology? In this regard, his new interpretations of Aristotle were just the first step in a long pathway of thought. That Heidegger consciously chose to take this step in this way is shown by the introduction to his *Aristotles-Interpretationen,* the manuscript that Heidegger sent to Paul Natorp. I obtained a copy from Natorp at that time; it was an analysis of the "hermeneutical situation" for interpretating Aristotle. And with whom did it begin? With the young Luther, precisely the Luther who demanded of anyone who really wanted to be Christian that he or she foreswear Aristotle—this "great liar." I still remember very clearly the names that followed:[1] Gabriel Biel, Petrus Lombardus, the master of sentences, Augustine, and finally Paul. There is no doubt that Heidegger's old, well-documented concern with the original Christian message motivated his endeavors with Aristotle.

Not that Heidegger would have expected Aristotle to address directly his concern. The contrary is true: His awareness that the theology which he had studied and which found its support in Aristotle's metaphysics did not correspond in the least bit to the true motives of Greek thinking must have been sharpened by his exchange with these thinkers. This understanding of time that was so viable with St. Paul and that Heidegger had rediscovered was not

---

1. Although the text has not yet been edited, one should be able to obtain a copy of it—at least in the form of a typscript—without the innumerable additions on Natorp's copy made in his handwriting.

Greek at all. The Greek concept of time, which Plato and Aristotle had formulated as the unit and number of movement, held sway over all conceptual possibilities of later times, from Augustine through Kant until Einstein. Thus, the question that plagued him at the deepest level, the question concerning the Christian expectation of the end of time, must have remained viable: Did the force that Greek thought exerted on the Christian experience of faith distort the Christian message so much that it was unrecognizable and alienate Christian theology from its own task? In fact, not only was St. Paul's and Luther's doctrine of exoneration important to him; he also took up again Harnack's theme of the calamitous Hellenization of Christian theology. In the end he not only found justification for his own perplexity concerning the appropriateness of his theological upbringing, but he also recognized in the Greek legacy, with which all contemporary thinking is burdened, the origin of all the confusion concerning Being and the historicality of human Dasein, a confusion that dictated to him the epigram for *Being and Time.*

It was precisely the aporia of modern thought, which he came across with Bergson, Simmel, Lask, and above all Dilthey, that weighed heavily on his mind during the most decisive years of his development, that is, the period during World War I. Therefore, it was the case for him, as it was for Unamuno, Haecker, Buber, Ebner, Jaspers, and many others, that Kierkegaard's concept of existence [*des Existierens*] became a new password. Kierkegaard's writings were just then coming to have an effect, due to the recent release of a German edition by Dieterichs. There, in those brilliant essays, Heidegger rediscovered his own theme. The polemic against Hegel—this last and most radical Greek, as Heidegger had named him—must have been interesting to Heidegger not only because of its religious motivations and because it pointed out how the either/or character of human existence had been veiled; the specific countering of the Greek concept of "memory" [*Erinnerung*] must have been illuminating as well. Kierkegaard's category of repetition was defined precisely by the notion that it would fade into memory, into the illusion of the return of the same, if it was not experienced as the paradox of historicality, as the repetition of the unrepeatable, as time beyond all time.

This was the experience of time that Heidegger recognized in St. Paul; it is the Second Coming that cannot be expected, a coming that is meant as parousia and not as presentness. Above all,

Kierkegaard's religious oration, which became accessible then to German speakers under the title *Leben und Walten der Liebe,* must have been reassuring to him. There one finds the noteworthy distinction between "understanding from a distance" and understanding concurrently [*in Gleichzeitigkeit*]. Kierkegaard's critique of the church pointed out that it did not take the Christian message with any existential seriousness and that it eased the paradox of concurrence that is a part of the Christian message. When the death of Jesus on the cross is understood from a distance, then it loses all true seriousness, and the discourse about God and the Christian message as pursued by theology (and by the dialectic speculation of the Hegelians) was also definitely approached from a distance. Can one speak about God like one speaks about an object? Is that not precisely the temptation of metaphysics to lead us into arguments about the existence and characteristics of God as if we were arguing about an object of science. Here, with Kierkegaard, lie the roots of dialectical theology, which found its beginning in 1919 with Karl Barth's commentary on the Epistle of St. Paul to the Romans. During the years of Heidegger's friendship with Bultmann in Marburg, his primary concern was with giving an account of "historical" theology and learning how to think about the historicality and finitude of human Dasein in a more radical way.

During this period Heidegger referred repeatedly to the religious historian Franz Overbeck, the friend of Nietzsche. Overbeck's polemical essay on the "Christian Spirit of Theology" [*"Christlichkeit der Theologie'*] expressed these deepest doubts that animated Heidegger, and it confirmed completely his own philosophical experience of the inappropriateness of the Greek concept of Being for the Christian idea of *eschaton* [the last or ultimate], which is no way an expectation of a coming event. When he wrote in a letter to Löwith, "I am a Christian theologian," he must have meant that he wanted to defend the true task of theology, that is, "To find the word that is capable of calling one to faith and preserving one in faith," against the appropriated Christian spirit of today's theology. (I heard him use these words in a theological discussion in 1923.) But this was also a task for thinking.

This he had learned not only from Aristotle, but also from Husserl, whose masterful analysis of temporal consciousness had formally demonstrated the burden left behind by Greek thinking.

The schooling by Husserl had made him immune to the danger of underestimating the solidity of transcendental idealism, and it had also made him impervious to the temptation of trying to oppose it with a naive realism using references to catch words of phenomenology. Thus, he knew that it would not work to assume a position like that of Pfänder or the young Scheler and insist that things are what they are and that they are not produced through thought. Neither the Marburg conception of production nor Husserl's disputed concept of the constitution <of the transcendental ego> have anything to do with Bishop Berkeley's metaphysical idealism or the epistemological problem concerning the reality of the external world. Husserl was intent on making the "transcendence" of things, their Being-in-themselves, understandable in a transcendental way; he wanted to give them an "immanent" foundation, so to speak. The doctrine of the transcendental ego and its apodictic evidence was nothing other than an attempt at founding all objectivity and validity. But precisely this attempt became more and more entangled in the detailed analyses of the structure of time in subjectivity. The constitution of the transcendental ego, the disclosure of which was recognized as the task at hand, lead to paradoxical conceptual formulations, such as the self-constitution of the stream of consciousness, the self-appearance of the stream, the primeval presence, and original change. This must have confirmed for Heidegger that neither the concept of the object nor that of the subject would be applicable to his problem, that is, the issue of the facticity of human Dasein. In truth, he had already begun making his way, starting from the character of the consummation of the concern of Dasein [*Vollzugscharacter der Daseinsbekümmerung*]—later called *care*—instead of beginning with the visualizing consciousness and, then, proceeding to characterize existence in terms of futurity. Therefore, it was by way of his theological intentions that the historicality of Dasein became an issue for him—thereby remaining outside the influence of historicism—and this issue guided his question concerning the meaning of Being.

But how could theology be thought of as a science [*Wissenschaft*][a] without it losing its Christian spirit and without falling under the spell of the concepts of subjectivity and objectivity again? As I recall, Heidegger had already begun thinking along those lines in the early Marburg years. In the *Tübinger Vortrag* given in 1927, it was formulated as follows: Theology is a positive science because it deals with something as a being; namely, with the Christian spirit. Theology must be considered as a conceptual explication of faith. Thus, it stands closer to chemistry or biology than to philosophy, for philosophy, as the sole science, deals not with beings (that which is given—even if it is merely given in faith) but with Being: It is the "ontological" science.

One can easily see the conscious provocation found in Heidegger's hypothesis concerning theoretical basis of this "science." In faith, one also encounters that which is believed in faith <i.e., a content of faith, of belief>—and this can also be given a conceptual explication, if it is a faith at all. But is the belief an object or a field of objects like chemical substances or living beings? Or does it not rathr refer to—as does philosophy—the whole of human Dasein, including its world? On the other hand, Heidegger must have maintained that the ontological base-constitution of human Dasein, as recognized by philosophy, was the corrective for the conceptual explication of faith. Philosophy, which sees the "existentiell" of guilt as having its source in the temporality of Dasein, certainly can present only a formal indication for the sin that is experienced in faith.

Heidegger is using here the well-known concept of the "formal indication" [formale Anzeige] that was often used by him earlier. It is almost the equivalent of Kierkegaard's "making one attentive" [Aufmerksammachen], and one certainly is not making a mistake to recognize in this an intention that runs contrary to the a priori framework Husserl's "ontologies" claimed to provide for the empirical sciences. With the concept of the formal indication, one recognizes that a philosophical science can certainly take part in the conceptual explication of faith—in theology—but it cannot take part in the consummation; that is the affair of faith itself. And lurking behind this there must have been the deeper awareness that in the end the question concerning Being was no scientific question; rather, it "folds back into the Existential."

It is well known that this careful limitation of phenomenological apriorism has provoked a good deal of criticism. Is the guilt characteristic of Dasein really independent of and neutral with regard to the history of Christian faith? What about the desire-for-a-conscience or the advancement toward death? Heidegger would hardly be able to deny this with reference to himself or his experience-base [Erfahrungsboden]; he would be able to maintain only that finitude and "Being-towards-death" can be redeemed from any base of human experience and that this gives everyone some direction for the conceptual explication of the experience of faith.

Of course, the whole confrontation between philosophy and theology remains awkward so long as there is an uncertainty about one fundamental assumption: Is theology a science at all (see Heidegger, *Phänomenologie und Theologie,* p. 25)? Indeed, is faith really to be imposed upon by theology? And even more awkward is the question: Is the concretization of the factical consummation of Dasein in the form of "care" really capable—as is claimed—of leaving behind the ontological anticipation [*Vorgreiflichkeit*] of transcendental subjectivity and thinking temporality as Being? Care is ultimately a concern about one's self, just as consciousness is certainly self-consciousness. Heidegger had correctly accentuated this as the tautology of Being-a-self [*Selbstsein*] and care, but he also believed that the concept of care as the original temporization [*Zeitigung*] had overcome the ontological narrowness of "Saying-I" [*Ich-Sagens*] and the thereby constituted identity of the subject. Meanwhile, what is the authentic temporality of care? Does it not appear as a self-temporalization? *"Dasein is authentically itself* in the primordial individualization of reticent resoluteness that exacts anxiety of itself" (*Sein und Zeit,* paragraph 64). The later Heidegger made the comment concerning "angst," "that it is the clearing of Being as Being." Would he be able to say that Dasein itself exacts the clearing?

Just as the later Heidegger no longer wanted to ground the thinking of Being as time on the transcendental analytic of Dasein and, therefore, spoke of the turn that he had gotten himself into, so too could the relationship between philosophy and science no longer be thought of along the lines of the assumption that one was dealing with a relationship between two sciences. It was already noticeable in the text of *Tübinger Vortrag* that theology was characterized not only as "historical" in a radical sense, but that it was also characterized as a "practical science." "Every theological tenet and concept as such repeats its contents, and this happens *not* simply in a supplemental way in terms of the so-called practical application to the pious existence of the individual human in the community." Therefore, it is not surprising when Heidegger later (in 1964) concludes one of his comments to the essay "Nonobjectifying Thinking and Speaking" with the negative sounding question, "Can theology still be a science, since it presumably cannot be *permitted* to be a science at all" (*Phänomenologie und Theologie*, p. 46).

So, ultimately it was not with the help of theology, but rather through a turn away from it and the metaphysics and ontology that it so dominated, that the religious dimension in Heidegger was able to begin its search for a language. The religious dimension found its language, inasmuch as it was found at all, via Nietzsche and the freeing of Heidegger's tongue that occurred as a result of his explication of Hölderlin's poetry.

It is really misleading to think that Nietzsche was important to Heidegger because of the atheistic implications of his thought. The contrary is the case. The radicality of Nietzsche's thought left such atheistic dogmatism far behind. Rather, Heidegger was attracted to the desperate boldness with which Nietzsche questioned the foundations of the whole of metaphysics and with which he recognized everywhere the "will to power." Not the reevaluation of all values— this seemed to him to be a superficial aspect of Nietzsche—but rather that human beings in general were thought of as the being that set and estimated value. This was the birth of the well-known Heideggerean expression of "calculative" thinking, which computes the value of everything and which has become the fate of human culture in the form of technology and the technological institutions of Being-in-the-world. What Nietzsche described as the surfacing of European nihilism was understood by Heidegger not as a process of reevaluating all values, but on the contrary as the final establishment of thinking in values—and he called it the *forgetfulness of Being*.

However, Nietzsche was for Heidegger not simply the one who diagnosed nihilism—with the surfacing of "nothing," Being becomes visible. This is why Heidegger cites the scene with the mad man in *Holzwege*. In this scene the mad man enters the market with the multitude of people who do not believe in God and screams, "I am seeking God, I am seeking God!" and he knows that "We have killed him." But the one searching for God—and this is Heidegger's point—"knows" of God; those who attempt to prove his existence are those who kill him in precisely this way. Seeking presupposes measuring, as does measuring knowing—that which is absent, granted, but that which is absent is not not. It is "there" [*da*] as absence.

And this is what Heidegger rediscovered with Hölderlin: an ode to the existence [*Dasein*] of the disappeared gods. For Hölderlin, the last god of the old world was Christ, the last one to tarry "among the humans." All that is left are traces of these gods who have escaped, "but of the divine much remains."

This was the model Heidegger followed as he attempted to think thinking anew; that is, thinking not in the sense of metaphysical or scientific thinking. Just as one can know of the divine without grasping and knowing God, so too is the thinking of Being not a grasping, a possessing, or a controlling. Without forcing the parallel with the experience of God or the Second Coming of Christ, which can indeed be thought more correctly from this vantage point, one could say that Being is more than simple "presence" [*Präsenz*] (let alone a "representation" [*Vorgestelltheit*])—it is also just as much "absence," a form of the "there" [*da*] in which not only the "there is" but also withdrawal, retreating, and holding-within are experienced. "Nature loves to conceal itself"—these words of Heraclitus were often drawn on by Heidegger. They do not invite one to attack and attempt to penetrate; rather, the invitation is for waiting—and Rilke was right when he complained in his elegies about the inability to wait. Therefore, Heidegger spoke of remembrance, which is not only thinking about something that was, but also thinking about something that is coming, something coming that allows one to think about it—even if it comes "like a thief in the night."

What is prepared for in such thinking is not an ontology and certainly not theology. In spite of this, it should be remembered in closing that Heidegger once said—when thinking about a poem by Hölderlin—"The question, 'who is God?' is too hard for human beings. At most they are capable of asking, 'What is God?'" With this he hinted at the dimension of the hallowed and the holy and commented, "The loss of the dimension of the hallowed and the holy is perhaps the authentic unholiness of our age." What he meant by that is that we are incapable of reaching God because we speak about God in a way that can never be helped by the self-understanding of faith. But that is the affair of theology. My affair, that of the philosopher, is—and this Heidegger could have said with complete justification, and it would have been valid for everyone, not just for Christians or theologians—to sound a warning that the customary ways of thinking will no longer suffice.

Chapter Fifteen

Being Spirit God (1977)

Anyone who has been touched by Martin Heidegger's thinking can no longer read the title of this chapter, these three words that lie at the foundation of metaphysics, in the same way that they have been read within the metaphysical tradition. One would like to find oneself in accord with the claim made by the Greeks and Hegel that Being is spirit, and we are told by the New Testament that God is spirit. Thus, the occidental tradition [*überlieferung*] converged within the older <way of> thinking to form a self-evident question of meaning. And yet, this older <way of> thinking perceives a new challenge; it sees itself as being put into question by the new concept of knowledge that modern science has developed through its methodological asceticism and new critical standards. Philosophical thinking can neither ignore the existence of modern science, nor can it really incorporate it. Philosophy alone is no longer the whole of our knowledge, nor is it a knowing whole. Since the cockcrow of positivism, metaphysics has lost its credibility with many; like Nietzsche, these individuals tend to view "Hegel and the other Schleiermachers" as merely delaying the advent of what Nietzsche called *European nihilism.*[a] It seemed as though metaphysics had unfurled into a state of rest, following a path dictated by the way that it had formulated its own question. Thus, it could not have been expected that

181

metaphysics would charge itself once again with a new tension, enabling it to continue henceforth as a valid corrective to modern thinking. All of the efforts made in the twentieth century to renew metaphysics—as in the long line of concept creators and system fabricators who have been around since the seventeenth century—were attempts in one way or another at reconciling modern science with the older metaphysics. But that metaphysics itself could once again become a question, that its question, that is, the question concerning Being, which had already been given a 2,000-year-old answer, could once again be posed as if it had never been posed before—this could not have been foreseen. And when the uncommon sounds first began to ring out from the young Heidegger's podium and kindle a new fascination, they reminded people of Kierkegaard, Schopenhauer, Nietzsche, and all the other critics of academic philosophy. Indeed, even after the appearance of *Being and Time,* whose whole orchestration was expressly geared toward reawakening the question of Being, people still allied him more with the critics of this tradition than with the tradition itself.

This, however, is not surprising when one recalls that the young Heidegger himself had turned the phrase *destruction of metaphysics* into a password and warned his own students not to put him in the ranks of the "great philosophers." In a letter to Karl Löwith in 1921 he said of himself, "I am a Christian theologian."

This alone suggested that it was Christianity once again that challenged the thought of this man and held him in suspense; it was once again the old transcendence and not the modern worldliness [*Diessetigkeit*] that spoke through him. Yes, a Christian theologian who, in an effort to do justice to that which is called *faith,* wanted to achieve a knowledge thereof superior to that offered to him by the then modern theology. But why, in contrast to so many who were driven by the same desire and who as modern human beings could not turn away from the foundations of science, did he become a thinker instead of a Christian theologian? Because thinking was his affair [literally, he was a thinkinger/*Denkender*]. Because it was thinking at work within him. Because the passion of thinking made him quake—stirred as much by the force exerted on him by this passion as by the boldness of the questions that this passion compelled him to ask.

Not a Christian theologian, he did not feel qualified to speak of God. It was clear to Heidegger that it would be intolerable to speak of God like science speaks about its objects; but what that might mean, to speak of God—this was the question that motivated him and pointed out his way of thinking. Thinking is reflecting on something that one knows. It is a movement of thought to and fro, a being moved to and fro by thought, by possibilities, offers, doubts, and new questions. There were two offers in particular that, because he could neither simply accept nor reject them, Heidegger had to take into consideration from early on: Aristotle and Hegel. He himself told of how Aristotle gained importance early on, showing him the way with his explication of the multiple meanings of being [Seiende] that Aristotle had laid out, a multiplicity that resisted all efforts geared toward fitting it together into the unity deemed by many to be necessary. And the conclusion of his book on Duns Scotus is a testimony to the challenge presented to him by Hegel's philosophy, that colossal "system of a historical world-view [Weltanschauung]" as he called it; Hegel delineated for Heidegger the tense space between Being and spirit that—as the young Heidegger put it—"the living comprehension of the absolute spirit of God" came to inhabit during the age of metaphysics. It was necessary to take the measurements of this space, not to facilitate his search for an anser to his own question, but to make a judgment about what must be asked so that the question itself is not misunderstood again, eliciting a false desire to know. This was a questioning behind the question concerning Being—the question posed by metaphysics that had then received as its response that Being was to be conceived of as essence and as spirit—and, like every question that requires reflection, Heidegger's question was one in search of itself.

The tense space that this questioning behind metaphysics was to admeasure was itself an oddity: time. Not the measurable dimension that we measure out when we want to determine what we encounter in our experience as being [seiend]; rather, here the issue is that which constitutes Being itself: Presence [Präsenz], presentness [Anwesenheit], and contemporariness [Gegenwärtigkeit]. It was time that offered the various meanings of being [Seiende], as they had been differentiated by Aristotle, their true foundation, and by disclosing this foundation, Heidegger's interpretations of Aristotle gained their own peculiar clarity, and Aristotle became a formally pressing issue for people. These were truly philosophical questions, for they strengthened Aristotle, strengthened him before the whole tradition of metaphysics and, above all, strengthened him against the continued progression of metaphysics toward the subjective thinking of the modern era. The truly foundational [*das Zugrundeliegende*], the permanent presence of "substance," the maintaining-of-itself-in-Being of "*entelechie*," the self-showing of truth—all of these articulate the strength of Aristotle's answer in which Being is thought as presentness. And Hegel's magnificent effort to think the concept of Being as spirit—rather than as an object whose objectivity is grasped or constituted by the subjectivity of consciousness—was yet another offer. The historicality of spirit, its coming down into time, the disconcertedness of a self-reflective, historical consciousness—all of this seemed to raise spirit, which knows itself in its contemporariness, beyond the particularity of the subjective consciousness and then to bring it together within itself. As the last Greek, Hegel thinks Being within the horizon of time as the all-encompassing presentness. The *logos* of Being, about which the Greeks had inquired, and reason in history, about which Hegel inquired, formed the two great hemispheres of this spiritual whole.

One underestimates Heidegger's mission, that is, the task of overcoming metaphysics, if one does not first see how such an inquiry into the temporal character of Being furbishes metaphysics itself with its full strength and raises it above the subjective thinking of the modern age into a new contemporariness. There was the *analogia entis* [analogy of Being] that allows for no general concept of Being, and there was also the analogy of the Good and the Aristotelean criticism of the Platonic Idea of the Good, where the generality of the concept found its essential limit. From early on these were the key witnesses in Heidegger's thought experiments. And the ontological primacy of "true-Being" [*Wahr-sein*] ('όν ώς αληθές), of *nous* [intellect or spirit, see note a to Chapter 6], that Heidegger derived from the final chapter of book Θ of the *Metaphysics,* made Being as the presentness of that present, as essence, completely visible. This robbed self-consciousness and its immanent reflection of the primacy it has had since Descartes, and it returned to thinking the ontological dimension that had been lost in the modern philosophy of consciousness.

Likewise, Hegel's concept of spirit regained its substance in light of this newly reformulated question concerning Being. The concept also went through a process of "despiritualization." Through the process of dialectically unfolding spirit into itself, it came to be thought of as *pneuma* in a more original way. It came to be thought as the breath of life that blows through everything extended and distributed or, as Hegel put it, as the common blood that holds the cycle of life together within itself. This general concept of life is certainly thought at the peak of modernity, that is, with reference to self-consciousness, but it also implies a clear progression beyond the formal idealism of self-consciousness. The shared sphere that prevails between individuals, the spirit that combines them, is love: I, the you and you, the I, and you and I—all of these unite to constitute the we. With his understanding of the objective spirit—a concept that even today holds sway over the social sciences, regardless of how it is understood—Hegel not only found access to the existence of the social reality above any subject, but he also found an authentic concept of truth that, above and beyond all limitations, brought the absolute in art, religion, and philosophy to light. The Greek concept of *nous*—reason and spirit—remained the final word in Hegel's system of science. For him this was the truth of Being, the essence, that is, presentness, and the concept, that is, the selfness of that present which grasps everything within itself.

The power of this answer by metaphysics, which stretches from Aristotle to Hegel, is stronger than the flippant calls that people sometimes make to Heidegger's task of overcoming metaphysics. Heidegger always took issue with those wishing to interpret him as if he meant that metaphysics had been overcome and tossed away. Although his question probes behind the question of Being as found in metaphysics and brings to consciousness the horizon of time in which Being is thought, it still recognizes in metaphysics a preliminary answer, a response to the challenge in which Being is presented as the totality of beings. The question breaking forth in Heidegger's thought experiments allows the answer of metaphysics to speak anew. .

Heidegger saw in *Being and Time* nothing more than just such a preliminary preparation for the question of Being. However, what pressed to the foreground of his work was certainly something else; namely, his critique of the concept of consciousness found in transcendental phenomenology. This meshed well with the then-contemporary criticism of idealism, which had been formulated by Karl Barth, Friedrich Gogarten, Friedrich Ebner, and Martin Buber and which brought to completion the revival of Kierkegaard's criticism of Hegel's Absolute Idealism. "The essence of *Dasein* lies in its existence." This sentence was understood to mean that *existentia* takes precedent over *essentia,* and from just such an idealistic misunderstanding of the concept of "essence" sprang Sartre's existentialism, an intermediate entity formed by uniting the speculative motives of Fichte, Hegel, Kierkegaard, Husserl, and Heidegger into a new striking force for moral philosophy and social criticism. In contradistinction, Oskar Becker attempted to play down <the significance of> *Being and Time* by reading it as a further concretization of the basic transcendental-idealistic orientation of Husserl's *Ideas.* The Heideggerian paradox of a hermeneutics of facticity is not, of course, an explication that claims to "understand" facticity as such—that would be a true contradiction, to want to understand the "nothing"-as-factical [*Nichts-als-Faktische*], which itself is closed off to all meaning. The hermeneutics of facticity meant rather that existence itself is to be thought as the consummation of understanding and explication, and that by way of this consummation existence gains its ontological distinction. Oskar Becker then coupled this with a transcendental-philosophical conception of Husserl's phenomenological program, thereby reducing it to a hermeneutical phenomenology. But even if one took Heidegger's claim seriously, that is, to understand the existentiell analytic of Dasein as fundamental ontology, the whole could still be understood within the questioned horizon of metaphysics. It could be presented at best as a type of counterpart to classical metaphysics, or as a reconstruction of the same—a finite metaphysics based on the existential radicalization of historicality. In fact, Heidegger tried to integrate the critical element of Kant thinking—the very element that had blocked Fichte's attempt to reconstruct his work—into the formulation of his own question when writing his book on Kant in 1929.

Of course, this must have come across as a dismissal of classical metaphysics, for metaphysics is based on the infinity of the *intellectus, nous,* or the spirit, in which the truth of Being presents itself as the essence and to which all that is is attributed and arranged according to its particular sense of Being [*Seins-Sinn*]. By contrast, here it seemed that the eternal had been grounded on the temporal, truth on historicality. In this way, the secularization of the Christian legacy, such as in Hegel's dialectical synthesis of the absolute spirit, was outdistanced by the resoluteness of "nothing." People began to turn away from the *Angst* before death and search for more positive, less unpleasant moods of Dasein, or they tried to smother earthly despair with a renewed Christian hope. But either way, the thought impulse that stood behind Heidegger's effort as a whole had been misunderstood. For Heidegger, the issue had always been one dealing with the *"Da"* in the Dasein of human beings; it had to do with this characterization of existence, this being outside of itself and exposed like no other living being. But this exposedness meant, as displayed by the "Letter on Humanism" written to Jean Beaufret that humans, as humans, stand out in the open, that they are in the end more proximate to the furthermost, to the divine, than they are to their own "nature." In the humanism letter, Heidegger speaks of the "disconcerted of the living beings" and of our "barely conceivable, unfathomable physical kinship with animals."

Heidegger's effort to think this *"Da"* takes place in a long history of suffering permeated by philosophical passion. It was a history of suffering inasmuch as even Heidegger, with his unconventional, originary, bold, and speculative linguistic powers, had to battle against a resistent language, one whose opposition was constantly being renewed and was often overpowering. He himself described this as the risk, the risk that accompanied him every step of the way, even in his own thought experiments, that thinking might fall back into the language of metaphysics and the way of thinking delineated by its conceptual terms. But it was more than that. It was the language itself, his own as well as all of ours, against which Heidegger raised his voice, often violently, to wring from it the expression he sought.

It is certainly correct to say that the language and concepts of metaphysics dominate all of our thinking. This was the way taken by Greek thinking—the thinking that cultivated metaphysics: To question the statement or proposition, to query about the objective content of a judgment, and ultimately to become aware of the Being of beings, the Being-What or the essence as mirrored in a definitional proposition. And it was definitely one of Heidegger's greatest insights to recognize in this early answer of metaphysics the origin of the type of desire for knowledge that led to occidental science, to its ideal of objectification and the global technical culture that it founded. It is also apparent that the linguistic family to which Greek belongs— and Greek is the language from which European thinking emerged— functioned like a mold for metaphysics. Because Greek distinguishes the subject from its predicates, it was predisposed to the thinking of substance and its attributes. Thus, the fate of European thinking, that it develop metaphysics, logic, and ultimately modern science, was already determined by its ancient linguistic history. But the essence of language itself causes the most confusion. It seems almost impossible to think of language, regardless of which one in particular, in such a way that it would not perform the function of presencing, and similarly, it seems intrinsic to reason, regardless of how it is thought, that it question the present or that made present [*das Gegenwärtige oder Vergegenwärtigte*] and treat everything as if it were held in common—regardless of whether that occurs in mathematical equations, in a compelling series of conclusions, in related similes, or in aphorisms and wise sayings.

It is obvious that even Heidegger's attempt to raise the event of the *"Da"*—which first creates a place for thinking and speaking—into thought was still an attempt to find articulation through a concept, even if it was striving to avoid the language of metaphysics. It is equally clear that he has no choice but to continue speaking of the essence of the thing—in contrast to the scientific grasping of the empirical world—even though the term *essence* [*Wesen*] does not, even in this usage, carry with it the new verbal accent of "being present" [*Anwesen*] that Heidegger's attempt to think Being as time had conferred upon it. Here, with reference to Heidegger, Eugen Fink's observation first made about Husserl, that is, that certain basic concepts of thought often remain unthematic and exist only in an operative use, was proved to be correct. Yet, it is no less true that Heidegger's whole endeavor during the progression of his thought remained true to his resolve to resist the temptation to conform to the language of metaphysics and to endure the ensuing poverty of language, a poverty that he had gotten himself into with the question concerning the Being that was no longer the Being of beings.

This resolve manifested itself initially in his turn away from the transcendental constitution of the self found in his fundamental ontology, an approach that he still adhered to in *Being and Time*. The basic structure of temporality fundamental to the human Dasein may well have been capable of encompassing temporal modes of beings as the condition for their possibility—the contingent as well as the necessary, the passing as well as the eternal—but, on the other hand, Being, which itself constitutes Dasein, the Being of this *"Da,"* was not a transcendental condition for the possibility of Dasein. Rather, it was Being itself that occurs [*sich ereignet*] whenever Dasein is, or, as Heidegger expressed it in one of his first formulations, "when the first human being lifted its head." We spent a week after Heidegger first used this expression arguing over who was meant by this first human being—Adam or Thales. You can see that our understanding left something to be desired in those early Marburg days.

Of course, European thought did not have at its disposal the conceptual means needed to avoid this transcendental conception of the self. Nevertheless, Heidegger was able to find some articulate metaphors with whose help he instilled new meaning into the basic logical and ontological concepts of metaphysics, such as Being and thinking, or identity and difference. He spoke of the clearing, of the resolution [*Austrag*], and of the event. With these metaphors he tried to grasp that which glimmered through the earliest documents of Greek thinking, documents associated with the names of Anaximander, Parmenides, and Heraclitus. These were the first steps taken on the way to classical metaphysics, and with these steps, these originative thinkers were trying to meet the challenge put to their thinking—the great challenge of the *Da*.

One gets a hint of this from the Judeo-Christian theological doctrine of creation, for this thinking that had been molded by the Old Testament, that had heard God's voice or experienced his mute refusal, had developed much more of a receptivity to the *"Da"* (and its obfuscation) than to the organized forms and the "what-content" of *Da*-beings [*Was-Gehalt von Da-Seiendem*]. Heidegger was thus truly fascinated when he saw how Schelling had tried to grasp conceptually the mystery of revelation in his theosophical speculations on the ground in God and the existence in God. Schelling's astonishing ability to verify in and to draw from the human Dasein the basic concepts of this occurence in God made visible the existential experiences that pointed beyond all of the boundaries of spiritistic metaphysics. And because it saw the law of the day as being limited by the passion of the night, this was an area where Heidegger could show some sympathy for Karl Jasper's thought. However, freedom from the language of metaphysics as well as from its inherent consequences was to be gained from neither Schelling nor Jaspers.

A renewed encounter with Friedrich Hölderlin enabled him to make a genuine breakthrough to his own language. Hölderlin's poetry was always close to him, not only because he was a compatriot of the poet, but also because Hölderlin was a contemporary during World War I (this was, in fact, the period when the later Hölderlin became well known). From then on, Hölderlin's poetic works were to accompany him as a constant reference point in his search for his own language. This is shown not only by the fact that, after recognizing his political mistake in 1936, he came forth with his own *Hölderlin-Interpretationen,* but also by his endeavor in the same year to understand the work of art as its own eventing [*Sich-Ereignen*] of truth and to try to think the tense field spanning "world" and "earth." The use of the term *earth* here as a philosophical concept was something almost stunningly new. Certainly Heidegger's analysis of the concept of world, which he first drew out of the structure of Being-in-the-World and then clarified as the structure of the worldliness of the world by way of the referential contexts of ready-to-handness, brought about a real transformation in the way that this concept is understood in the philosophical tradition. It shifted the emphasis from a cosmological problem to its anthropological counterpart. Of course, there were theological and moral-philosophical precursors to this; but that "earth" was to become a philosophical theme—this transfer of a word poetically charged to a central conceptual metaphor—this really was a breakthrough. As a counterconcept to "world," "earth" was not simply referential field related solely to human beings. It was a bold stroke to claim that only in the interplay between earth and world, in the shifting relationship between the sheltering, concealing earth and the arising world, could the philosophical concept of *"Da"* and truth be gained. This opened up new ways of thinking. Hölderlin had freed a tongue for Heidegger's thinking.

That was in essence what Heidegger had been searching for from early on. His concern centered of the question concerning Being. That the Being of beings was characterized by the Greek concept of *aletheia* itself, of unconcealedness or truth, and that its place was not defined entirely by the way that humans relate to beings—in a "judgment"—this was one of the first points that Heidegger insisted on as a teacher. Truth was in no way centered on a judgment. This, of course, implied that the logical and epistemological concept of truth needed to be deepened, but beyond that it pointed toward a completely new dimension. This privative concept of *aletheia,* this thief which draws that concealed out of the darkness and into the light—and which ultimately leads to the move of European science toward clarification [*Aufklärungszug der europäischen Wissenschaft*]—requires its countersupport if it is really to make contact with Being. The self-showing of what is, of that which shows itself as that which is, includes—if it is—a holding within and a self-restraint. This is what gives the being that shows itself the weight of Being in the first place. We know from our own personal, existential experiences [*Existenzerfahrung*] of Being how fundamentally interconnected the "*Da*" of human Dasein is with its own finitude. We know it as the experience of darkness, a darkness in which we stand as thinking beings and back into which all that we raise up into light falls. We know it as the darkness from which we come and into which we pass. But this darkness is not merely a darkness opposed to the world of light; we are ourselves shrouded in darkness, which merely confirms that we *are*. Darkness plays a fundamental role in constituting the Being of our Dasein.

The earth is not only that which resists the penetration of the beams of light. This darkness that conceals is also one that shelters, a site from which everything is brought into brightness—like a word from silence. What Kierkegaard used to oppose the self-transparency of absolute knowledge, that is, existence, as well as what Schelling characterized as the unpreconceivable [*das Unvordenkliche*], which lies out in front of all thinking, belonged to the truth of Being itself. For Heidegger, Hölderlin's invocation of the earth came to symbolize this poetically.

Within the framework defined by the question concerning the origin of the work of art Heidegger was able to point out for the first time the ontologically constitutive (and not only privative) function of the earth. Here it became crystal clear that the idealistic interpretation of the work of art was indebted to the work of art itself for its own distinguished way of Being: to be a work, either to stand there or to tower like a tree or a mountain, and yet to be language as well. This "*Da*" of the work, which bowls us over with its self-sufficient presence, does not merely share itself with us. Rather, it draws us entirely outside of ourselves and imposes its own presence on us. This no longer has the character of an object that stands over and against us; we are no longer able to approach this like an object of knowledge, grasping, measuring, and controlling. Rather than meeting us in our world, it is much more a world into which we ourselves are drawn. Thus, the work of art is an exceptionally tangible event of the *"Da"* into which we are all placed.

From this vantage point, the next two steps that Heidegger's thinking must take stand out clearly. The artwork cannot be considered an object, as long as it is allowed to speak as a work of art and is not forced into the alien relationships such as commercial trade and traffic. This ultimately forces an awareness that even the thing [*das Ding*], as something of ours, possesses its own original worldliness and, thus, the center of its own Being so long as it is not placed into the object-world of producing and marketing. Rilke's poems on the thing makes mention of something like this. The Being of this thing cannot be accessed by objectively measuring and estimating; rather, the totality of a lived context has entered into and is present in the thing. And we belong to it as well. Our orientation to it is always something like our orientation to an inheritance that this thing belongs to as an heirloom from a relative, be it from a stranger's life or from our own.

Although one may feel at home in these worlds filled with works and things, this sense of "being-at-home" is by far the strongest when one is at home in the word, this most intimate home for all who speak. The word is not limited to its function as a means of communication. It is not merely a gobetween that makes reference to something else and that one uses as a sign that can be redirected to something else. As a single word or as the unity of a discussion, it is an area in which we are so thoroughly at home that we remain completely unaware of our living in the word. But even there, where it exist in itself as a work—as in a poem or a collection of thoughts—it emerges as that which it always fundamentally is. It takes us captive. To linger immersed in the word means to let it be and to keep ourself within the *"Da"* of Being.

This is a far cry from that which prescribes the daily routine and life-style of today's human beings. Yet, are these not precisely the phenomena that, even though they have been pushed to the fringes of our world and deprived of all legitimacy, display to this thinking the experience of Being of concealment, revealment, and sheltering? The world of the work of art comes across like a world gone by, or perhaps one passing away or closed off to the present, one without a place in our own world. Today's withering aesthetic culture, to which we are deeply indebted for the sharpening of our senses and of our spiritual receptivity, has more of the character a well-cared-for sanctuary than something that belongs in our world and in which we would feel at home. It is definitely a fundamental characteristic of the industrial age that we live in—and one that will inevitably become increasingly more prominent—that things are gradually losing their standing in Being and in life, caught up in the flood of articles of merchandise and the pursuit of the newest fashion. Even language, this most flexible and pliable possession of any speaking being, grows visibly stiff as it moves toward stereotypes and adapts to the general leveling of life. Against this backdrop Heidegger's orientation, which endowed his question concerning Being with an identifiable content, may appear to be nothing more than a romantic evocation of worlds passing away or already gone by.

However, anyone acquainted with Heidegger knows that the revolutionary pathos of his thinking was directed toward contemplatively penetrating the events of our world and was far removed from attaching any real meaning to the worthy endeavor of preserving that which is passing away. What distinguishes his thinking is the radicality and boldness with which he depicted the progression of occidental civilization into the technical omniculture [*Allkultur*] of today as our fate and as the necessary consequence of occidental metaphysics. But this means that all the benign attempts to slow down this gigantic process of calculating, empowering, and producing—which we call *cultural life*—did not have a place in his thought. To him, the boldest and most radical planning and projecting amounted to only what it was, the fateful answer of our time to the challenge we humans must face. It <this planning> presents itself to this human race that has been released into the world [*Ausgesetzheit des Menschens*] as a human endeavor more serious than any other. Heidegger foresaw some time ago something that is only today beginning to seep slowly into the general consciousness: With the bold onslaught of technical know-how, which has forced a realignment of humanity itself, human beings are courting an unavoidable challenge that they have been subjugated to. Heidegger names this challenge *Being,* and he calls this way of humanity, which has been developed under the auspices of technical civilization, the way to the most extreme forgetfulness of Being. In the same way that metaphysics oriented itself within the Being of beings, in the Being-What [*Was-Sein*] or the essence and, thus, misconstrued its own character of being-released [*Ausgesetztsein*] into the *"Da,"* today's technology penetrates into the fartherest reaches of the world's establishments and thereby determines the way that that which *is* will generally be experienced. But naturally the concealed presence of that forgotten is a part of all forgetfulness. The forgetfulness of Being is always accompanied by the presence of Being, sporadically illuminating in the instance of loss and constantly superjacent to Mnemosyne, the must of thinking. This is also true for a thinking that holds that this most extreme form of forgetfulness of Being, the one toward which we are now drifting, is itself the fate of Being. Heidegger also described his own thinking-out-ahead *[Vorausdenken]* into that which is as a step back, one attempting to think anew the beginning as a beginning. Thinking-out-ahead is not planning, calculating, estimating, and managing; rather, it is thinking what is and what will be. Therefore, thinking-out-ahead is necessarily a thinking back to the beginning, for the beginning is ultimately the starting point from which even the very last possible step originates, and thus, that last step can be seen as an outcome of the beginning. Thinking is always thinking the beginning. When Heidegger interprets the history of philosophical thought as the history of the alterations in Being and as the thoughtful responses to the challenge of Being—as if the totality of our philosophical history was nothing but a growing forgetfulness—he nevertheless knew that all of the great attempts at thinking were seeking to think the same *[das Selbe zu denken]*. They are efforts to remain proximate to the beginning, to address and answer the challenge of Being. So, it is not another story that must be told if one wants to run through the history of remembering Being; it is rather the same story. The recollection of Being is the contemplative accompaniment of the forgetfulness of Being. We are entrusted to the partnership that unites all thought experiments with one another. Heidegger saw clearly that we are all bound together by such a conversation. It is precisely for this reason that he placed—with a growing resoluteness—markers in his own contribution to this conversation. These markers point out the way of the history of Being, that is, our own fate, so that we are directed in every possible way to the openness of the one question.

He did not conclude the dialogue, regardless whether it is named the dialogue of metaphysics, of philosophy, or of thinking. He also never found an answer to his original and constantly advancing question; namely, How can one speak of God without reducing him to an object of our knowledge? But he posed his question with such breadth that no God of philosophy and perhaps not even one of theology can serve as an answer, and we should certainly not presume to have one either. Heidegger considered the poet Friedrich Hölderlin to be his closest partner in this dialogue that is thinking. Hölderlin's lamentation over the abandonment, his call to the disappeared gods, and on the other hand, his awareness that "we still have access to much of the divine" were like a pledge to Heidegger that the dialogue of thinking can still find a partner even on the eve of the world's complete homelessness and remoteness from the gods. We all take part in this dialogue. And the dialogue continues, for only in a dialogue can a language arise and continue to develop—a language in which we, in a more and more estranged world, are at home.

NOTES

1. EXISTENTIALISM AND THE PHILOSOPHY OF EXISTENCE

a. The Greek term *pathos* is used in this text more in the German sense, meaning "emotiveness," with more of an emphasis on strong emotions or passions per se and not so much in the more restricted sense, meaning "feelings of pity or sympathy," which is the more common meaning in English. Perhaps an English speaker can best get some feeling for what is meant here by considering what is suggested by the morpheme *path* in the word *apathy*.

b. The German word that I am translating here as "ways," *Wege*, has occasioned more controversy and discussions than any other word in the text. In itself, *Wege* is not a difficult word to understand; it corresponds fairly nicely with the English word *ways*. My concern was that the word *way* might be interpreted too subjectively, as a method or manner of being that is developed by and characteristic of a certain person—and this especially because the title of the book is *Heidegger's Ways*. The other option would have been "paths," something that one discovers or stumbles upon, but does not create oneself. In a discussion with Gadamer it became clear that he meant something between these two extremes. He described what he meant with *Wege* by way of the Greek term ʾατραπός, as that from which one cannot deviate. He went on to talk about this in terms of a direction in which one is compelled to go due to external circumstances, the natural environment, for example. His specific example had to do with the general direction that one hiking might be forced to take because of the shape of a certain mountain range: This direction is one more or less determined for the hiker. Yet, the particular way that one might get through the mountains would be dependent on decisions made by the individual. Thus, *Heidegger's Ways* were ways determined in part by circumstances larger than any "subject"; yet, they are also inextricably bound up with and were determined to a certain extent by an individual person.

2. MARTIN HEIDEGGER—75 YEARS

a. The noun *Anschauung* (from *anschauen,* to look at, to view or observe) has presented somewhat of a problem for this translation. It is traditionally translated as "intuition," especially with reference to Kant and Husserl, but neither Gadamer nor I am very happy with this choice. The word *intuition* comes from the Latin *intueor* meaning "I look at, I view or observe." But as I understand it, *intueri* meant "to look at" more in a mental or spiritual sense, which led to its English cousin taking on the meaning that it now has, namely, to have insight into something, to grasp something mentally or by way of feelings without being able to explicate rationally how one arrived at those insights. It is precisely because it is associated with either a mental image in the Kantian sense or with these insights with hidden origins, i.e., a type of incomplete seeing, that the word *intuition* is not entirely suited here. When Gadamer talks about Heidegger's *"Anschauungskraft,"* his intuitive powers or powers of viewing, he is talking about Heidegger's ability to see something vividly and in its totality and then to portray that vision in a concrete and graphic language so that others could see it just as vividly. In a discussion I had with Gadamer on March 16, 1992, we discussed this ability of Heidegger's at length: the word *concreteness* came up frequently, and Gadamer described this ability as Heidegger's "powers of plasticity." What is lost in the translation of *Anschauung* as "intuition" is precisely this emphasis on Heidegger's ability to communicate what he saw so vividly; "intuitions," as insights with hidden origins generally resist this kind of communication. For various reasons I have decided to stick with *intuition,* not the least of which being that this is an established tradition, but I wanted to make the reader aware of this deficiency.

b. *Dasein* is a term that, in the normal usage of German, refers to existence in a more informal sense, such as in "Does such a thing actually exist?" or "We want our children to have a better existence than ours." It is formed by joining *da,* "there," with *Sein,* the infinitive of "to be." Therefore, it was quite appropriate for Heidegger's endeavor in *Being and Time* because it makes a direct appeal to what is "there," i.e., existence. I have used the

German *da* instead of "there" in the translation so that the play on words
would not be lost.

c. The German reads, "Wer den Bereich, in dem Denken und
Gedachtes allerest als Bezung auseinandertreten, denken will, scheint sich
ins Undenkbare zu verlieren." Gadamer mentioned that he was referring
here to Heidegger's *Austrag* (see Heidegger's "The Onto-Theo-Logical
Constitution of Metaphysics"), which Derrida later developed into his notion
of "*différance.*"

3. THE MARBURG THEOLOGY

a. The Greek translates: "There is indeed a forgetting of states of
this sort (i.e., of reasoned states concerning opinion), but not of practical
wisdom."

b. See Johannes Duns Scotus, *Super universalia,* q. 14, nr. 4.

c. I have decided to translate *existenziell* as "existential," and
existenzial as "existentiell," thus reversing the precedent set by John
Macquarrie and Edward Robinson in their translation of *Sein und Zeit.*
Heidegger's use of *existenziell* seems to me to be very close to the
everyday use of *existential* in English, whereas the word *existential* is a
technical term of Heidegger's; I thought it less confusing to render
existential "existentiall" so that there would be less chance of confusing
the technical meaning which the more common meaning associated
with "existential."

d. More literally, the understanding, thought, or perhaps, mind of
the author.

4. "WHAT IS METAPHYSICS?"

a. I have translated *das Nichts* as "nothing," more or less following
the example set by David Krell. I do deviate a bit from Krell's translation in
that I have left "nothing" in quotation marks when it refers to "*das Nichts*" to
distinguish the substantive from the indefinite pronoun, i.e., *nichts,* which is
also translated as "nothing." (See "What Is Metaphysics?" in Martin
Heidegger, *Basic Writings from 1927 to 1964,* ed. and trans. David Farrell Krell
[New York: Harper and Row, 1977], pp. 95–112.)

b. I think the essay that Gadamer is referring to here was
actually published in 1931. See Rudolf Carnap, "Überwindung der
Metaphysik durch logische Analyse der Sprache," *Erkenntnis* 2 (1931):
219–241, esp. par. 5, pp. 229–233.

6. THE THINKER MARTIN HEIDEGGER

a. Perhaps one could translate voῦς with "intellect" or "spirit." It stems from the verb voεῖν, meaning to think or perceive, and the noun refers to the ability to perceive intellectually and to will as well as to the capacity to have feelings and moods.

9. THE TRUTH OF THE WORK OF ART

a. See Paul Ernst, *Der Zusammenbruch des deutschen Idealismus* (Munich: G. Müller, 1918).

b. See Martin Heidegger, "Über den Ursprung des Kunstwerks," in *Holzwege* (Frankfurt: Klostermann, 1950), pp. 7–68.

c. Gadamer is referring to the angel motif in Rilke's *Duino Elegies.*

d. See Heidegger, *Die Frage nach dem Ding: Zu Kants Lehre von den transzendentalen Grundsätzen* (Tübingen: Max Niemeyer, 1962.) English translation: *What Is a Thing?* trans. Barton and Deutsch (Chicago: Henry Regenery, 1967).

10. MARTIN HEIDEGGER—85 YEARS

a. Often German verbs that have the prefix *ver* have a negative connotation. The verb *verheideggert,* which I have translated here as "Heideggerized," seems to me to be fit into that category; I think it is suggesting that the students language was not improved by Heidegger's influence.

b. The term *Holzwege* refers to trails in the forest, usually built and used by the timber industry, which neither begin nor end in any significant place. In common usage, *Holzweg* functions like a "deadend street."

12. THE GREEKS

a. The German text reads: *"dass das immer Anwesende das am meisten Seiende ist."*

b. The Greek translates: "whoever is ruling as king at the time."

c. The German translates: "whoever is currently king."

d. The following translation corresponds roughly with Diels's translation into German (see footnote 2): "Becoming as well as passing away, Being as well as Nonbeing, the altering of place as well as the changing of the radiant color."

13. THE HISTORY OF PHILOSOPHY

a. The Greek phrase could also be translated as "a being as true, unconcealed."

b. *Entis* is the present participle in the active voice from *esse,* the Latin verb "to be." Although Gadamer seems to be interpreting it to mean "Being," the more obvious translation based upon the grammatical structures would seem to be (to or of a) "being."

14. THE RELIGIOUS DIMENSION

a. The German word for science, *Wissenschaft,* is much broader in scope than its English counterpart, which usually refers to the empirical study of natural phenomena. In German, any system of knowledge that has been acquired through methodological study can be referred to as a science, including theology and philosophy.

15. BEING SPIRIT GOD

a. There is a play on words here that may escape the English-speaking reader. Schleiermacher was, of course, a philosopher and theologian who was a contemporary of Hegel, but his name also means a "maker of veils." Gadamer mentioned that this was a quotation taken from Nietzsche, but he was unsure where it was to be found. I have been unable to find this exact quotation; the closest facsimile that I have been able to locate is in Nietzsche's *Ecce Homo,* "The Case of Wagner," par. 3.

GLOSSARY

die Abwesenheit absence

das Abwesende that which is absent

abwesende absence, absent
das An-denken rememberance or recollection (Linge)
die Anschauung intuition

anschaulich intuitional
das Ansichhalten holding within
die Anwesenheit presentness

die Anwesung presencing

das Anwesende that which is present
die Anzeige indication
der Apriorismus apriorism
das Aufgehen coming up (with reference to seeds) or arising
die Auslegung explication

auslegen explicate
der Austrag resolution
berechnen compute
bergen sheltering

Sich-Bergen self-sheltering
die Bewegtheit motility
die Befindlichkeit disposition
die Begrifflichkeit conceptuality
der Bildungsidealismus educational idealism
die Christlichkeit Christian spirit
da there
der Denkversuch thought experiment

der Denkentwurf thought projection
diesig hazy
dunstig misty
die Eigentlichkeit authenticity

eigentlich authentic

eigensten innermost or own most
die Eignung suitability
die Entbergung revealment
die Entschlossenheit resoluteness
entstehen emerge
der Entwurf projection or project
der Entzug withdrawal
das Ereignis event, happening, or occurence

ereignen occur or happen
erkenntnis-theoretisch epistemological-theoretical
erklären explain
erschliessen disclose
die Existenz existence

das Existieren "to exist"

existenzial existentiell

existenziell existential
die Fragestellung formulation of a question
freilegen expose
der Gegenbegriff counterconcept

der Gegenentwurf counterprojection
die Gegenwärtigkeit contemporariness

gegenwärtig contemporary
der Geist spirit, intellect
die Geisteswissenschaften the humanities
das Gemeinte that which is intended or (occasionally) meant
die Geschichtlichkeit historicality
das Gespräch dialogue or conversation
die Geworfenheit thrownness
die Grenzsituation boundary situation
die Grundstimmung basic mood
die Historizität historicity
das Ich the I or ego
die Jemeinigkeit mineness
die Jeweiligkeit currentness
Machen-Können constructive capacity (Linge)
prägen form or coin (with reference to words)
nebelig foggy
das Nichts nothing or the nothing
die Problematik problematic or difficulty
die Problemgeschichte history of problems
die Präsenz presence
rechnend calculating, calculative
der Rückzug retreat
die Sache thing, matter, or affair

die Sache des Denkens the matter for thinking

die Sache selbst the thing itself
die Schulwissenschaft pedagogy
das Sein Being
das Seiende being or entity
sich-Zurückhalten self-restraint
die Sorge care
die Sprachnot poverty of language or deficiency in language,
        linguistic barrier
der Stoss thrust

die Uneigentlichkeit inauthenticity
die Unverborgenheit unconcealedness
das Unvordenkliche the unpreconceivable, the unprethinkable, or that
    which cannot be prepared for in thought

das Denken des Unvordenklichen thinking of what cannot preconceived
die Verbergung concealment

die Verborgenheit concealedness
die Verdecktheit coveredness, Hiddenness (Kayser)

die Verdeckung covering (over)
die Verfügbarkeit having at one's disposal or availability
die Vergessenheit des Seins the forgetfulness of Being
das Verschliessen closing off
der Vollzug consummation
das Vorausdenken thinking out ahead
die Voreingenommenheit bias
das Vorhandensein being present-at-hand
das Was-Sein What of Being
weilen tarrying
die Wirkungsgeschichte effective history
die Widerständlichkeit resistant character
zeitigen temporalize
die Zukünftigkeit futurity
zumuten exact
das Zurhandsein being ready-to-hand

INDEX